SMALL PRESS

GUIDE
2002

The complete guide to poetry &
small press magazines.

- 7th Edition -

© Writers' Bookshop 2001
ISBN 1-902713-11-7

First published by Writers' Bookshop
Remus House, Coltsfoot Drive,
Woodston, Peterborough PE2 9JX

Edited by James Feeke

Acknowledgements

Thanks to all who generously shared their information and ideas to make this book possible.

A note from the Publisher

This is the seventh edition of this small magazine guide, which we hope will help both magazine editors and writers wishing to submit work for publication.

The information used has been supplied by the magazine editors themselves.

The Small Press Guide is updated annually. If you feel we have omitted useful information or that the Guide could be developed further, we would like to hear from you.

Good Luck!

Aiming High with Something Small

Welcome to the Small-Press Guide 2002, the definitive gateway to the publishing world

Most small things are often seen as insignificant. Yet a closer look at most of the things we deem small and insignificant are usually the opposite. An apple seed is small, but when planted, grows into an enormous tree bearing delicious fruit. Likewise, we as humans started out as small, and by God, look at us now!!! In saying that, not everything began small. Certain aspects of technology started out big and gradually over the years has reduced in size, yet at the same time, has increased in ability: 12 inch vinyl records are now CDs; videos, dvds; computers, which were once the size of your average drawing room with precious little memory are now the size of your average hardback novel with tuns of memory crammed into a small space. Scientists call this progress.

Given the above examples, would it now be unwise of us to view the Little Magazine as insignificant, something of little value and unworthy of our attention? The late Raymond Carver said in his 1980 essay on the poetry magazine: "Most of the good writing being done is being done in the little magazines." A cursory glance at any Small-Press journal/anthology will verify this. Don't forget, quite a number of our best-selling authors grew out of the Small-Press. For example, earlier work by Phil Ford, who began his career in education, appeared in Lexikon Magazine way back in 1997. Today, he writes regularly for the tv soap, Coronation Street.

Noteworthy is the comments made by the Poetry Library, who incidentally carry every Small-Press magazine ever published in the UK: "The little magazine is a phenomenon which has been peculiar to poetry throughout this century, and it is hard to overestimate its importance to and influence on poetic movements and development over the past eighty odd years. Famous for their individuality and independence, they are infinite in their variety, range, quality, intention, audience and appeal." That being the case, then it is imperative that you study them carefully before making the decision to submit examples of your work. In this way you'll most definitely increase your chances of getting published. Read the magazines first. Indeed, why waste time and money targeting avant-garde poetry to a magazine that only wants sonnets.

This wonderfully produced guide carries in excess of 330 names and addresses of all sorts of Small-press magazines. Choose carefully and submit wisely.

Finally on this point, a number of budding authors often make the mistake of targeting major publishers before they've even tested the waters, so to speak, and wonder why they receive endless rejections. It is a good idea to wait until you have amassed several magazine credits first. Not only is this good practice, but it will provide you enough time in which to hone your craft, establish an audience, and get some feedback on your work. Publishers are more likely to be impressed by poetry/short-fiction that has already shown clear signs of having literary promise.

Choosing Your Market

The Small-press is no doubt the best opening for any new writer. They're usually always looking for new material and yours might be just what they want. But before you submit anything, consider the following.

1   Many Small-press magazines are often run by volunteers with small budgets. This means that their response time maybe longer. However, try to be patient and avoid bothering them with loads of telephone/e-mail enquiries as to the progress of your submission, else you'll only succeed in jeopardising your chances of ever getting published at all.

2   Small magazines are often short-lived. This means they could fold at any time without notice. Always bare this in mind when submitting work. Always try and support them if you can by offering to pay for a couple of back issues instead of expecting them for free.

3   Don't always expect to earn money from your poem/story. Payment usually takes the form of a complimentary copy or two of the magazine in which your work appears. However, there's no reason why you shouldn't target some of the more prestigious high-paying magazines. When doing so, please bare in mind that competition will be great and the chances of getting published will be less.

4   Always adhere to magazine guidelines. If an editor says 30 lines max for poems, then don't submit 33 lines. The same goes for short stories. If an editor asks for 2,000 words, then 2,002 is two too many. Remember, an editor knows how much space he/she has got and how much work will fit into that space. Therefore, don't annoy them by going against their wishes. Send for their guidelines first before submitting anything, remembering to enclose a suitably sized stamped addressed envelope for their reply.

✳✳✳

Now that you have decided to submit samples of your work to a select group of magazines, your next task is to choose those best suited to your writing. As I have already mentioned, it is simply no good targeting those magazines which only accept love poetry if all you write is humour.

A couple of magazines which take a variety of styles are: Purple Patch edited by Geoff Stevens; Poetry Now; Envoi; Candelabrum, The Red Candle Press; Raw Edge, edited by Jonathan Davidson, and Breakfast All Day. Check through this guide and after finding the ones which you feel best suit you, then make a list and start submitting.

For those of you who write short stories, then the list is somewhat limited. This is because more people write poetry than short fiction. Breakfast All Day, New Fiction, Lexikon Magazine Online and Raw Edge, all accept short fiction. You'll find more in the Writers Handbook.

Then what about those of you who write exclusively for the women's market? An excellent, well-produced magazine is QWF, (Quality Women's Fiction) edited by Jo Good. Launched in December 1994, this smartly produced journal was born out of Jo Good's ambition to profile some of the best fiction written exclusively by women. "I want something which pushes the boundaries of women's fiction," she said; "something which goes a few steps further than the fiction found in women's magazines."

Writers and The Internet

The internet is fast becoming one of the most sharpest tools in a writer's toolkit. Accessing a world of information has never been easier. With well over 1 million new members joining every week, one can't start to imagine the sheer volume of electronic media that is presently available at the click of a mouse. For writers and publishers, the opportunities are endless. Indeed, findings of a recent survey revealed that over 75% of publishers have already embraced this new media and that book sales are on the up. But whilst the internet is still relatively new, writers and publishers need to be aware of the cons as well as the prose. For now, I simply want to focus on the prose as I feel these far outweigh the cons.

Online Resources

There is simply hundreds of Usenet Groups online that are of particular interest to writers. These groups enable writers to team up with thousands of budding authors, exchange ideas, share their work, and critique one another's manuscripts.

The two main resources for writers that allow you to achieve this successfully are Internet Mailinglists and Usenet discussion groups.

1   Internet Mailinglists

The internet Mailinglists are e-mail based and are made up of individual subscribers. These individual lists are usually manned by an editor or co-ordinator who vets and collates information they receive from subscribers before sending them out.

Via these lists, writers can receive articles and practical advice from other subscribers. In turn, you can reciprocate by posting messages, articles and comments. Beware, there are simply hundreds of these Usenet groups on the internet, so pick ones which best suit you as you could find yourself desk-top deep in megabytes of continuous text, and unable to cope.

Finally, these lists are also used to promote special announcements, new book/magazine titles, competitions, breaking news, and much more. I currently edit such a list which carries mainly literary news, reviews, announcements and regular features.

For more information on these lists and Ezines, visit HYPERLINK *http://www.ezinepublisher.com*

2 Usenet Groups

Usenet Groups are not too dissimilar to Mailinglists mentioned above. The only difference being, they're not e-mail-based. Basically they are interactive websites where writers can post samples of their work, critique existing examples, exchange ideas, etc. These groups reach a wider audience and no subscription is required.

A couple of groups which you might like to try: alt.prose, misc.writing, and alt.journalism. Here you'll be able to meet writers, editors and receptive readers. As well as posting your work, reading sample manuscripts by other writers, you will find lists of other resources of interest to writers, including: internet mailing list addresses, publications looking for submissions, e-mail addresses of editors, and much more.

Ezines

Ezines are now one of the biggest market that can be contacted over the internet. These can be found in a variety of locations including FTP sites and Usenet groups. They provide a dynamic mix of prose and poetry, and are often found in or near universities. The most effective way to approach the editor of one of these Ezines is to familiarise yourself with the publication. Then when you have decided that your writing has a place in that journal, you can submit it to the editor by e-mail in accordance with their guidelines.

Payment is usually limited to recognition, but the chance of developing an audience for your work is priceless.

Preparing Your Work for Publication

Before submitting your poetry/story to an editor, it is important that it is well presented and in a legible format. Below is a set of guidelines generally recognised and respected by most professional editors.

1   Your manuscript should be typed/wordprocessed on one side of an A4 sheet of good quality white 80/90GSM paper.

2   Type your name, address and e-mail and phone number, single spaced, in the top left-hand corner.

3   Make sure that the spelling and punctuation are exactly as you want them.

4   Never put more than one poem on a page.

5   Do not send your only copy as editors cannot be held responsible for work lost/damaged in the post.

6   Stories need to be double-line spaced and each page numbered with the title of your story centred at the top of every sheet and the word end on the concluding page.

7   Always enclose an A4 stamped addressed envelope with your work for the safe return of your manuscript or for an acknowledgement.

8   Always enclose a covering letter which should not contain superfluous information about your favourite pop group or why you dislike women drivers. Rather it should include relevant information about your poem/story and a short biography listing previous publication acceptances.

9   Be patient. Never expect to receive an immediate reply. Replies can often take anything from seven days to three months, (or in my case when I submitted my first article to the Times, two years).

Good luck with your writing!

Francis Anderson
Freelance Journalist

10TH MUSE

10th Muse is the leading international forum for nonist poetics. Nonism is the only contemporary experimental genre which is progressive and radical in outlook. Nonists overturned the conservatism of the experimental milieu by embracing non-experimental traditions within a precursor aesthetic. That which was 'hidden' within the experimental milieu became simultaneously realised and superseded with nonism. Within nonist culture, belief is amplified into its antithesis. It is not negated within contradiction, nor realised. Culture is expressed (it is not defined, nor described) as a verb. In this refraction of belief, the ideology of particularities is revealed as mythic. So too is the ideology of Universalism. Notions of 'power in belief' are thus rendered absurd. The nonist reconstructs the 'self' according to this knowledge and thus is free. We walk a lit 'ground', even in the 'valley'.

Poetry, prose, graphics; nonist cultural criticism; false landscape exposé; lyrical simulation. This does not describe 10th Muse.

Editor Name(s): Andrew Jordan
Address: 33 Hartington Road, Southampton SO14 0EW
Mag Frequency: Occasional
Subscription: £7.50 for 3
Single Issue: £3
Back Issue: £1.50
Overseas: 8 US dollars, in cash
Payment in: Cheques (if drawn from UK accounts)/or US dollars (cash)
Payable to: 10th Muse
Inserts accepted: Yes
Terms: Ask first
Circulation approx: Mythical
Payment terms to contributors: 'Free' complimentary copy
Accept/rejection approx times: 1-3 months

3RD STONE

3rd Stone is an illustrated miscellany covering the archaeology and folklore of ancient sites and landscapes. Contributions span the academic and fringe worlds, and each issue includes news, abstracts, an events listing, extensive reviews and lots of other stuff that you wouldn't come across elsewhere.

Editor Name(s): Neil Mortimer
Address: PO Box 961, Devizes, Wiltshire SN10 2TS
Telephone: 01380 723933
Fax: 01380 730136
Email: neil@thirdstone.demon.co.uk
Website: www.thirdstone.demon.co.uk
Mag Frequency: Bi-annual
Subscription: £10
Single Issue: £5
Overseas: $25 or £15
Payment in: UK or US cheque - visa/mastercard
Payable to: 3rd Stone
Inserts accepted: Yes
Terms: Two weeks prior to publication
Advertising Rates: Variable, depending on day of week
Circulation approx: 2250
Payment terms to contributors: Expenses plus free subscription
Accept/rejection approx times: 1 month

A 1 WASTE PAPER CO LTD

Various mail art publications since 1980 including U-Mak-It, Christmas Catalogue, 20 Years in the Mail, Do Wonders Invention Manual and Particulary, Curios Thing, a small xeroxed 16 page booklet of crazy cut up collage and non-sense poetry gleaned from charity shops and car boot sales. Curios Thing is in it's 16th year and collaborative off-shoots have included Curios Radio, Curios Snail, Curios Dog, Curios Ads and Curios Nahpro. All are hand stamped and coloured and usually have a free badge or stickers.

Editor Name(s): Michael Leigh
Address: 33 Shipbrook Road, Rudheath, Northwich, Chesire
Telephone: 01606 436670
Mag Frequency: When enough material is gathered
Subscription: Negotiable
Single Issue: Negotiable
Back Issue: Negotiable
Overseas: Negotiable
Payment in: Kind
Inserts accepted: No
Circulation approx: 50 - 100 copies

A BARD HAIR DAY

A.B.H.D magazine is a general poetry and short story publication that awards prizes for the best pieces in each issue. A bi-annual publication alternating with the Poet Tree.

Editor Name(s): Ian Deal
Address: 289 Elmswood Avenue, Feltham, Middlesex TW13 7QB
Telephone: Approach in writing please
Fax: www.homestead.com/partners_writing_group
Email: partners_writing_group@hotmail.com
Mag Frequency: Bi-annual - Apr 30th and Oct 30th
Subscription: England £5 sterling, Europe £6 or $10, International £8 or $12
Single Issue: England £2.50 sterling, Europe £3 or $5, International £4 or $6
Back Issue: £2.50 - same
Overseas: (Per issue) Europe £3/$5 International £4/$6
Payment in: Sterling only - Cheques or Postal Orders/Abroad American Dollars acceptable
Payable to: I Deal
Inserts accepted: Yes
Terms: £50 per 1000 or complimentary advertising
Advertising Rates: £50 full page, £25 half page, £10 quarter page - page size 148mm x 211mm
Payment terms to contributors: None
Accept/rejection approx times: 2 weeks - 4 when busy

AABYE (Formerly New Hope International)

A gathering of talented poets from around the globe; new and old together; traditionalists meet the avant-garde; haiku to long poems; translations; a collage of writing that consistently surprises. Submissions arriving without return postage are not considered. AABYE is a printed magazine. The ezine AABYE's Baby found at http://www.aabyesbaby.ukpoets.net/ is an electronic magazine only. The two are separate and there is no shared content.

Editor Name(s): Gerald England
Address: 20 Werneth Avenue, Gee Cross, Hyde, Cheshire SK14 5NL
Email: newhope@iname.com (no email submissions)
Website: http://www.nhi.clara.net/nhihome.htm
Mag Frequency: Irregular (not more than one per year at present)
Subscription: Send £10 or more and receive current and future issues of Aabye plus other books published by New Hope International to the value of 133% of your payment
Single Issue: £4.50
Back Issue: £3 each or 6 for £10
Overseas: £6 or $10 cash
Payment in: Overseas: cash or sterling cheques - foreign cheques add $20 to cover bank charges
Payable to: G England
Inserts accepted: No
Advertising Rates: No ads
Circulation approx: 600
Payment terms to contributors: Contributor's copy
Accept/rejection approx times: May-Nov: up to 6 weeks, Dec-Apr: up to 6 months

ABRAXAS

Founded November 1991, Abraxas is an exciting quarterly magazine with a growing readership, incorporating The Colin Wilson Newsletter, bringing together poetry and fiction, philosophy and meaphysics. On the philosophy side, it has published essays by Colin Wilson on Jacques Derrida, Alfred North Whitehead and Edmund Husserl, while on the literary front it has featured translations of stories from Pablo Palacio, Jose de Cuadre and poems from DM Thomas and Zofia Ilinska. Articles have varied, from a penetrating study of criminal messiahs to an analysis of the angel craze sweeping America and probing, sceptical reflections on the UFO abductee syndrome. Furthermore there are book reviews, readers' comments and artwork. Abraxas includes a booklist of Colin Wilson titles, enabling readers to obtain personally-signed copies of his works.

Editor Name(s): Paul Newman and Pamela Smith-Rawnsley
Address: 57 Eastbourne Road, St Austell, Cornwall PL25 4SU
Telephone: 01726 64975
Fax: Same as phone
Email: palnew7@hotmail.com
Website: abrax7.stormloader.com
Mag Frequency: Twice a year at present (intended quarterly)
Subscription: £14 (four issues)
Single Issue: £3.50
Back Issue: £3.50
Overseas: USA $32
Payment in: Sterling preferred
Payable to: Paul Newman
Inserts accepted: Yes
Terms: £10 (small insert) to £100 (full page)
Advertising Rates: Same as 'insert' terms
Circulation approx: Exclusive
Payment terms to contributors: Free copy of mag

ACORN

Acorn is a 40 page colour glossy magazine. Our aim is that writers should be read, so we welcome articles, stories and poems from subscribers. Subscribers are invited to submit their work for free publication on our website. Acorn also contains tuition by professionals on fiction writing and poetry, as well as interviews with published authors.

Editor Name(s): Beth Rudkin
Address: South Scarle, Newark, Notts NG23 7JW
Telephone: 01636 893118
Email: Acornmag@aol.com
Website: http://www.members.aol.com/Acornmag
Mag Frequency: Bi-monthly
Subscription: £16 one year, £8.50 six months
Single Issue: £2.95
Overseas: Europe: £20, USA and Australia: £25
Payable to: Acorn Publications
Inserts accepted: Yes
Advertising Rates: £10 for 1/16 page
Circulation approx: 500
Payment terms to contributors: £5 per article or story, £2 per poem
Accept/rejection approx times: 2 weeks

ACUMEN

Acumen is a literary magazine with an emphasis on poetry. It seeks to please the intelligent reader with high-quality, well-written prose and poetry. In addition it has an extensive reviews section devoted mostly to poetry publications; and a recent innovation has been the issue of a free focus sheet and poster combined that provides a sampler of the poetry of an individual poet. Its overall aim is to emphasise the continuity of English poetry and literature into the present age.

Editor Name(s): Patricia Oxley
Address: 6 The Mount, Higher Furzeham, Brixham, Devon TQ5 8QY
Reviews to: Glen Pursglove, 25 St Albans Road, Brynmill, Swansea SA2 0BP
Mag Frequency: 3 times per year
Subscription: £12.50
Single Issue: £4.50
Back Issue: Various
Overseas: $35-45
Payment in: Cheque/PO/IMO
Payable to: Acumen
Inserts accepted: Yes
Terms: £100 per 1000
Circulation approx: 750
Payment terms to contributors: Under review
Accept/rejection approx times: Rejections 2 weeks/Acceptances 3 months

ADVOCIST DEMOCRATIC FRONT (ADF) DIGITAL PUBLICATIONS

ADF Digital Publications run an occaisional circulation off floppy disks, compatable for HTML for PC, to promote the views of the late radical Satanist and philospher, Tim Telsa. These publications are complete copies of his essays, concerning anarchism, Satanism, revolution and Satanist chauvanism. These disks are free, and are completely non-copyright, allowing people to copy, publish, sell or disseminate as you wish. Tim Telsa killed himself on Halloween 2000, and his ashes were spread as a ritual Satanic magical Circle. R. I. P.

Good contacts are honoured... hisssssssssssss

Editor Name(s): Lucifer Elite
Address: BM Betelguise, London, WC1N 3XX
Website: www.geocities.com/CapitolHill/1843
Mag Frequency: Very random, sometimes occaisional
Subscription: Free
Single Issue: Free
Back Issue: Free
Overseas: Free
Payment in: Donations of stamps are always welcome
Inserts accepted: No
Circulation approx: Unknown (People are welcome to copy our files)
Payment terms to contributors: Sadly not!

THE AFFECTIONATE PUNCH

Now in its 7th year and part-funded by the National Lottery-A4E, The Affectionate Punch is a stylish compendium of new unpublished poetry and fiction from new and established writers. £10 is paid for the piece of work receiving the most accolades in a given issue. Well thought-out poetry and fiction by people who care is most welcome. Poetry: 40 lines max. Fiction: up to 1400 words. Book reviews: 500 words. SAE essential with all submissions. 'Quality writing, well presented' - Zene.

Editor Name(s): Andrew Tutty
Address: 35 Brundage Road, Manchester M22 0BY
Website: www.affectionatepunch.co.uk
Mag Frequency: Bi-annual (summer and winter)
Subscription: £6 plus 50p p&p
Single Issue: £3 plus 25p p&p
Back Issue: £2 plus 50p p&p
Overseas: £6 - sterling only
Payment in: Cheque/PO (sterling)
Payable to: The Affectionate Punch
Inserts accepted: Yes
Terms: By arrangement
Advertising Rates: By arrangement
Circulation approx: 300
Payment terms to contributors: Free copy (plus £10 for vote winner)
Accept/rejection approx times: 1-4 months

AGENDA

My editorial criteria are personal - to print a poem I have to some degree be moved by it. A great poem must remain a mystery. In every age it is a rare event. I look for poems that can be lived with over years rather than work of immediate impact. Agenda does not believe poetry should be affected by fashions. Lasting poems remain timeless - they do not date, unlike the ephemera - often the most popular in whatever era. Editing Agenda is for me rather like making a book which gradually takes shape throughout a lifetime. The magazine's growth is thus organic like a tree...

Editor Name(s): William Cookson and Assistant Editor Patricia McCarthy
Address: 5 Cranbourne Court, Albert Bridge Road, London SW11 4PE
Telephone: 020 7228 0700
Fax: Same as phone
Email: agendapoetry@btinternet.com
Mag Frequency: Quarterly
Subscription: £26 (Individual)
Single Issue: Varies £5-£6
Back Issue: Varies but generally £5
Overseas: £28 Europe/£30 Overseas (for individuals)
Payment in: Cheque/Credit card
Payable to: Agenda
Inserts accepted: Yes
Terms: £80 per 1000
Advertising Rates: Varies: £250 full page
Circulation approx: 1200
Payment terms to contributors: £15 per page of poetry/£10 per page of prose - but only when we can afford it
Accept/rejection approx times: 3 months

AIREINGS

Poetry magazine - accepts short prose pieces. We welcome poetry and prose on all subjects. Only 40 pages so we do have to reject much of what we are sent.

Editor Name(s): Jean Barker/Linda Marshall
Address: 24 Brudenell Road, Leeds, West Yorkshire LS6 1BD
Telephone: 0113 2785893
Mag Frequency: Twice yearly
Subscription: £6 pa
Single Issue: £3
Back Issue: £2.50
Overseas: £7.50
Payment in: £ Sterling
Payable to: Aireings Publication
Inserts accepted: No
Circulation approx: 300
Payment terms to contributors: Free copies
Accept/rejection approx times: Editorials July and January

ALBEDO ONE

Albedo One is Ireland's only current fiction magazine specialising in science fiction, horror and fantasy. It started life as an A5 digest sized magazine and changed to A4 in 1996. It has won 3 European SF Awards, including Best Small Press and Best Publisher. Published regularly since 1993, it has featured stories from Brian Stableford, Anne McCaffrey, Ian McDonald, Gill Alderman, the ubiquitous DF Lewis, Norman Spinrad and Jeff Vandermeer as well as instantly recognisable small press names and new writers. Each issue carries an author interview, extensive book reviews, a comment piece (usually 2000 words) and readers' letters. We are always looking for thoughtful, well-written fiction. Our definition of what constitutes SF, horror and fantasy is extremely broad and we love to see material which pushes at the boundaries. We are also looking for interviews with high profile authors and book reviews. Our comment section is open to anyone who feels they have something to say (we don't need to agree with what they say but we do have to agree that it's worth saying) and the more keenly felt the emotion the better the chances are of publication. To get a real feel for what we are about, other than buying a copy of the magazine, you could visit our website at www.yellowbrickroad.ie/albedo. The site features a selection of stories from past issues plus interviews, book reviews and other wonderful stuff.

Address: Albedo One, 2 Post Road, Lusk, Co Dublin
Reviews to: Robert Neilson, 8 Commons Road, Loughlinstown, Co Dublin
Email: bobn@eircom.net (BOBN)
Website: www.yellowbrickroad.ie/albedo
Mag Frequency: 3 times per year (4 monthly)
Subscription: £12 per 4 issues
Single Issue: £3.50 (incl p&p)
Back Issue: Cover price
Overseas: IR£18 Europe; IR£22 RoW (all airmail)
Payable to: Albedo One
Inserts accepted: No
Circulation approx: 900
Payment terms to contributors: IR£5 per story or artwork used/Comp copy. Best story in issue £25 prize
Accept/rejection approx times: 12 weeks

THE ALCHEMY PRESS

The Alchemy Press was established in 1998 to take an idiosyncratic approach to publishing SF, fantasy and horror - in other words, at the whim of the Editor-in-Chief. So far, four titles have been published , THE PALADIN MANDATES (short story collection) by Mike Chinn; SHADOWS OF LIGHT AND DARK (poetry) by Jo Fletcher; WHERE THE BODIES ARE BURIED (short story collection) by Kim Newman; and SWORDS AGAINST THE MILLENNIUM (Swords and Sorcery anthology) edited by Mike Chinn, with a fifth title, BENEATH THE GROUND (horror stories edited by Joel Lane), in the pipeline. The Alchemy Press has co-produced three of the above books with Airgedlamh Publications and Saladoth Productions. Write, email, or visit our website for further details.

Single issue details: Paladin Mandates £6.00 paperback; Shadows of Light and Dark (signed by author), Neil Gaimen (introduction), Les Edwards and Seamus Ryan (illustrations), Michael Marshall Smith (designer) £12.99 hardcover; Where the Bodies are Buried (signed by author), Peter Atkins (introduction), Sylvia Starshine and Randy Broeker (artists), £17.50 hardcover; Swords against the Millennium £9.95 (paperback) and £25.00 (hardcover signed by editor and contributors: Cherith Baldry, Ramsey Campbell, Adrian Cole, Pauline E Dungate, Anne Gay, Simon R Green, Joel Lane, Paul Lewis, Chris Morgan, Stan Nicholls, Lisanne Norman plus artists David Bezzina, Bob Covington, Jim Pitts).
Address: Peter Coleborn, 46 Oxford Road, Acocks Green, Birmingham B27 6DT
Subs to: Please write/email with ideas first; do not send unsolicited manuscripts
Email: peter@alchemypress.demon.co.uk
Website: http:/www.alchemypress.demon.co.uk
Mag Frequency: Variable
Subscription: No subs
Payable to: The Alchemy Press
Terms: Dealers' rates apply
Circulation approx: 250 - 750 depending on title
Accept/rejection approx times: Please write with ideas first; do not send unsolicited mss

AMBIT

Ambit publishes a wide range of experimental new poetry, short fiction, fine art and illustration, plus a vigorous and stimulating reviews section. Established writers appear alongside up-and-coming new talent and hitherto unpublished writers. Ambit, now funded by the Arts Council of England, was started in 1959 and has been published quarterly without interruption since. Meticulously edited by Martin Bax, Carol Ann Duffy, Henry Graham, J G Ballard, Geoff Nicholson and Mike Foreman; you can expect a consistently exciting and important selection of work in every issue.

Address: 17 Priory Gardens, London N6 5QY
Mag Frequency: Quarterly
Subscription: UK £24 (institution £35)
Single Issue: £6 (institution £9)
Overseas £8/$16 (institution £11/$22)
Back Issue: £10 (institution £12)
Overseas £12/$24 (institution £14/$28)
Overseas: £26/$52 (institution £37/$74)
Payment in: Cheque/PO/Visa/Mastercard
Payable to: Ambit
Inserts accepted: Yes
Terms: £170 per 1000
Circulation approx: 3,000
Payment terms to contributors: £5 per printed page
Accept/rejection approx times: 3 - 4 months

AMERICAN MARKETS NEWSLETTER

Highlights American and international markets accepting articles and stories from writers. Gives press tips, book reviews, writers' tips, guidelines of the month, and readers' letters. Free syndication of articles is offered to all subscribers.

Editor Name(s): Sheila O'Connor
Address: 175 Westland Drive, Glasgow, Scotland G14 9JQ
Telephone: 415 753 6057 (USA)
Fax: 415 753 6057 (USA)
Email: sheila.oconnor@juno.com
Mag Frequency: 10/year
Subscription: £34
Single Issue: £3.95
Overseas: £42
Payment in: £ sterling
Payable to: S O'Connor
Inserts accepted: Yes
Terms: £25 per issue
Advertising Rates: 25p per word
Payment terms to contributors: 3 months sub extension
Accept/rejection approx times: 2 months

AMMONITE

Ammonite has become known for publishing the unexpected, the surprising, the unusual. Contributors stretch their imaginative boundaries when writing for Ammonite. A wealth of new writing imagination beyond the straight rules of the speculative genre. Ammonite brings new dimensions to the thinking of all those who seek the challenge of ideas and images that stir the human mind and spirit to part the veil of mundane, accepted views of reality. Ammonite is presented in A5 format with 36 pages of poetry, fiction and ideas within a decorative art card cover.

Address: Ammonite Publications, 12 Priory Mead, Bruton, Somerset BA10 0DZ
Mag Frequency: Occasional
Subscription: £5
Single Issue: £3
Back Issue: £2.50
Overseas: £8
Payment in: Cheque/IMO/PO/ Discount of 20% of total order value if 5 or more copies ordered
Payable to: Ammonite Publications
Inserts accepted: No
Circulation approx: 200
Payment terms to contributors: 1 free copy
Accept/rejection approx times: 8 weeks

ANGEL EXHAUST

The space, normally 128 pages, is divided equally between poetry and documentation on poetry. We are interested in the realm where formally innovative work overlaps with socially radical ideas, also in Gothic and New Age poetry. We do not publish work comfily snuggled inside the behavioural rules established before 1970. Ideal poets for this magazine would be Allen Fisher, Denise Riley, Maggie O'Sullivan, and JH Prynne. The prose arm aims at making visible the achievements of the British Poetry Revival as the history of the present, via interviews, survey articles, and in-depth reviews of new books. Special issues have been on the schools of Cambridge poetry, and London; an anthology of new poets; art and politics; the history of Cambridge poetry; and Socialist, Northern poetry. Special interests include Scottish informationism, socialist poets of South Wales, Gothic poetry of the Seventies, the Left, the critique of subjectivity, navigating in new information landscapes, the milieu of the text and peripheral or minority traditions, neoprimitivism, sociobiology, the periodization of the past 30 years of style history, and the nincompoop school of poetry. An elite team of reviewers is dedicated to the unswathing of brilliance, the massacre of the insignificant, and the incomprehension of the incomprehensible.

Address: 35 Stewart's Way, Mannden, Nr Bishop's Stortford, Herts CM23 1OR
Mag Frequency: Twice yearly
Subscription: £7
Single Issue: £4
Back Issue: Two for £7, one for £4
Overseas: £9 for a year
Payable to: Angel Exhaust
Inserts accepted: Yes
Circulation approx: 300
Payment terms to contributors: In offprints
Accept/rejection approx times: 1 week

ANSIBLE

Informal newsletter edited by David Langford, covering doings in the science fiction community, primarily in Britain. The first series ran from 1979 to 1987; the current incarnation (2pp A4 each issue) has appeared since 1991. Ansible received Hugo awards - the international SF 'Oscars' - in 1987, 1995, 1996 and 1999. Coverage includes events, meetings, gossip, award results, authors' and publishers' misbehaviour, humorous items of related interest (eg examples of grotesquely bad writing from current SF/fantasy), and whatever else suits the editor's whim. Many noted SF authors have contributed. Ansible may be examined on the web at the site below - no charge.

Editor Name(s): David Langford
Address: 94 London Road, Reading, Berks RGI 5AU
Subs to: SAEs to above address
Fax: 0705 080 1534
Email: ansible@cix.co.uk
Website: http://www.dcs.gla.ac.uk/SF-Archives/Ansible
Mag Frequency: Monthly
Subscription: Free
Single Issue: Send SAE
Back Issue: N/A (available on World Wide Web)
Overseas: US & Australian details on request
Inserts accepted: Flyers for non-commercial, non-profit SF events etc only - by arrangement
Circulation approx: 2600 plus unknown on web
Payment terms to contributors: Free copies and drinks only
Accept/rejection approx times: 1 month

AQUARIUS

A serious poetry magazine bought by individuals and institutions world wide. Has featured work from George Barker to Fay Weldon. This magazine is one of the essential outlets for poetry. The editor likes writers who have bought and studied the style and form of the work published in the magazine.

Editor Name(s): Eddie S Linden
Address: Flat 4, 116 Sutherland Avenue, London W9 2QP
Telephone: 020 7289 4338
Mag Frequency: Yearly
Single Issue: £5 plus 70p p&p
Overseas: $17
Payable to: Aquarius
Inserts accepted: Yes
Terms: £50
Circulation approx: 2000
Payment terms to contributors: By arrangement

THE ARCADIAN

The Arcadian was founded in 1991, and includes editorial, reviews, news, readers' letters, as well as poems and essays. A regular feature is a chronological history of the Poet Laureates, with the work and life of a different incumbent highlighted in each issue. The editor has a blind spot concerning haiku, but otherwise all forms of poetry are considered. However most of the poems accepted tend to come out of a traditional/ mainstream background.

Editor Name(s): Mike Boland
Address: 11 Boxtree Lane, Harrow Weald, Middlesex HA3 6JU
Mag Frequency: Bi-annual
Subscription: £2 per issue
Single Issue: £2
Back Issue: Out of print
Overseas: £2 plus IRC
Payment in: Sterling
Payable to: Mike Boland
Inserts accepted: Yes
Terms: Reciprocal
Circulation approx: Healthy and growing
Payment terms to contributors: 2 free copies of magazine
Accept/rejection approx times: Variable

AREOPAGUS MAGAZINE

Areopagus is an A4-sized 32-page special interest magazine, aimed mainly at Christian writers. Established in 1990, it covers market news and writing events, and focuses on issues which will be of interest to writers of all backgrounds. Published material is sourced exclusively from subscribers, and there is also a subscribers-only competition in each issue, with £28 prizes. Areopagus also publish an annual Guide to (UK) Christian Publications (price £3 from same address).

Editor Name(s): Julian Barritt
Address: The Membership Secretary, Areopagus Magazine, 17 Mayfield, Barnard Castle, Durham, DL12 8EA
Email: jbarritt@areopagus.freeserve.co.uk
Website: http://www.churchnet.org.uk/areopagus/index.html
Mag Frequency: Quarterly
Subscription: £10
Back Issue: £1
Overseas: Europe £12.50/USA $17 - write or email first for postal details/RoW £15
Payment in: Cheque/PO - sterling (UK and non-USA); dollars (USA)
Payable to: Areopagus Publications
Inserts accepted: Yes
Advertising Rates: 10p per word; £4 per half page A4
Circulation approx: 150
Payment terms to contributors: From £3 - £7
Accept/rejection approx times: 2 weeks

ARETÉ

Areté publishes fiction, poetry, reportage, reviews, interviews, drama. Contributors include: T S Eliot, William Golding, Boris Pasternak, Harald Pinter, Patrick Marber, David Lodge, Ian McEwan, William Boyd, Martin Amis, James Fenton, Blake Morrison, Christopher Logue, Christopher Reid, Simon Armitage, Frederic Raphael, Dorothy Gallagher, Rose Tremain, Rosemary Hill, Peter Foster, Peter Morris, Ralph Fiennes, Adam Thorpe and Ben Rice.

Editor Name(s): Craig Raine
Address: 8 New College Lane, Oxford, OX1 3BN
Telephone: 01865 289193
Fax: 01865 289194
Email: craig.raine@new.ox.ac.uk
Website: aretemagazine.com
Mag Frequency: 3 times a year
Subscription: (3 issues) £21 or US $45, Libraries: £30/$50
Single Issue: £7.99
Back Issue: £7.99 plus p&p
Overseas: US $45 Libraries and Institutions: $50
Payment in: Sterling or dollars
Payable to: Arete Magazine
Inserts accepted: No
Advertising Rates: Full Page Ad: £125, Full Page x3 issues: £300
Circulation approx: 2000
Payment terms to contributors: Negotiable
Accept/rejection approx times: One month

ART BEAT READER MAGAZINE

Career overview of pop musicians, jazz and rock stars, writers poets. Reviews of CD and books. Advance information on Agenda Books who publish titles of lesser known stars such as: Mike Bloomfield, Al Kooper, Captain Beefheart, Tom Waits, Nick Drake, Tim Buckley etc. The magazine also updates the books with 'readers' input. The magazine has ten pages at rear with CDs, books, LPs for sale usually 1000 plus items in each issue.

Editor Name(s): Ken Brooks
Address: 54 The Avenue, Andover, Hampshire SP10 3EP
Telephone: 01264 335388
Fax: 01264 335270
Email: Paul@dmac.co.uk
Website: http://www.dmac.co.uk/Agenda.html
Mag Frequency: Quarterly
Subscription: £8
Single Issue: £2
Back Issue: Same
Overseas: Same
Payment in: £ Sterling, US Dollars
Payable to: K Brooks
Inserts accepted: Yes
Advertising Rates: £30 per page
Circulation approx: 500
Payment terms to contributors: 30 days

ASWELLAS

Aswellas, now in its seventh year, aims to give new writers (poetry and prose) a voice alongside the more well known - particularly writers who have an oblique and quirky view of life. We also feature drawings and black and white photographs.

Address: John Steer, 69 Orchard Croft, Harlow, Essex CM20 3BG
Mag Frequency: Yearly
Subscription: £3 per copy
Single Issue: Same
Back Issue: £1.50
Overseas: £4 - £2 Back Issue
Payment in: Sterling cheque
Payable to: West Essex Literary Society
Inserts accepted: No
Circulation approx: Growing all the time
Payment terms to contributors: Free copy of magazine
Accept/rejection approx times: Approx 3 - 4 weeks. Greater favour shown to those who subscribe

B

BACK BRAIN RECLUSE (BBR)

BBR publishes some of the most startling and daring SF currently being written, and has developed a cult following around the world through a policy of emphasising the experimental and uncommercial end of the form. Recent contributors have included Richard Kadrey, Paul Di Filippo, Michael Moorcock, Misha, Don Webb and Mark Rich, as well as many exciting new names making their first professional appearance. 'If you think you know what science fiction looks like, think again' - Covert Culture Sourcebook.

Address: BBR, PO Box 625, Sheffield S1 3GY
Email: magazine@bbr-online.com
Website: www.bbr-online.com/magazine
Mag Frequency: Irregular
Single Issue: UK £4
Payment in: Ireland/USA/Australia enquire with SAE for local agents
Payable to: Chris Reed
Inserts accepted: No
Circulation approx: 3000
Payment terms to contributors: £10 ($15) per 1000 words, on publication
Accept/rejection approx times: 2 months

BAD POETRY QUARTERLY

Bad Poetry Quarterly is a weekly poetry magazine with an open door publishing policy. Submissions are invited from anywhere in the known universe and beyond provided suitable means of replying are supplied (eg SAE, IRCs). Payment to contributors is one complimentary copy. Subscriptions are even more welcome provided payment is in sterling, cheque or PO. Poems can be in any language as long as it is English. We look forward to hearing from everyone. Earthlings are especially welcome as they are currently under-represented among our subscribers/contributors.

Editor Name(s): Gordon Smith
Address: Bad Poetry Quarterly, PO Box 6319, London E11 2EP
Mag Frequency: Weekly
Subscription: 99p plus 1st class stamp or equivalent
Single Issue: 99p plus 1st class stamp
Overseas: 99p plus 50p p&p (sterling only)
Payment in: Sterling - Cheque/PO
Payable to: G Smith
Inserts accepted: Yes
Terms: Swap
Advertising Rates: Full page £80 and pro rata
Circulation approx: 500
Payment terms to contributors: Complimentary copy
Accept/rejection approx times: 4 weeks. Keep a copy - with your name and address on each copy. Thank you

B
BANGMAN

Bangman is a Bang Bang Machine fanzine. Bang Bang Machine were a band that officially existed from 1991-1996. Bangman features photos and articles on the band or inspired by the band! Also covers related themes such as Geek Love (the book!), Freaks (the film!), The Elephant Man (the film!), Dark City (the film!) and any other dark media similar to Bang Bang Machine! Bang Bang Machine's back catalogue is ironically available from Ultimate Records, the record company that caused the band to prematurely split up! Half the band have formed a new band called Bluemouth. Bang Bang Machine were great guitars/vocals/beats! Any info, articles or photos of Bang Bang Machine, Bluemouth or the individual members needed! Hopefully will become a fan club for the band!

Editor Name(s): Leigh Smith
Address: Leigh Smith, 16 Bridge Street, South Quay, Maryport, Cumbria CA15 8AE
Mag Frequency: Now and again!
Subscription: Free!
Single Issue: Free!
Back Issue: Free!
Inserts accepted: No
Circulation approx: 100
Payment terms to contributors: Depends how juicy the contribution is!
Accept/rejection approx times: 1 week

BEAT SCENE

Beat Scene is the magazine about America's Beat Generation. That is writers such as Jack Kerouac, Charles Bukowski, William Burroughs, Allen Ginsberg, Lawrence Ferlinghetti, Harry Crews, Gary Snyder, Hunter S. Thompson, John Fante, Diane di Prima, Kenneth Rexroth, Philip Whalen, Ruth Weiss, Kenneth Patchen and many others. The magazine is a mix of interviews, profiles, features, the jazz, news, reviews, photos. We try and explore the legacy and the ongoing output of the Beats, Michael McClure, Ken Kesey et al. No 35 included some previously unpublished full colour photos of Charles Bukowski at the races from 1979, an interview with Bukowski previously unpublished, articles on William Wantling, Elise Cowen, Leroi Jones, John Fante, William Burroughs and more besides. We are not a poetry magazine but rather consider it a news magazine. We publish in full sized format, full colour covers, 68 pages, with 12 pages of full colour inside. We are now working on issue No 39.

Editor Name(s): Kevin Ring
Address: 27 Court Leet, Binley Woods, Nr Coventry CV3 2JQ
Telephone: 02476 543604
Email: kev@beatscene.freeserve.co.uk
Website: www.beatscene.freeserve.co.uk
Mag Frequency: Quarterly
Subscription: £17 for 5 issues payable to M Ring
Single Issue: £4
Back Issue: £4 in UK
Overseas: $38 for a 5 issue subscription - payable to Mr D Hsu, PO Box 105, Cabin John, Maryland 20818, USA
Inserts accepted: No
Payment terms to contributors: Negotiable
Accept/rejection approx times: 1 week

THE BETTER BOOK COMPANY LIMITED

The company specialises in helping authors to self publish their work. We are not a 'vanity' publisher and we work with our authors honestly and professionally to produce and market books of which both of us can be proud.

Editing, design, print, marketing and distribution are all part of an integrated service. We have had some notable successes.

Editor Name(s): Jude James Garvey
Address: Warblington Lodge, The Gardens, Nr Havant, Hampshire, PO9 2XH
Telephone: 023 9248 1160
Fax: 023 9249 2819

BILL LANCASTER

A twice yearly journal at appox 150 pages devoted to cultural, social and political affairs of Northern England. Described by Ian Jack as Britain's best regional journals recent emphasis on Northern literature and the politics of devolution.

Editor Name(s): Bill Lancaster
Address: Centre for Northern Studies, University of Northumbria, Newcastle upon Tyne, NE1 8ST
Telephone: 0191 227 3738
Fax: 0192 274187
Email: william.lancaster@unn.ac.uk
Mag Frequency: Twice yearly
Subscription: £18 per annum
Single Issue: £8.99
Overseas: £25 per annum
Payment in: Sterling
Payable to: University of Northumbria
Inserts accepted: Yes
Terms: £50
Advertising Rates: £50 per page A5
Circulation approx: 300
Payment terms to contributors: N/A
Accept/rejection approx times: Two months

BISHOP STREET PRESS

We are not a magazine but a small press. We publish religious books with a humorous/ serious slant. Titles include: 'Yours Reverently' (as reviewed in the Daily Telegraph) and the 'Parson Knows' and now 'The Vicar Calls', completing the humourous Parish Notes of the Rev. Oliver Willmott. Further titles published 'Heavy on the Tree' poetry by Brenda Whincup, 'Admiring the View' poetry by Kevin Bamford. 'Makings' by Justinian, an eclectic collection by a Shropshire poet who prefers to remain anonymous, and 'A Nurse from the Hills' by Margaret Jones describing the work and life of a midwife on the hills around Stiperstones. Unsolicited mss, synopsis and ideas welcome, if accompanied by SAE.

Editor Name(s): Mike Willmott
Address: 8 Bishop Street, Shrewsbury SY2 5HA
Telephone: 01743 343718
Fax: 01743 231826
Email: mcbwillmott@lineone.net
Payment in: Sterling
Payable to: Bishop Street Press
Accept/rejection approx times: 3 months

BLACK CAT BOOKS

B

Calling all authors - Black Cat Books need your tales. Authors, become published this year 2000. Send SASE for information on being published with us this year. Black Cat Books need new authors for our 2001 edition, Traveller's Tales 2001. We will accept short stories, on any subject, for this latest edition. Most publishers won't take new authors on. We will give you the chance to see your book in print. Don't worry if you haven't been successful with your tales, we are here to help. Once you have a novel/ short tale, under your belt you can be positive about your new career.

Novels: It is almost impossible for new authors to have their work published, we are making an outlet for you. It is an opportunity for all new authors to be published and read. Over 250,000 faithful followers wordwide! Established since 1994. We are now reading novels for publication later in the year. We work with the authors to produce their book. Do not send in unrequested work, send a SASE first. We are looking forward to seeing your stories and helping you in your new career. The more your stories are seen the better chance you have of being recognised. Don't leave them in a dusty drawer. 191 authors published since 1995. Our 13th Edition Traveller's Tales 2000 out now.

Books recently published - 'A Candle for Rosie', Mark Carter, 'Stranded', Jason Toyn,'Firebrimstone', D B Gregory and 'Whispers' Paul Ward, all copies £6.25 inc post.

Authors do not send in your tales until you receive our reply!

Editor Name(s): Neil Miller
Address: Mount Cottage, Grange Road, St. Michaels, Tenterden, Kent TN30 6EE
Subs to: No unrequested tales please
Mag Frequency: 2-3 a year
Single Issue: £3.25 - £5.75
Overseas: $7
Payment in: UK Cheque/Cash/Postal Orders
Payable to: Neil Miller Publications
Inserts accepted: No
Circulation approx: 3000
Payment terms to contributors: Free copy
Accept/rejection approx times: 2 - 6 - 8 weeks

THE BLACK ROSE

The Black Rose is a UK ONLY quarterly magazine featuring poetry from talented writers both new and accomplished.

Although no payment is made at present, readers vote for their favourite poems and the winning poem receives £10. Each issue also features a free pull-out reviews section.

Poetry of all styles, up to a maximum of 80 lines will be considered for publication, both published and un-published and from subscribers and non-subscribers alike.

Reviews and material to be reviewed are also welcome.
Editor Name(s): Bonita Hall
Address: 56 Marlescroft Way, Loughton, Essex, IG10 3NA
Email: CoolVamp@btinternet.com
Website: http://expage.com/blackrosepoetry
Mag Frequency: Quarterly
Subscription: £8 per annum
Single Issue: £2.50
Overseas: Not available overseas
Payment in: Cheque
Payable to: Miss B Hall
Inserts accepted: Yes
Terms: Free, but no larger than A5 (fold A4 sheets in half)
Advertising Rates: Free, reciprocal advert appreciated if possible
Circulation approx: Around 100
Payment terms to contributors: None, but each issue awards £10 + free copy of magazine for Readers' vote winner. All published reviews also earn a free copy of magazine.
Accept/rejection approx times: Usually within one week, always within three

BLADE

Now in its sixth year. Poetry and reviews of clarity and incisive nature. Occasional free supplement with news and extra reviews. Editorial-based, each issue attacks and explores different facets of the UK poetry scene. 56 average pages. New and well-known names. No-one sensitive to strong criticism should submit work. 'One of Britain's gutsiest poetry magazines' - Neil Astley. 'I both admire and am provoked by its ebullience' - G Allnutt, Poetry Review. Magazine currently on go-slow while editor (Jane Holland) is at university.

Editor Name(s): Jane Holland
Address: 'Maynrys', Glen Chass, Port St Mary, Isle of Man IM9 5PN
Mag Frequency: No set frequency/irregular
Subscription: No sub
Single Issue: £5
Back Issue: £3
Overseas: £15 Sterling
Payment in: Cash or IMO
Payable to: Blade Press
Inserts accepted: No
Circulation approx: 170-200
Payment terms to contributors: 1 copy
Accept/rejection approx times: Up to 6 months

BLITHE SPIRIT - Journal of the British Haiku Society

Journal containing original haiku, senryn, tanka, renga in English, with learned articles in this field. Published by The British Haiku Society, it accepts only haiku and haiku-related material from members of the society. We welcome diverse statements about the writing and appreciation of haiku as well as poetry, on the understanding that none of the work submitted is under consideration elsewhere. Please provide publication details of any item submitted which has already appeared in print.

Editor Name(s): Colin Blundell
Address: Colin Blundell, Longholm, Wingland, Sutton Bridge, Spalding, Lincs, PE12 9YS
Subs to: Arwyn Evans, 13 Ty Brachty Terrace, Kendon, Crumlin, Gwent, NP1 4BU
Mag Frequency: Quarterly
Subscription: £20 pa Society membership/£16 magazine only
Single Issue: £4
Back Issue: Some years £3.50
Overseas: £26 (US $40) Society membership/£20 (US $30) magazine only
Payment in: Sterling/US bills
Payable to: The British Haiku Society
Inserts accepted: No
Advertising Rates: No ads
Circulation approx: 500
Payment terms to contributors: None
Accept/rejection approx times: 1 month

BOGG

Uses contemporary poetry, short prose, articles, reviews, letters, graphics. It is actually an American publication. George Cairncross is purely the British editor.

Address: John Elsberg, 422 N Cleveland Street, Arlington VA 22201 USA/George Cairncross, 31 Belle Vue Street, Filey, North Yorkshire YO14 9HU
Mag Frequency: Irregular
Subscription: £8
Single Issue: £3.00
Back Issue: £2.50
Overseas: $12 (US)
Payment in: Cheque or Postal Order
Payable to: George Cairncross
Inserts accepted: No
Circulation approx: 700
Payment terms to contributors: Two free copies of magazine
Accept/rejection approx times: As soon as possible

BORDERLINES

Magazine published by Anglo-Welsh Poetry Society, a group founded to promote poetry in the Marches/Welsh border area. Open to contributions from anyone. No axe to grind. The editors say 'We try not to have preconceived ideas about what poetry should be and try to be catholic in our choice of material - more instinctive than analytical. We are aware of needing to maintain a reasonable standard while providing encouragement where possible. We always seem to end up with a magazine with plenty of variety, a generally high standard and some first class material.' Orbis said, 'This excellent magazine lives up to everything the editors say about it.' Peter Finch says, 'Well worth the £1.50 asked for it.'

Editor Name(s): Dave Bingham/Kevin Bamford
Address: Nant y Brithyll, Llangynyw, Welshpool, Powys SY21 OJS
Telephone: 01938 810263
Mag Frequency: Twice yearly
Subscription: £3
Single Issue: £1.50
Overseas: £5
Payment in: Sterling IMO
Payable to: Anglo-Welsh Poetry Society
Inserts accepted: Yes
Terms: Negotiable
Circulation approx: Print run 200
Payment terms to contributors: Complimentary copy of magazine

BRANDO'S HAT

A5 format, 44 pages. Poetry only. Groups of poems by individual writers, poetry sequences or slightly longer individual poems. The standard is high and authors are encouraged to read the magazine before submitting.

Editor Name(s): Seán Body, Francesca Pridham, Steven Waling
Address: Flat 1a, 17 Mauldepth Road, Manchester, M20 4NE
Telephone: 0161 792 4593
Fax: Same as phone
Email: tarantulapubs@lineone.net
Mag Frequency: 3 times a year
Subscription: Annual subscription £10 (p&p free) (3 issues)
Single Issue: £4 incl p&p
Overseas: Europe + £1.30, RoW + £2.50
Payment in: Sterling only
Payable to: Tarantula Publications
Inserts accepted: Yes
Terms: Free on exchange basis
Advertising Rates: £20 full page, £10 half page, £30 back cover
Circulation approx: 250
Payment terms to contributors: Complimentary copy
Accept/rejection approx times: 1 - 3 months

B

BRAQUEMARD

Like all magazines, Braquemard has its own distinctive flavour, and it is obviously best to see a copy before submitting. There are no style limitations - I have used sonnets, villanelles, haiku etc as well as free verse. I try to avoid politics, explicit religion, ecology and PC attitudes; I like bad taste, black humour and the sick side of human nature. Quality, however is the watchword - tastelessness is not a substitute for talent. Short story writers should be just that, very short, no more than 1000 words; some issues are poetry only because of a dearth of excellent micro-fictions. These notes are by no means limiting - they are more a hint at editorial prejudices and obsessions. Basically, if I like it and it fits then a piece stands a pretty good chance of being accepted, even if it has been published elsewhere. My advice to contributors is: send me your best. Correspondence should always include an SAE, as no reply can be given if this is omitted. I also strongly recommend that each item carry the name and address of the author to avoid filing system confusion and catastrophe. E-mail submissions are acceptable.

Editor Name(s): David Allenby
Address: 20 Terry Street, Hull HU3 1UD
Email: braquemard@hotmail.com
Website: www.braquemard.fsnet.co.uk
Mag Frequency: Twice yearly (in theory)
Subscription: £5 per 2 issues
Single Issue: £2.90 (incl p&p)
Back Issue: £1.50
Overseas: £8 subs, £5 single
Payment in: Sterling cheques
Payable to: David Allenby
Inserts accepted: Yes
Terms: On application
Circulation approx: 200
Payment terms to contributors: Copy of the magazine
Accept/rejection approx times: Up to 6 months

BREAKFAST ALL DAY

Breakfast All Day, aka BAD, is now a bi-annual magazine of fiction, comment, poetry, humour, cartoons and graphics, drawing contributions from Britain, mainland Europe and North America. A4, 90-100pp, perfect bound, black and white pages, coloured cover. We publish short fiction (up to 4000 words), poetry (maximum 50 lines), articles (up to 1500 words, any subject matter, but preferably with an original viewpoint, or humorous slant. Articles on art, language, and social issues are especially welcome, but they shouldn't depend on topicality). Fillers, short items, interesting quotations. Cartoons, comic strips, line illustrations and black and white photographs very welcome. Written contributions should be in clear black typescript on white paper, or saved as an ASCII file on a 3.5" disk. Line art and cartoons should be sent as good quality photocopies. Contributions should be accompanied by one or more IRCs. We do not usually return manuscripts unless particularly requested, in which case sufficient return postage must be sent. Send £4.50 for a sample issue by post.

Editor Name(s): Philip Boxall, Mary Wraight
Address: 43 Kingsdown House, Amhurst Road, London E8 2AS or 4 rue Bonne Nouvelle, 76200, Dieppe, France
Fax: +33 (0)2 35 40 33 26
Email: boxall@badpress.com
Website: www.badpress.com
Mag Frequency: Bi-annual
Subscription: £7.50
Single Issue: £3.90
Overseas: US $20 / Europe £9
Payment in: Sterling cheques, or cash in any major currency
Payable to: BAD Press
Inserts accepted: Selectively
Terms: By arrangement
Advertising Rates: £50 per page, and pro rata
Circulation approx: 500
Payment terms to contributors: 1 free copy of magazine
Accept/rejection approx times: 2-3 months

B

BREATHE POETRY MAGAZINE

Founded August 2000, Breathe has quickly gained recognition as a quality small press poetry magazine. Submissions are on-going for poetry and poetry related articles. Breathe also features one cartoonist per issue. Reviews by commission only. All submissions must be clearly typed and sent with a SAE for reply.

Payment - Subscribers - receive their usual one copy of the magazine plus inclusion in the Reader's Favourite Poem vote. If a subscriber is chosen as the winner of the Favourite Poem Vote of a particular issue, they receive the prize of £12.50
Non subscribers - receive one complementary copy of the magazine plus inclusion in the Reader's Favourite Poem Vote of a particular issue, they receive the prize of £7.50

Editor Name(s): Mrs Sharon Sweet
Address: C/O 2 Grimshoe Road, Downham Market, Norfolk, PE38 9RA
Email: breathemag@email.com
Website: www.breathepoetry.co.uk
Mag Frequency: Bi-monthly
Subscription: £10.00 (6 issues)
Single Issue: £2.00
Overseas: On application
Payment in: £ sterling by cheque or postal order
Payable to: S Sweet
Inserts accepted: Yes
Terms: Subscribers only
Advertising Rates: N/A
Circulation approx: 100

THE BRITISH FANTASY SOCIETY NEWSLETTER

There is a group of people who know all the latest publishing news and comment. They enjoy the very best in fiction from some of the hottest new talents around. They can read articles by and about their favourite British Fantasy Society. Foremost amongst the BFS's publications is the acclaimed Newsletter. Published on a bi-monthly schedule, it contains genre news, exclusives, publication information, interviews, features and other items of interest to members. The Newsletter also contains informed book reviews, and reviews of all other genre-related material including films, magazines, fanzines, small press magazines, television and radio productions, video and much more. There are regular celebrity columns, members' letters, artwork and lots more besides. Members also receive magazines of fiction and comment as well as occasional 'specials.' These have included free BFS-published/funded paperback books. Members also receive discounted attendance to the BFS' FantasyCon event. The BFS is dedicated to genre works of all ages, so accepts material on authors old and new, classic and forgotten, popular and unknown. The BFS enjoys the patronage and participation of many established authors, artists and journalists. The BFS' own publications are regularly looked to by editors when selecting material for numerous 'Best Of' anthologies and numerous members have gone on to become published authors in their own right. FantasyCon is the convention organised by the BFS. Guests and attendees travel from around the world to take part, meet old friends and make new ones. Recent Guests of Honour have included Christopher Fowler, Graham Joyce, Raymond Feist, Robert Rankin, Graham Masterton, Mike Tucker and Louise Cooper.

Address: The Retreat, Barry, Angus DD7 7RP
Subs to: 201 Reddish Road, Stockport SK5 7HR
Mag Frequency: Bi-monthly
Subscription: £20 UK - £25 Europe - £40 RoW
Back Issue: Write for details
Payable to: The BFS, 201 Reddish Road, Stockport SK5 7HR
Inserts accepted: Yes
Terms: £60 per mailing (plus pro rata postage if insert pushes rate up)
Circulation approx: 500 and rising steadily
Payment terms to contributors: Complimentary copy of work
Accept/rejection approx times: Variable - ideally 1 month from receipt

B

BRITTLE STAR

Now in our 2nd year - we publish poetry and short stories, under 2000 words, which we feel perhaps would not get published in other magazines. We are looking for stuff with an edge - new and different - but nothing too weird.

Editor Name(s): Nigel Kemp, Sue Richmond, Cathy Jeffries, Jo Ward, Ray Wilmot
Address: 73 Lyal Road, London, E3
Email: brittlestar@poetic.co.uk and susrichands@yahoo.co.uk
Mag Frequency: Twice a year
Subscription: £5.00 for year inc postage
Single Issue: £2.00
Payable to: Brittle Star
Circulation approx: 100
Payment terms to contributors: None
Accept/rejection approx times: 3 - 5 months

BUZZWORDS

'The title helps sum up the entertaining content and the magazine has attracted international contributions - In short a newcomer which should cause a stir in the Small Press world and set it humming.' Carole Baldock - Orbis.

'Well thought out, full of helpful advice... a seriously intentioned though light-heartedly produced magazine.' Ann Stanbury - Writers Bulletin.

BuzzWords is a relatively new magazine, born out of the BuzzWords '99 Short Story and Poetry competition. Our tag line is BuzzWords wants you and your writing. That says it all. Our aim is to offer new writers the opportunity to see their work published alongside more established writers, many of whom are subscribers.

We're on the lookout for fresh and original fiction and poetry, and also feature topical interviews and articles of interest to writers. Since our inception, our circle of contributors and readers has grown, and we have featured work from across Europe, America, Canada and India.

We would always advise would-be contributors to see an issue of BuzzWords, and our contributors' guidelines before submitting. Preference will be given to subscribers. Please enclose SAE with all queries.

Editor Name(s): Zoë King
Address: Calvers Farm, Thelveton, Diss, Norfolk IP21 4NG
Email: zoeking@calversfarm.fsnet.co.uk
Website: www.buzzwordsmagazine.co.uk
Mag Frequency: Bi-monthly
Subscription: £18 pa
Single Issue: £3
Overseas: £23
Payment in: Sterling Cheques/POs only please for UK and Europe, but contact me for US agent details where applicable
Payable to: Calvers Farm
Inserts accepted: Yes
Terms: Reciprocal
Advertising Rates: Lineage ads free, other prices on application
Circulation approx: Growing
Payment terms to contributors: Two copies of relevant magazine. Payment position regularly reviewed
Accept/rejection approx times: 2-3 months, but please be patient as my aim is never to send out a rejection slip without advice as to how pieces might be brought to publishable standard

C

CADENZA

A new quarterly magazine publishing the winning entries in the Focus on Fiction short story competition as well as short stories, articles, poetry, interviews and markets of interest to fiction writers. Cadenza is A5 format, perfect bound with glossy cover, and 80 pages of content.

Editor, Jo Good, is looking for unique 'voices' - writers who can produce cracking, vibrant prose who aren't afraid to take risks. Inventive use of language is important. Word limit is 4,000 words for stories. Fiona Curnow is the poetry editor. Poems up to 40 lines.

Editor Name(s): Jo Good
Address: PO Box 1768, Rugby CV21 4ZA
Telephone: 01788 334302
Fax: 01788 334702
Email: jo.good@dtn.ntl.com
Mag Frequency: Quarterly
Subscription: £15.50 (4 issues), £7 (2 issues)
Single Issue: £3.95
Back Issue: £2 UK (£2.75 Europe / £3 RoW)
Overseas: £17 Europe (4 issues), £18 RoW (4 issues), £7.50 Europe (2 issues), £8 RoW (2 issues)
Payment in: UK Sterling, cash, postal orders, cheques
Payable to: Focus on Fiction
Inserts accepted: Yes
Terms: Negotiable
Advertising Rates: Negotiable
Payment terms to contributors: Voucher copies
Accept/rejection approx times: 2 months

CALABASH

'...full of interesting and valuable information...' - Senior Marketing Executive, Longmans. 'We all here are highly impressed with Calabash!' - Prof. Markham, Sheffield University. Calabash aims to be an information provider for those interested in literature by writers of African and Asian descent and writers from these cultural backgrounds. Calabash is a free A3 black and white newsletter published 2 times a year. 5000 copies are distributed comprehensively throughout London using the library distribution service as well as targeted arts venues in the capital, writing organisations publishers and academic institutions within and outside London. This profile gives it a substantial readership ration 6:1.

Editor Name(s): Editors change each issue, Contact: C Johnson
Address: Calabash, Centerprise, 136-138 Kingsland High Street, London E8 2NS
Telephone: 020 7254 9632 x 214
Fax: 020 7923 1951
Email: cath.centerlit@care4free.net
Mag Frequency: 3 times a year
Single Issue: Free
Overseas: Postage only
Payment in: Stamps
Payable to: Centerprise Trust Ltd
Inserts accepted: No
Advertising Rates: Phone for details
Circulation approx: 3000 - 5000
Accept/rejection approx times: No more than 8 weeks

CAMBRENSIS

A quarterly magazine, founded 1988, devoted solely to short stories by writers born or resident in Wales; no payment offered other than writers' copies; short stories under 2500 words; only other material used - book reviews and features of Anglo-Welsh literary interest; art-work, mainly cartoon and line-drawings by Welsh artists; SAE with submissions or IRC with overseas inquiries; not more than one manuscript at one time; the magazine is supported by The Arts Council of Wales.

Address: 41 Heol Fach, Cornelly, Bridgend, CF33 4LN
Telephone: 01656 741 994
Mag Frequency: Quarterly: Spring/Summer/Autumn/Winter
Subscription: £6 for year's 4 issues, post paid
Single Issue: £1.50 post paid
Back Issue: £1.50 (some available)
Overseas: Via Blackwell's Periodicals, Oxford or Swets & Zeitlinger BV, PO Box 800, 2160 Lisse, Holland
Payment in: Overseas: Sterling via these two companies
Payable to: Cambrensis Magazine
Inserts accepted: Yes
Terms: Negotiable
Circulation approx: Print run 450
Payment terms to contributors: Copies to writers
Accept/rejection approx times: By return of post mainly

C

CANDELABRUM POETRY MAGAZINE

CPM is Britain's longest established Traditionalist fringe poetry publication. For authors offering work:- Please note that there are two yearly numbers, and space is eagerly competed for; so that accepted work almost never appears in the issue immediately following the date of acceptance. A5 saddle-stitched 40pp; established 1970. Preference for metrical and rhymed poetry, but free verse not excluded. English 5/7/ 5 haiku accepted. Any subject but NB no racialist, sexist or ageist matter. SAE essential. Overseas poets IRC and self addressed envelope. NB IRC must be stamped on the left side by the issuing post office. 'A magazine of well-crafted poetry, and not one a dud' New Hope International. 'Well crafted writing' 10th Muse.

Editor Name(s): Leonard McCarthy
Address: 9 Milner Road, Wisbech, Cambs PE13 2LR
Email: rcp@poetry7.fsnet.co.uk
Mag Frequency: Twice yearly (April and October)
Subscription: £13.50 Volume 10 (2000-01); and for Volume 11 (2002-04)
Single Issue: £2.50
Overseas: US $27 the volume - single copy US $5
Payment in: British: Cheque/PO; USA & Canada: US $ bills only - no cheques
Payable to: The Red Candle Press
Inserts accepted: No
Circulation approx: 900
Payment terms to contributors: Complimentary copy
Accept/rejection approx times: 8 weeks

CARILLON MAGAZINE

A new, A5 40+ pages containing short stories, poetry, articles, and a prize competition. Writing Groups' news, comment and submissions.

Requirements: Stories/articles/fillers to a maximum of 1200 words. Poetry to maximum of 32 lines. Articles must be factually correct with sources acknowledged. Submissions: Single sided, typed on A4 white paper. Include a stamped self-addressed envelope. Subscribers will be made for unpublished items, initially at the following rates: Stories/Articles: £1.00 - £2.00 according to length (rates will be increased as circulation grows).

Not required: 'Bad' Language, pornography, anything socially offensive, cliched writing and unreadable texts.

Editor Name(s): Graham Rippon
Address: 19 Godric Drive, Brinsworth, Rotherham, South Yorks, S60 5AN
Website: http://www.carillonmag.org.uk
Mag Frequency: Three per calender year
Subscription: 3 issues £7.25 + 60p postage
Single Issue: £2.50 + 30p postage
Payment in: Cheques/POs payable to Carillon Magazine

CENCRASTUS

Cencrastus covers Scottish and international literature, arts and affairs. Submission of articles, short stories, poetry and reviews welcomed speculatively, payment by negotiation. Editor: Raymond Ross; Managing Editor: Richard Moore. The magazine was first published in 1979 and takes its name from the Curly Snake, the Celtic serpent of wisdom, the symbol of energy and infinity as embraced by Hugh MacDiarmid in his poem 'To Cicumjack Cencrastus'. The magazine also took its international motto - 'If there is ocht in Scotland that's worth ha'en/There is nae distance to which it's unattached' - from the same poem. Cencrastus is at the cutting edge of literary, artistic and political affairs. The magazine constantly publishes unseen material from established writers and new writers.

Editor Name(s): Raymond Ross, Editor, reviews and subs to Kate Kelman, Managing Editor
Address: Cencrastus, Unit 1 Abbeymount Techbase, 2 Easter Road, Edinburgh EH8 8EJ
Fax: 0131 661 5687
Mag Frequency: Three times a year
Subscription: £12 (4 issues) £15 (institutions)
Single Issue: £2.95
Overseas: £15 (4 issues) £17 (institutions)
Payment in: In advance
Payable to: Cencrastus
Inserts accepted: Yes
Terms: Negotiable
Circulation approx: 2000
Payment terms to contributors: Negotiable
Accept/rejection approx times: Approx 6-8 Weeks

C

A CHANGE OF ZINERY ON-LINE

Peterborough Science Fiction Club's website at www.btinternet.com/~c.ayres/ psf.htm and part of this is the online fanzine A Change of Zinery. We post SF, fantasy and horror short stories and poetry. We tend to use work from the Peterborough area (North Cambridgeshire, East Northamptonshire, Rutland, South Lincolnshire and West Norfolk), though this has flexible boundaries. Check out the site first and ask the Site Manager (Chris Ayres) about submitting on either disk, down the wire or in hardcopy. We are especially interested in using pieces that have previously been printed elsewhere due to the very nature of the internet.

Address: 58 Pennington, Orton Goldhay, Peterborough PE2 5RB
Website: www.btinternet.com/~c.ayres/psf.htm
Mag Frequency: Constantly updated
Payment terms to contributors: None

C

CHAOTIC ORDER

Started in April 1999 Chaotic Order was first envisaged as a publication to promote such underground media as the Cinema of Transgression, and has since grown to become a reflection of all alternative culture, stretching through film, music, art, fiction and culture. With respected contributors such as Jack Sargeant, Rik Rawling, Richio Johnson, Bob Rosen, Martin Jones, Gary Simmons and many others. Chaotic Order has become a respected publication going beyond it's relatively small print run. New issues are set to include an ever wider range of subject matter although I have now limited the print run to allow a more personally controlled approach. NO poetry though... Bob Smith - editor

Editor Name(s): Bob Smith
Address: 15 Digby Close, Doddington Park, Lincoln, LN6 3PZ
Email: bob@chaoticorder.freeserve.co.uk
Website: www.insound.com/zinestand/co
Mag Frequency: Thrice yearly (February, July, October)
Subscription: £5.00 for 3 issues (1 year)
Single Issue: £2.00/$3.50
Back Issue: Issues 10/11 - £2.00/$3.50, issues 8/9 - £1.50/$2.50
Overseas: $10.00 for 3 issues (1 year)
Payment in: UK - cheques/PO's made payable to 'Chaotic Order', cash sent at own risk. Overseas: Cheques drawn on UK banks as above, cash in US Dollars or Pound Sterling only sent at own risk.
Payable to: Chaotic Order
Inserts accepted: No
Advertising Rates: £20/£30/£50 for quarter, half and full pages respectively. Trades welcome.
Circulation approx: 500
Payment terms to contributors: There are no strict payment terms, complimentary copies of completed issues are available as are trades for advertising (where relevant), otherwise just forward your ideas.
Accept/rejection approx times: Within a week

C

CHAPMAN

Chapman is Scotland's leading literary magazine, controversial, influential, outspoken and intelligent. Founded in 1970, it has become a dynamic force in Scottish culture, covering theatre, politics, language, and the arts. Our highly-respected forum for poetry, fiction, criticism, review and debate is essential reading for anyone interested in contemporary Scotland. Chapman publishes the best in Scottish writing - new work by well-known Scottish writers in the context of lucid critical discussion. With our strong commitment to the future, we energetically promote new writers, new ideas and approaches. Several issues have been landmarks in their field, in Scots language, women's writing, cultural politics in Scotland, and we have published extensive features on important writers: Hugh MacDiarmid, Tom Scott, Iain Crichton Smith, Ian Hamilton Finley, Alasdair Gray, Naomi Mitchison, Hamish Henderson, Jessie Kesson, to name but a few. We also publish poetry and short fiction by up-and-coming writers, as well as critical articles, book reviews and items of general cultural interest. Our coverage includes theatre, music, visual arts, language, and other matters from time to time. Each issue includes Scots and Gaelic, as well as English although most of the work is in English. Although the focus is on Scotland, Chapman has a long history of publishing international literature, both in English by non-Scots and in translation from other languages. Chapman will interest anyone researching British and Scottish literature. It has a natural outlet in universities and institutions of secondary education. With its emphasis on new creative writing, it is of interest to anyone with a love of literature. We also publish poetry collections and plays under the heading of Chapman Publishing. Our New Writing Series is dedicated to giving first publications to promising young writers. The Theatre Series brings the best of Scottish theatre before a wider audience.

Editor Name(s): Joy Hendry
Address: 4 Broughton Place, Edinburgh EH1 3RX
Telephone: 0131 557 2207
Fax: 0131 556 9565
Email: editor@chapman-pub.co.uk
Website: www.chapman-pub.co.uk
Mag Frequency: 3 x P.A.
Subscription: £17
Single Issue: £5.50 inc p&p
Back Issue: £4.00 inc p&p
Overseas: £23
Payment in: Cheque/PO/IMO
Payable to: Chapman
Inserts accepted: Yes
Terms: £50 per 1000
Circulation approx: 2000
Payment terms to contributors: Copies
Accept/rejection approx times: 1-3 months

CINEMA EXHIBITOR

A quarterly publication for the British and European exhibition industry which exists to publish news, insights and current opinion on issues affecting all aspects of cinema exhibition for Britain and Europe under a single banner. Cinema Exhibitor is aimed at cinema management at all levels, also projection room and technical staff, wether actively or otherwise employed or involved within the cinema exhibition, film distribution seasons, also entertainment architects, cinema suppliers and members of film and cinema societies interested in architecture, projection, showmanship and nostalgia.

Editor Name(s): Philp Turner
Address: PO Box 144, Orpington, Kent, BR6 6LZ
Telephone: 01689 833117
Fax: 01689 833117
Email: TBA
Website: TBA
Mag Frequency: Quarterly
Single Issue: £5.00
Back Issue: £5.00
Overseas: £28
Payment in: Sterling
Payable to: The Knolic Press
Inserts accepted: Yes
Advertising Rates: TBC
Circulation approx: Est 40,000+
Payment terms to contributors: To be negotiated
Accept/rejection approx times: TBC

$\mathcal{C}$
THE COFFEE HOUSE

The Coffee House is a meeting place for the arts. The Coffee House is Charnwood's international journal of poetry, short prose and visual art. The only manifesto held by the journal concerns the concept of giving a platform to fresh, well-wrought pieces. 'They publish poems with meaning and feeling, poems that move the reader...' (Barry Tebb, Poetry Now Newsletter).

Editor Name(s): Deborah Tyler-Bennett
Address: Charnwood Arts, Loughborough Library, 31 Granby Street, Loughborough, Leics LE11 3DU
Telephone: 01509 822558
Fax: 01509 822559
Email: charnwood.arts@virgin.net
Website: www.cuttlefish.com/charnwood-arts
Mag Frequency: 2 x year (spring/autumn)
Subscription: £8.50 for 4, £4.50 for 2
Single Issue: £2.50
Back Issue: £2.50
Overseas: Add postage (International Coupon)
Payment in: Sterling
Payable to: Charnwood Arts
Inserts accepted: Yes
Terms: 1 page of A5
Advertising Rates: Negotiable
Circulation approx: 300
Payment terms to contributors: Free copy of relevant journal
Accept/rejection approx times: One month

C

COMPETITIONS BULLETIN

Up to date details of UK (and some other) writing competitions: short stories; poetry; plays; collections... you name it, we list it. Competition organisers send details to the editor. Listing is free. Approx £100,000 prize money up for grabs in each issue.

Editor Name(s): Carole Baldock
Address: 17 Greenhaw Ave, West Kirby, Wirral, CH48 5EL
Telephone: 0151 625 1446
Email: carolebaldock@hotmail.com
Website: www.cherrybite.co.uk
Mag Frequency: Bi-monthly
Subscription: £2 per issue
Single Issue: £2
Overseas: Add 50p Eur. add £1 Row
Payment in: Sterling in Dollar Bills
Payable to: Cherrybite Publications, 45 Burton Road, Little Neston, Chesire, CH64 4AE
Inserts accepted: Yes
Terms: Reciprocal
Advertising Rates: Lineage is free. £20 per full page
Circulation approx: 500 +

C

CONNECTIONS

Connections publishes new work - articles, short stories (up to 2500 words), poetry - anything to do with writing matters including reviews, letters, information on events and competitions. There are also articles from professional writers, and we hold our own annual competitions each year. We welcome submissions from the UK and abroad but we do advise those wanting to send work to us to see a copy of the magazine first.

Editor Name(s): David Shields
Address: Gambia, 2 Ship Street, Aberaeron, Ceredigion, SA46 0RS
Mag Frequency: 4 a year
Subscription: £9.50
Single Issue: £3.25
Back Issue: £2.50
Overseas: £14
Payment in: Overseas - IRCs
Payable to: Connections
Inserts accepted: Yes
Advertising Rates: £50 back cover/£25 half/£20 quarter inside pages
Circulation approx: 350
Payment terms to contributors: Over 1000 words £10/under £5 plus complimentary copy (unsolicited). Solicited by arrangement
Accept/rejection approx times: 6 weeks

CORRIDOR PRESS

Corridor Press is a voluntary, non-profit making Community publisher which 'opens doors to peoples stories and poems' in Berkshire. Founded in 1992, its major publications have included a book about food - 'See it, Want It, Have It!' One about Buildings in Reading 'Bricks and Mortals' and the story of Football in Reading 'Moments of Glory'. More recent books have included stories of gardens and gardeners in Berkshire. 'A Book of Cuttings'; traditional remedies from far and wide 'Potions and Notions'; and a millenium topic - people and music in Berkshire 'Airs and Places'. School and Community groups anthologies have been interspersed between these along with the publishing of local individual poets' work. During the past year, Corrider Press has moved to new premises, courtesy of Berkshire County Blind Society, with which it hopes to produce some Talking Books.

Editor Name(s): Daphne Barnes-Phillips
Address: Midleton House, 5 Erleigh Road, Reading, Berkshire, RG1 5LR
Telephone: 0118 987 2017
Email: corridorpress@yahoo.co.uk

C

COUNTRYSIDE TALES

Countryside Tales is a Quarterly magazine containing short stories on any subject but preferebly with a rural setting. Articles and poetry about the countryside are also welcome. Regular competitions are held with cash prizes. The magazine is in A5 format and illustrated with line drawings. The usual writer's guidelines apply, but further details may be obtained by sending an SAE to the editorial address or by telephoning for a chat about your work. We publish two small mags - 'Scribble' and 'Countryside Tales'. We hold several writing competitions every year, (2002 over £600.00 of prizes). An anthology is published each year containing the shortlisted stories in an annual themed competition. Details of all of our competitions can be obtained by sending an SAE to the editorial address or by logging on to our website.

Editor Name(s): David Howarth
Address: Park Publications, 14 The Park, Stow On The Wold, Cheltenham, Glos GL54 1DX
Telephone: 01451 831053
Email: parkpub14@hotmail.com
Website: www.parkpublications.co.uk
Mag Frequency: Quarterly
Subscription: £10 (4 issues incl p&p)
Single Issue: £3 (incl p&p)
Back Issue: £2 (incl p&p)
Overseas: As above
Payment in: Sterling
Payable to: D Howarth
Inserts accepted: Yes
Terms: Usually free
Advertising Rates: Negotiable
Circulation approx: 2000+ magazines sold per annum
Payment terms to contributors: Cash prizes
Accept/rejection approx times: 2 weeks

CREATIVE WOMEN'S NETWORK JOURNAL & WEBSITE

Material accepted: We accept articles, advertising, stories, poetry and information on anything relevant to creative women (see below).
*Make friends and contacts*Learn how others do it*Share experiences, ideas and tips*Exchange/advertise your services*Give and receive support.

The journal and web site cover the following subjects:

Women for creative living, the arts, design, crafts, publications writing, novels, stories and poetry, getting out there, being reclusive, expression, career, home and family, self-employment, exchanging services, voluntary work, health and fitness, travel, study, spirituality, courses, advice, living your art, new possibilities, psychology and personal development, sharing personal experiences, teaching and learning, helping others,cross-culture, being a mother and not, women's roles - challenging them, understanding them, transforming business, unique women, inspiring women - words to share, challenging the norm, down shifting, up-grading, being human, living the ideal, seeing the extraordinary in the everyday.

Where possible, please e-mail submissions, typing and pasting into an e-mail document. No attachments please. All writing must be of good quality and acceptance for publication is at the editor's discretion.

Members of the Creative Women's Network receive free web and journal advertising (up to two ads of 40 words each, with extra space for address/contact details), plus a copy of our inspiring journal, every six months - and lots of other advantages. See our web site for more details plus details on our special free introductory advertising offer.

Note: Web link exchanges welcome!
Editor Name(s): Jane Reid
Address: 5 Grosvenor Close, Great Sankey, Warrington, Chesire, WA5 1XQ
Telephone: 01925 574476
Email: CWN@themutual.net
Website: www.creativewomensnetwork.co.uk
Mag Frequency: Journal published twice yearly
Subscription: Membership of network and to receive journal is $15 per year
Payment in: Sterling
Payable to: Jane Reid

C

CRIMEWAVE

Modern crime fiction gives writers the freedom to discuss ideas, to create characters and explore locations, and above all to investigate human psychology and society. The genre is broader in scope than others, humour, horror, satire, escapism and political analysis are all encompassed in crime fiction and Crimewave aims to cover the entire territory, from the misnamed 'cosy' to the deceptively subtle 'hardboiled'. Every issue contains stories by authors who are household names in the crime fiction world (Ian Rankin, Julian Rathbone, Maureen O'Brien, Michael Z Lewin, etc), but we also constantly find room for lesser-known or even unknown writers. The magazine is beautifully designed in a unique and colourful B5 format, with at least 132 pages per issue.

'Crimewave offers the best in cutting-edge crime fiction and delivers it in a sleek, slick package that is a pleasure to see and hold.' Ed Gorman, Mystery Scene.

Editor Name(s): Mat Coward, Andy Cox
Address: TTA Press, 5 Martins Lane, Witcham, Ely, Cambs CB6 2LB
Telephone: 01353 777931
Email: ttapress@aol.com
Website: http://www.tta-press.freewire.co.uk
Mag Frequency: Quarterly
Subscription: £22 (4 issues)
Single Issue: £6
Overseas: Europe £7/£24; USA $12/$40; RoW £8/£28
Payment in: Cheque/PO/Eurocheque, etc
Payable to: TTA Press
Inserts accepted: Yes
Terms: Negotiable
Advertising Rates: Query with SAE
Payment terms to contributors: Contract on acceptance, payment on publication
Accept/rejection approx times: 6 weeks

CURLEW

A5. Founded 1975. Contributors from Britain and America. Poetry, fiction, reviews, graphics. Contributors please note: authors' own originals used in production process so accepted mss not available for return. Publishes without grants or Arts Council money.

Editor Name(s): Jocelynne Precious
Address: Hare Cottage, Kettlesing, Harrogate HG3 2LB
Mag Frequency: 1-2 a year approximately
Subscription: £1.50
Single Issue: £1.50
Back Issue: On request
Overseas: £5 (no dollars or US cheques)
Payment in: English Sterling only
Payable to: P J Precious
Inserts accepted: Yes
Terms: Negotiable
Advertising Rates: Free
Circulation approx: Small
Payment terms to contributors: One complimentary copy
Accept/rejection approx times: From return of post up to 3 months

C

CURRENT ACCOUNTS

Features work by members of Bank Street Writers alongside poetry and prose by outside contributors. Previously unpublished work is preferred. No restriction on subject matter apart from usual considerations of taste and decency. Previous contributors include M R Peacocke, Pat Winslow and Gerald England. Please read a copy before submitting work!

Address: 16-18 Mill Lane, Horwich, Bolton BL6 6AT
Email: rodriesco@cs.com
Mag Frequency: 2 per year
Subscription: £4
Single Issue: £2.00
Overseas: £6.00
Payment in: Sterling cheque/PO/cash
Payable to: Bank Street Writers
Inserts accepted: Yes
Terms: Free
Circulation approx: 50 plus
Payment terms to contributors: Free copy of magazine
Accept/rejection approx times: 1 month

C

CUSTARD PIE - The Magazine of Funny Stuff

Fresh, light, genuinely funny and flavour-filled magazine. Contains the very best cartoons, poems, short stories and oddments. Some of the humour is dark, some is risqué. Comments: 'Had me in hysterics'... 'Excellent magazine'... 'Try this one for size'... 'It did tickle the old funny bone.'

Editor Name(s): Jason Ingham
Address: 76c Granville Road, Finchley, London N12 0HT
Mag Frequency: Annual
Subscription: £4 for 2 issues
Single Issue: £2.20
Overseas: Plus IRC if outside EU
Payment in: Cheque/PO
Payable to: Jason Ingham
Inserts accepted: Yes
Terms: Negotiable
Advertising Rates: Negotiable
Payment terms to contributors: Copy of magazine
Accept/rejection approx times: 1 month

C

CUTTING TEETH

Cutting Teeth is a magazine of new writing by a mixture of well established and previously unpublished writers. High profile Scottish names such as Edwin Morgan and Janet Paisley as well as international writers such as Alan Kauffman from USA and Hwang Suk Yong from Korea have featured alongside newcomers. Three issues are published each year, edited and produced by the Arts and Cultural Development Office. Contributions to Cutting Teeth are now received from throughout the world.

Editor Name(s): John Ferry
Address: 17b Castlemilk Arcade, Castlemilk, Glasgow G45 9AA
Telephone: 0141 634 2603
Fax: 0141 631 1484
Email: info@fringemedia.co.uk
Website: www.fringemedia.co.uk
Mag Frequency: 3 per year
Subscription: £7.50
Single Issue: £2.50
Back Issue: £2.50 inc p&p
Overseas: £3.50 inc p&p
Payable to: Cutting Teeth Literature Magazine
Inserts accepted: Yes
Advertising Rates: Available on request
Circulation approx: UK wide and USA
Payment terms to contributors: £15 per short story, £5 per poem
Accept/rejection approx times: Up to 6 months (back log!)

DADAMAG

Whether or not Dadamag exists is of course without question.

To ask yourself why, you need to understand how the random tossing of a coin or roll of some dice can result in a division of results.

When you have achieved that, you are ready to operate diverse results from a uniform action.

From Dadamag non-general thesis vol ix.

Address: PO Box 472, Norwich NR3 3TS
Mag Frequency: Sometimes, perhaps
Subscription: N/A will vary
Single Issue: N/A
Payment in: ££'s/cheques/PO only
Payable to: W L Walker
Accept/rejection approx times: Don't send unsolicited work. Enquiries only for now with SAE

DANDELION ARTS MAGAZINE

Dandelion Arts Magazine is an international non-profit making publication created and founded in 1978 in London by Jacqueline Gonzalez-Marina who has been the publisher ever since. Its aims have always been to provide an outlet for poets, journalists and illustrators world-wide. Contributions are welcome but subscription is a must if seeking publication. All submissions should be accompanied by a SAE. Personal advice will be gladly given on an individual basis.

Editor Name(s): Jacqueline Gonzalez-Marina
Address: Fern Publications, Casa Alba, 24 Frosty Hollow, East Hunsbury, Northants NN4 0SY
Fax: 01604 701730
Mag Frequency: Bi-annual
Subscription: £12 UK
Single Issue: Half subscription cost
Back Issue: Half subscription cost
Overseas: £18 Europe/£20 RoW
Payment in: Sterling by cheque, bankers draft or postal order
Payable to: J Gonzalez-Marina
Inserts accepted: Yes
Terms: £8 per 100/£80 per 1000
Advertising Rates: It varies according to text or photos included. Request of an estimate is desirable
Circulation approx: About 1000
Payment terms to contributors: No payment given, just the publicity and advice
Accept/rejection approx times: 2 weeks

DARK HORIZONS

Dark Horizons is the journal of the British Fantasy Society. It publishes a mix of fiction (stories and poetry) and non-fiction, covering all aspects of fantasy, horror and SF. The definitions of these three words are as wide as the authors' imaginations - although we tend not to publish gratuitous matter for its own sake. A story can be of any style, but ultimately it must entertain. In the past, Dark Horizons has published material by professionals (such as Ramsey Campbell, Thomas Ligotti and Storm Constatine) and non-professionals. Although we do publish poetry, only a few poems are included each issue. We encourage new writers. Dark Horizons also publishes artwork, ranging from that produced to illustrate specific stories and articles, to 'spot' pieces.

Editor Name(s): Peter Colborn, Mike Chinn, Helen Knibb
Address: British Fantasy Society, 201 Reddish Road, South Reddish, Stockport SK5 7HR
Subs to: 2 Harwood Street, Stockport, Cheshire SK4 1JJ
Email: peter@alchemypress.demon.co.uk
Website: www.geocities.com/SoHo/6859
Mag Frequency: 1-2 times a year
Subscription: £20 in UK
Single Issue: £4-£6 depending on issue
Back Issue: £3-£4
Overseas: £30
Payable to: The British Fantasy Society
Inserts accepted: Yes
Terms: £25 min depending on size etc
Advertising Rates: £25 minimum for small press, more for professionals
Circulation approx: 500-600
Payment terms to contributors: Contributor copies
Accept/rejection approx times: Varies

DATA DUMP

This publication gathers and disseminates information on genre poetry - science fiction poetry as a priority, but also fantasy and horror. Topics covered include new collections/anthologies, articles on the field, early work, novels incorporating poetry, poetry in fantasies, humorous SF poetry, SF poetry on the net, picturesque/human-data, SF poetry in unusual settings (media, film, opera, radio). Aim is an ongoing update on the field, plus a backfill of its past, with a preponderance of attention to the UK but some coverage of USA, Australia, Europe etc. Information on any of these topics welcomed/credited. Otherwise no unsolicited MSS. Original poetry is not sought.

Editor Name(s): S Sneyd
Address: 4 Nowell Place, Almondbury, Huddersfield, West Yorkshire HD5 8PB
Mag Frequency: 6 Monthly (approximately)
Subscription: See payment details
Single Issue: 70p incl p&p
Back Issue: Ordinary issues - photostat reprints only. Special double issues, send SAE for details
Overseas: Individual copies US $2 cash or small denomination (50¢ or less) US stamps to that amount. For Special Issue prices enquire with SAE/IRC. Distribution in USA by NSFA
Payment in: No advance subscriptions as price/format may vary, but those wanting each copy as produced can place a 'till cancelled' order and pay for each issue when received
Payable to: S Sneyd
Inserts accepted: Yes
Terms: Exchange basis by prior arrangement
Circulation approx: 100
Payment terms to contributors: None
Accept/rejection approx times: No MSS accepted as such. Information of relevance welcomed, and as and when included, source acknowledged

DAY BY DAY

Founded 1963, Day By Day is a news commentary, digest of national and international affairs and review of the arts, independent of all major political parties, with an emphasis on non-violence and social justice. Anti-war and anti-racialist, it is concerned about conservation, pollution, cruelty to animals, the arms trade, poverty, unemployment, world debt, homelessness and moral and civilised values. It publishes short poems, reports cricket, reviews exhibitions, films, plays, opera and musicals. It very rarely publishes short stories. No illustrations. Reviews books on art, cricket and other sport, current affairs, economics, education, films, conservation, music, history, politics, religion, peace, non-violence, literature, war etc. Unsolicited manuscripts must be accompanied by a SAE. It is worth studying an issue or two first, since we like outside contributions to harmonise with the spirit of our editorials. Manuscripts cannot be considered if they are not accompanied by a stamped, addressed envelope.

Editor Name(s): Patrick Richards, Poetry and Reviews Editor: Michael Gibson, News Editor: Ronald Mallone
Address: Woolacombe House, 141 Woolacombe Road, Blackheath, London SE3 8QP
Telephone: 020 8856 6249
Mag Frequency: Monthly
Subscription: £11.60 in UK
Single Issue: 95p
Overseas: Europe £18/USA and RoW $28
Payment in: Sterling Cheque, International Money Order or Eurocheque
Payable to: Day By Day
Advertising Rates: Only small ads 50p per word
Circulation approx: 25,000

DIAL 174

An A5-size magazine of 60 plus pages with A4-sized large print version available. Wide variety: poetry, short fiction, articles, travelogues, book reviews, news. Artwork accepted, printed in colour, specially when accompanying and enhancing submissions. Resident artists illustrate suitable submissions for featuring on the cover or as centre pages spread. The editor's policy: to help and encourage those deriving pleasure from writing and reading the writing of others. Debate on the art of writing and social issues derives from the content of submissions, articles and readers' letters. Dial involves itself with charity work, including: discretionary free subscription or reduced rates to those not so 'financially fortunate', so mention your circumstances if you wish to be considered and would like to belong to this 'literary family'. The magazine reaches a wider audience than mere subscription, being on permanent display at the South Bank Centre Poetry Library, universities in the USA - and it is free to establishments such as schools and prison education departments. It also produces anthologies and books featuring selected subscribers.

Editor Name(s): Joseph Hemmings
Address: 21 Mill Road, Watlington, King's Lynn, Norfolk PE33 0HH
Telephone: 01533 811949
Mag Frequency: Quarterly
Subscription: £12 (£16 A4 format)
Single Issue: £3 (£4 A4 format)
Overseas: £16 or $30
Payment in: PO/Cheque/IMO/sterling, dollar, DM notes
Payable to: Dial 174
Inserts accepted: Yes
Terms: Exchange basis
Advertising Rates: Exchange basis
Circulation approx: 400
Payment terms to contributors: None (non-funded/non-profit)
Accept/rejection approx times: See 'publishing policy' sent with info pack

THE DRAGON CHRONICLE

The Dragon Chronicle founded in 1993 by Ade Dimmick. New Editor Kevin Matthews. Special interest journal dedicated entirely to dragons in all their forms and aspects. Features dragon-related and dragon-inspired myth, magic, paganism, astrology, folklore, fantasy, spirituality and tradition. Plus artwork and poetry. A dracophile's delight!

Editor Name(s): Kevin Matthews
Address: Dragonslair, 106 Oakridge Road, High Wycombe, Bucks HP11 2PL
Mag Frequency: 3 times a year
Subscription: £8 per 4 issues
Single Issue: £2.50
Overseas: $30/$8 Single Issue
Payment in: UK: cheques to Dragonslair / Overseas: cash only - dollars or sterling
Payable to: Dragonslair
Inserts accepted: Yes
Terms: Free to dragon-orientated flyers from subscribers/supporters
Advertising Rates: Upon request
Circulation approx: 100
Payment terms to contributors: Articles/features/poems/illustrations - free copy
Accept/rejection approx times: Generally acknowledged by return

D

DRAGON'S BREATH

The International Small Press review and independent monthly newsletter. Here's why you should subscribe... 'Comments definitely not sycophantic' - Dreamberry Wine / 'Well worth checking out' - ByPass / 'Handy and useful for budding writers and the like' - Monas Hieroglyphica / 'Micro reviews... wide net' - Fans Across the World / 'Genuine enthusiasm for the subject' - A Riot of Emotions / 'Stuffed with close-typed punchy reviews' - The Wizard's Knob / 'Reviews of the latest issues of most popular zines' - Sierra Heaven / 'Can be quite scathing... but useful and informative' - NHI Review / 'Densely packed with a swift content overview and Zine Kat's wry observations' - The BBR Directory / 'Information-dense, essential, and free' - Matrix / 'Does sterling service to the genre' - BFS Newsletter / 'Brings you sharp reviews of (the) Small Press' - Zine Zone / 'Comment on lots of magazines, excellent taster' - Iota / 'Pulls no punches so you can tell which is overpriced junk and which is good value... Try one - it's compellingly intriguing' - Krax / 'Gives you the rundown on many of the Small Press mags around. Always frank, never unfair' - Monas Hieroglyphica / 'Beware, the dragon doesn't pull its punches!' - The Doppelganger Broadsheet / 'Essential monthly roundup... Masses of info... Well worth £2.50' - Fanzine Fanatique / 'Listings and reviews... devoted to... popular esteric topics. Weird and wonderful' - Earthsongs.

Address: Zine Kat, c/o Pigasus Press, 13 Hazely Combe, Arreton, Isle Of Wight PO30 3AJ
Subs to: Tony Lee at Pigasus Press
Mag Frequency: Monthly
Subscription: £2.50
Single Issue: Sample free for SAE
Overseas: 1 IRC per issue
Payment in: Cheque/PO
Payable to: Tony Lee
Inserts accepted: Yes
Terms: See advertising rates
Advertising Rates: Available on request - send SAE/IRC
Circulation approx: Unknown
Payment terms to contributors: N/A
Accept/rejection approx times: N/A

DREAM CATCHER

Since its 1996 beginings Dream Catcher has grown to a twice yearly, perfectly bound eighty page magazine, committed to portraying the eclecticism of modern culture. Our policy is to welcome every literary style from minuature to film script. Motivated editors, with diverse expertise in poetry, prose and photography (b/w artwork, colour for cover is also considered) ensure the magazine's quality and that each submission is properly considered. Dream Catcher though focused on Britain increasingly receives works from international writers, particularly from Canada. This underlines the magazine's commitment to cultural diversity.

Editor Name(s): Paul Sutherland, Co-ordinator: Joe Warner, Eds: Chris Firth (fiction) Ian Parks (poetry)
Address: 9 Berkeley Drive, Lincoln,LN6 8BN. Address: 32 Queens Road, Barnetby-le-Wold, North Lincolnshire, DN38 6JH
Telephone: Co-ordinators number 0771 812 5880
Email: paul_sutherlanden-kesteven.gov.uk
Website: www.openingline.co.uk/magazines/dreamcatcher
Mag Frequency: Twice yearly, summer and winter issues
Subscription: £8 per year
Single Issue: £3.60 (plus 80p p&p)
Back Issue: 5 & 6 issues: £4, discount rates for back issue with present
Overseas: Europe £10, Canada and USA £16/Aust and Jap £17
Payment in: Sterling, Can dollars, US dollars
Payable to: Dream Catcher Literary Arts
Inserts accepted: Yes
Terms: £40 per insert
Advertising Rates: ¼ page £15, ½ page £40, whole page £75, inside cover £80, outside back cover £100
Circulation approx: 500 copies per issue
Payment terms to contributors: A free copy of issue in which they appear

THE DREAM ZONE

The Dream Zone is A4 in size and perfect bound and contains short stories of a dark bizarre nature.

Editor Name(s): Paul Bradshaw
Address: 44 Knowles View, Holmewood Estate, Bradford, BD4 9AH
Email: thedreamzone@btinternet.com
Mag Frequency: Triannual
Subscription: £7.50 for 3 issues
Single Issue: £3.00
Back Issue: Sold out
Overseas: $7.00 per copy
Payment in: Cheque, overseas cash only
Payable to: Paul Bradshaw
Inserts accepted: No
Advertising Rates: Reciprocal
Payment terms to contributors: Payment in copy
Accept/rejection approx times: 1 - 2 weeksAccept/rejection approx times: 4-6 months

EASTERN RAINBOW

Eastern Rainbow is a magazine which focuses on 20th century culture via poetry, prose and art. Will appeal to a wide range. Has featured Elvis Presley, Marilyn Monroe, George Best, Martin Luther King, George Orwell, Star Trek, Dr Who, The Prisoner, etc, in the past. Looking for enthusiastic work, but not hero-worshipping, deification of celebrities/TV programmes/films, etc. We also run poetry competitions and forms are available for an SAE/IRC. Full guidelines for contributions are available for an SAE/IRC.

Address: 17 Farrow Road, Whaplode Drove, Spalding, Lincs PE12 OTS
Email: peaceandfreedom@lineone.net
Website: http://website.lineone.net/~peaceandfreedom/
Mag Frequency: Once yearly
Subscription: £7.50 for 4 issues
Single Issue: £1.75
Back Issue: £1
Overseas: $16
Payment in: UK cheque/PO; Overseas IMO/banknotes
Payable to: Peace & Freedom
Inserts accepted: Yes
Terms: £20/$50 per 1000. Free to magazines who are willing to exchange circs
Circulation approx: 300
Payment terms to contributors: Free issue of magazine when work is published
Accept/rejection approx times: Less than 3 months

E
ECLIPSE POETRY MAGAZINE

Non-genre poetry magazine aimed at bringing new and untried poets into print. All forms of poetry accepted on any subject. All work is read and acknowledged. SAE must be supplied with all submissions.

Editor Name(s): Elizabeth Boyd
Address: Everyman Press, 53 West Vale, Neston, Chesire, CH64 9SE
Mag Frequency: Bi-monthly
Subscription: £3.00 per issue
Single Issue: £3 UK
Back Issue: £2.00
Overseas: £3.50 Europe, £4.00 RoW
Payment in: £ sterling
Payable to: Everyman Press
Inserts accepted: Yes
Terms: By arrangement
Advertising Rates: By arrangement
Payment terms to contributors: None - £25 for readers vote 'Best Poem'
Accept/rejection approx times: One month

ÉCORCHÉ
(Also DESCORCHE and RICOCHET)

écorché favours works whose avant-garde character is rooted in a violent collision with reality. Issue one included Bataille, Buck, Savitzkaya etc; issue 2 and interview with Kathy Acker and works from Noël, Mor and many others; issue 3 is devoted to the work of Paul Green while following issues, under the new title Descorche, will concentrate entirely on work from Latin America. A further offshoot will be the booklet-publishing press Ricochet, to begin with a limited edition publication of poems by Elizabeth Bletsoe. The magazine does not accept unsolicited material.

Editor Name(s): Ian Taylor
Address: 17 Eastfield, Thornford, Nr Sherborne, Dorset DT9 6PU
Mag Frequency: Irregular
Subscription: £10 for 2 issues
Single Issue: £5
Overseas: $10 incl p&p
Payment in: Cheque
Payable to: Ian Taylor
Inserts accepted: No
Circulation approx: 200
Payment terms to contributors: Free copy of issue
Accept/rejection approx times: Not applicable - unsolicited material not accepted

E

THE EDGE

The Edge is A4, at least 64 pages, designed by John Coulthart. The Edge discerningly publishes fiction, interviews, reviews, articles (book, film, video, music, the 'arts'). We've published a wide range of fiction. For example: Stephen Baxter, Steve Beard, Simon Clark, Christopher Fowler, Michael Moorcock, Alan Moore, Joyce Carol Oates, Kate Orman, Chris Petit, Nicholas Royle, James Sallis, Iain Sinclair and others; so high standards, but there's always space for new names.

We're looking for modern, unusual, experimental, interesting stories of any length (not novellas or novels). We want fiction that could be described as horror/fantasy/sf, slipstream, crime, erotica, cross-genre, transgressive; please note: we don't like cliches, and experimental work is welcome. Please send one story at a time.

If you want to write features or reviews for us, please send a sample of your work, published or unpublished. Our interviews tend to be long (up to 20,000 words). Please note that we've never published an unsolicited review.

Interior or cover artwork is no longer required. Comic strips (various lengths, not cartoons) may be considered. No poetry, please. We take the first rights only, so no reprints or simultaneous submissions, also please don't send submissions on disk or by email.

Return postage is essential with enquiries or mss (the only exception is if you want a reply by email, which we'll do to save you postage). UK: a stamped, self-addressed envelope for the return of your work and/or a reply. Europe/Republic of Ireland: 1 International Reply Coupon (an IRC) and disposable work, or as per the UK. (British stamps only...) USA/Australia/RoW: Disposable work with 2 IRCs or $2 (US, cash), or as per the UK (you need 64p in British stamps on a business sized envelope). All replies are sent by air mail.

Editor Name(s): Graham Evans
Address: The Edge, 65 Guinness Buildings, Fulham Palace Road, London W6 8BD
Telephone/Fax: 020 7460 9444
Email: grahamevans@lineone.net
Website: www.users.globalnet.co.uk/~houghtong/edge.htm
Mag Frequency: Quarterly
Subscription: £12 (4 issues), £7 (2 issues) (Sent post free)
Single Issue: £3.50 (this is the cover price)
Overseas: Europe: £4 one issue, £12 for 4, £8 for 2, USA: $7 one issue, $25 for 4, $14 for 2, RoW pay US prices or enquire for details
Payment in: US cheques or cash, Eurocheques, British cheques or cash, IMOs; or you can pay by cheque in most currencies, but send 2 IRCs or email for details
Payable to: The Edge
Inserts accepted: Yes
Terms: Enquire
Advertising Rates: £250 per page. Smaller sizes available at a substantial discount for small press publishers. Exchanges considered
Payment terms to contributors: Professional, negotiable (up to £60 per thousand words)
Accept/rejection approx times: Always within 3 weeks of receipt, usually within one week

EDIBLE SOCIETY

A web-based magazine presenting short stories, poetry collections (some with RealAudio sound), featured poetry and an art gallery. It publishes quality writing with hypertext and pictures, all attractively and accessibly designed. A creative newspaper is planned, inspired by the surrealist magazines of the 1930s, incorporating a personalised 'art trail' and video. Potential contributors must please view the site first, to see if their work is likely to be suitable, and read the submissions guidelines at the foot of the front page of the relevant section. The magazine is part of Black Cat Communications' multi-art website - hundreds of web pagges devoted to a 21st century art with vision and heart

Editor Name(s): Peter Frazer
Email: edsoc@threeface.co.uk
Website: http://www.threeface.co.uk/blackcat/edsoc
Mag Frequency: Updated regularly
Subscription: Send email to request site update notification
Single Issue: The price of local phone calls to your ISP.
Overseas: Local phone calls, request update notification by email
Inserts accepted: Art and literature links and information accepted
Terms: Links and information must be relevant
Advertising Rates: £50 per banner per quarter
Circulation approx: Unlimited
Payment terms to contributors: Inclusion in prestigious site
Accept/rejection approx times: Less than a month, sometimes a week

E
EDINBURGH REVIEW

This acclaimed literary and cultural review publishes a wide range of original and topical material with a new emphasis on the literary by both new and established writers. Lively, controversial and eclectic, Edinburgh Review is the only forum which positively asserts the rich diversity of Scottish arts and culture while attending to international literary and cultural events.

Editor Name(s): Alex Thomson
Address: Edinburgh Review, 22a Buccleuch Place, Edinburgh EH8 9LN
Telephone: 0131 651 1415
Email: Edinburgh.Review@ed.ac.uk
Mag Frequency: 3 times a year
Subscription: Individual £17/Institution £34
Single Issue: £6
Back Issue: £5
Payable to: Edinburgh Review
Inserts accepted: Yes
Terms: £135
Circulation approx: 800
Payment terms to contributors: By negotiation
Accept/rejection approx times: 3 months

EDUCATION NOW NEWS AND REVIEW

'News and Review' is the quarterley magazine/newsletter of the Education Now Publishing Co-operative LTD' which is a not-for-profit group devoted to promoting a more flexible, humane, democratic learning system with the slogan of 'alternatives for everybody, all the time'. A catalogue of books published is also available.

Editor Name(s): Paul Stanbrook, Mary Ann Rose, Roland Meighan, Janet Meighan, Chris Shute
Address: Education Now, 113 Arundel Drive, Bramcote Hills, Nottingham, NG9 3FQ
Telephone: 0115 925 7261
Fax: (Office) 0115 925 7261
Email: psi@btconnect.com
Website: www.gn.apc.org/educationnow
Mag Frequency: Quarterly
Subscription: £20 per annum (10 for non-waged)
Single Issue: £2.50
Back Issue: £5
Overseas: £20 per annum
Payment in: Sterling
Payable to: Education Now
Inserts accepted: Yes
Terms: £25 if 500 copies are supplied
Advertising Rates: No adverts! Inserts only
Circulation approx: 500
Payment terms to contributors: None
Accept/rejection approx times: One month

E

EM WRITING AND MUSIC

The latest issue of em writing and music consisits of over 250 pages of sudden fiction and a CD of eclectic music.

'threaded with keynotes of strung-out delicacy and vivid ingenuity, it can effortlessly transport the reader to avenues... em is still the real deal: startling fragments of expression scrapped together into a clever reflection of the pic and mix mash of contemporary culture.' Tina Jackson, The Big Issue

'a bang-on collision of music, prose and poetry, its intentions and content cannot be praised too highly' Jockeyslut

'great stories and an absolutely ace tape... eclectisism is the key' Nick Royle, Time Out

'A superb forum for new (and not so new) writers and musicians... em one is essential.' Muzik

Editor Name(s): Karl Sinfield
Address: PO Box 10553, London, N1 2GD
Email: karl@emwritingandmusic.com
Website: http://www.emwritingandmusic.com
Mag Frequency: infrequent - >2 years per issue
Subscription: N/A
Single Issue: $10 US
Overseas: $10 US + p&p
Payment in: (only available online)
Payable to: (only available online)
Circulation approx: 500

E

ENVOI

Current editor Roger Elkin. Subscription brings you * 176 pages each issue * Groups of poems (up to 8) by any one writer * Long(er) poems, over 40 lines of most magazine * Sequences, or extracts from longer sequences * Poems in collaboration * Poems in translation * First Publication feature for new writers * Articles on poetry, creativity and style * Competition and Adjudicator's Report each issue * Comparative reviews of current poetry publications * Letters and Comment* Free critical comment (3 poems per year) on request * And oodles of poems.

Editor Name(s): Roger Elkin
Address: 44 Rudyard Road, Biddulph Moor, Stoke-on Trent ST8 7JN
Mag Frequency: 3 issues per annum (Feb; June; Oct)
Subscription: £15 per annum
Single Issue: £5
Back Issue: Sample £3
Overseas: £20 or $40 pa/current copy £5 or $10
Payment in: Preferably in US dollar bills if sterling not available
Payable to: Envoi
Inserts accepted: Yes
Terms: £50 per 1000
Circulation approx: 800-1000
Payment terms to contributors: 2 complimentary copies
Accept/rejection approx times: 6-8 weeks

E
EPOCH

Epoch (founded 1991) features Scottish material in the context of European and world literature and art. Epoch is open to politics, philosophy, poetry. Leading article is usually on a major figure in Scottish literature (eg RB Cunninghame Grahame) plus articles on European artists (eg Goya) and writers (eg Victor Serge). Liberal/socialist ethos but not dogmatic - have carried articles on Nietszche in the past!

Editor Name(s): Neil Mathers
Address: 57 Murray Street, Montrose, Angus, Scotland DD10 8JZ
Telephone: 01674 672625
Mag Frequency: Depending on funds
Subscription: £9 for 5 issues
Single Issue: £2
Overseas: £20 Europe/America
Payment in: IMO/Sterling cheque/PO; foreign currencies must allow for exchange charge
Payable to: The Corbie Press
Inserts accepted: Yes
Terms: Free if reciprocated
Advertising Rates: Send for details
Circulation approx: 300 (increasing)
Payment terms to contributors: 1 copy
Accept/rejection approx times: Poetry only accepted from subscribers, but there is always a shortage of articles. Decision time about 6-10 weeks

EPOCH POETRY REVIEW

EPR is the sister publication of Epoch, totally devoted to poetry. The emphasis is on poetry from Scotland, but not exclusively. Prelim letter advised as there is always a glut of material for the editor. Also carries one article about poetry. The magazine is free to subcribers of Epoch (see separate entry).

Editor Name(s): Neil Mathers
Address: 57 Murray Street, Montrose, Angus DD10 8JZ
Telephone: 01674 672625
Mag Frequency: Depending on funds
Subscription: £4 for 5 issues
Single Issue: £1
Back Issue: £1
Overseas: £12 Europe/America
Payment in: IMO/Sterling cheque/PO allow for exchange charge
Payable to: The Corbie Press
Inserts accepted: Yes
Terms: Free if reciprocated
Advertising Rates: Send for details
Circulation approx: 300 (increasing)
Payment terms to contributors: 1 free copy
Accept/rejection approx times: 6-10 weeks

E
ERATICA

The Eratica began as a forum for Brighton Writers, but in its second issue expanded into perfect-bound and Europe-bound horizons. Initially a periodical for poetry and fiction, we welcome articles on music and the arts, 8pp of colour plates are included. The first new issue concentrates on the new Bavarian poetry, poetry of the 1940's, including unpublished poems by Vita Sackville-West, Drummond Allison, Michael Hamburger. There's a focus on modernism and non-mainstream poetry, music, painting- Alan Bush and Xenakis. Our taste is as catholic as the title suggests, the editors themselves both tend to the innovative that doesn't marginalise itself in ritual gardisms. Originality that can burn one's fingers is more fun, and needs less surgery. The poetry of one editor, Simon Jenner, is accused of density by lovers of the accessible, and accessible by some modernists as a term of abuse. He has two volumes out in Germany, and reckons he must have got the balance about right. At 270pp, we're more of a shelf life journal than mag, and cost reflects production! Pamphlet of Waterloo Press available SAE on request.

Editor Name(s): Dr Simon Jenner
Address: 51 Waterloo Street, Hove, Sussex BN3 1AH
Telephone: 01273 202876
Mag Frequency: Bi-annually
Subscription: £12 per issue
Single Issue: £12
Back Issue: Sold out
Payment in: Pounds Sterling
Payable to: Waterloo Press
Advertising Rates: £25 per half page
Circulation approx: 500
Payment terms to contributors: None
Accept/rejection approx times: Submissions: Please phone first - I tend to write friendly longish rejection letters and would find it easier over the phone! my BBC broadcasting poem surgery experience! Rejections: Attempt by return of post, and fail.

ESCAPED

Escaped is the regular magazine for members and supporters of Escape. Escape is a cutting edge campaign group which works for the freedom of animals, humans and the earth. Escape operates peaceful and legal public education campaigns, aimed at exposing and fighting against animal abuse, erosion of civil liberties, medical fraud and dangerous foods. Each issue of Escaped complements the Escape campaign work with in-depth articles about Escape's work, alternative health, animal liberation and other issues. Escaped is the magazine for the informed intelligent campaigner with the latest news, views, contacts and light-hearted features. Escaped - until all are free.

Address: Escaped Magazine, @ Escape, PO Box 2801 Brighton BN1 3NH
Mag Frequency: Quarterly
Subscription: £5 as membership of Escape campaign group
Single Issue: £1.50
Overseas: Overseas members £8 subscription
Payment in: Cheque/PO/Cash at own risk
Payable to: Escape
Inserts accepted: Yes subject to approval
Terms: Donation to Escape
Circulation approx: 260 copies currently increasing
Payment terms to contributors: No payment
Accept/rejection approx times: Replies within 1 month

Ɛ
ETHERIC REALMS

'Etheric Realms' incorporates 'Inner Sanctum Publications' and 'Living Sound Publications'. We publish works of a spiritual nature in the form of the written word and audio.

'There is a land suspended between Heaven and Earth, wherein all things are possible and all truth is told. This sacred domain is called The Etheric Realms and encompasses the wealth of mystical teaching, music and the written word. It is accessible through the many portals of our magazine and is blessed in the light and purity of the living spirit.'

Editor Name(s): Mary Hession
Address: Inner Sanctum Publications, 75 Greenleaf Gardens, Polegate, East Sussex, BN26 6PQ
Telephone: 01323 484058
Email: maryeethericrealms.com
Website: http://www.etericrealms.com
Mag Frequency: on line magazine continuosly updating
Inserts accepted: Yes
Terms: Inserts accepted provided that they are in harmony with our existing publications.
Advertising Rates: Free (if accepted)
Circulation approx: World wide
Accept/rejection approx times: ASAP

EXILE

Now in its 12th year, Exile promotes contemporary poetry, with an emphasis on new poets.
Contributions should be limited to 40 lines in English, with SAE. We hold occassional poetry competitions, with proceeds to local charities. Exile also reviews new poetry books, which are always welcome. We have recently expanded to the web, and will gradually include each issue in .pdf format, which may be downloaded free.

Editor Name(s): John Marr, Ann Elliott
Address: 1 Armstrong Close, Hundon, Suffolk CO10 8HD
Telephone: 01440 786937
Email: exile@2from.com
Website: http://www.2from.com/exile
Mag Frequency: Quarterly
Subscription: £8 for 4 issues (incl p&p)
Single Issue: £2.50 (incl p&p)
Back Issue: £2.50, as available
Overseas: £10 (incl p&p)
Payment in: UK £
Payable to: Exile
Inserts accepted: Yes
Terms: Free
Advertising Rates: None
Circulation approx: 300
Payment terms to contributors: No payment, free copy
Accept/rejection approx times: 6 months

F
FABRIC

Fabric welcomes poems from new and established writers. Submissions (up to a maximum of 5 poems) can be made by post (SAE required) or by email. The first issue includes work by poets from the UK, Canada, Japan, Samoa and elsewhere. Past contibutors include Ted Walters, Justin Hill and David Greig. The editor has a preference for shorter poems and for those of a whimsical, literary or urbane nature in either conventional or experimental forms.

Editor Name(s): M. Hogan
Address: 93 Holmdene Avenue, London, SE24 9LD
Email: fabricpoetry@aol.com
Mag Frequency: 1-2 times a year
Subscription: £4 per issue
Payment in: Sterling only
Payable to: M. Hogan
Circulation approx: 100 and growing
Payment terms to contributors: One complimentery copy
Accept/rejection approx times: 2-4 weeks

F

FACTS & FICTION

The magazine for everyone interested in oral stories and storytelling. F&F concentrates on the ancient art of oral storytelling with bias towards traditional stories but including storytelling in education; as a means of self expression and discovery; as a healing art and so on... We regularly feature interviews with tellers; news; views; reviews etc.

Editor Name(s): Pete Castle
Address: Facts & Fiction, c/o 190 Burton Road, Derby DE1 1TQ
Telephone: 01332 346399
Email: steelcarpet@lineone.net
Mag Frequency: Quarterly
Subscription: £10
Single Issue: £2.50
Back Issue: £1.50
Overseas: £11 Europe/£15 RoW
Payment in: £ Sterling only
Payable to: Steel Carpet Music
Inserts accepted: Yes
Terms: Enquire
Advertising Rates: £25 per A4 page pro rata
Circulation approx: 250 but growing
Payment terms to contributors: Nil

𝓕
THE FAIRACRES CHRONICLE

The journal of the Anglican contemplative religious community, The Sisters of the Love of God. A mix of community news and articles on prayer and spirituality with a bias towards contemplative prayer. Current books on Christian spirituality/prayer are reviewed. Poetry not accepted for publication.

Editor Name(s): Sister Isabel Mary S.L.G
Address: The Sister in Charge, SLG Press, Convent of the Incarnation, Fairacres, Oxford OX4 1TB
Telephone: 01865 721301
Fax: 01865 790860
Email: Orders only: orders@slgpress.co.uk
Mag Frequency: 2 issues per year
Subscription: £4.50 (p&p incl)
Single Issue: £1.50
Back Issue: As priced on cover
Overseas: Europe: £5.50, Surface Zones 1 and 2 £5/$9 (U.S), Air Zones 1 and 2 £6.50/$12 (U.S)
Payment in: Cheque or cash only (Sterling or U.S Dollars)
Payable to: SLG Press
Inserts accepted: No
Circulation approx: 1200-1300
Payment terms to contributors: No royalties. 2 complimentary copies of the Chronicle. Proportion of print run for publication
Accept/rejection approx times: By return or at earliest opportunity

FIRE

Fire is a magazine for new and experimental writing with a particular emphasis on new, young or little-known writers, though it does publish some better known writers from the 'alternative' end of the poetry spectrum. International and multicultural in outlook, it does not align itself with any particular group or style but will publish a broad range of work, mainly poetry but also some prose, from anywhere in the world. There is a strong belief in publishing work from the heart or soul, work in which what the writer needs to express is more important than following current trends and fashions or even than getting published at all.

Editor Name(s): Jeremy Hilton
Address: Field Cottage, Old Whitehill, Tackley, Kidlington, Oxfordshire OX5 3AB
Mag Frequency: 3 times a year
Subscription: £7 (3 issues)
Single Issue: £4
Back Issue: £3
Overseas: £10
Payment in: Sterling if possible
Payable to: Fire
Inserts accepted: No
Circulation approx: 300
Payment terms to contributors: 1 copy
Accept/rejection approx times: 5-8 weeks

F

THE FIRING SQUAD

A broadsheet of poetry of a complaint or protest nature.

Editor Name(s): Geoff Stevens
Address: 25 Griffiths Road, West Bromwich B71 2EH
Mag Frequency: Irregular
Subscription: 60p
Single Issue: 30p
Overseas: Not available
Payment in: Sterling
Inserts accepted: No
Circulation approx: 100
Payment terms to contributors: One copy
Accept/rejection approx times: 2 weeks

FIRST OFFENSE

The magazine is for contemporary poetry and is not traditional, but is received by most ground-breaking poets.

Editor Name(s): Tim Fletcher
Address: Syringh, Stodmarsh, Canterbury, Kent CT3 4BA
Mag Frequency: 1 or 2 yearly
Subscription: £2.75
Single Issue: £2.75
Back Issue: £2.50
Overseas: £2.75
Payment in: Cheque
Payable to: Tim Fletcher
Inserts accepted: No
Circulation approx: 300
Payment terms to contributors: N/A
Accept/rejection approx times: N/A

F
FIRST TIME

First Time has been referred to as 'The Consummate Magazine' for the publication of the first time poets and it will stay that way but the standard of work is so varied and of quality that many poets, who have used the magazine as a stepping stone, return time and time again. It is a well established magazine and too large to be called little. Note: 1. Poems submitted must not exceed 30 lines / 2. Poems must not have been published elsewhere and must be author's original work / 3. Name and address must be printed on each sheet / 4. Manuscripts cannot be returned unless SAE envelope enclosed / 5. The editor's decision is final. No correspondence can be entered into regarding choice for publication.

Editor Name(s): Josephine Austin
Address: 'The Snoring Cat', 16 Marion Park, Dudley Road, Hastings, East Sussex, TN35 5PU
Telephone: 01424 428855
Fax: Same as phone
Mag Frequency: Bi-annual
Subscription: £8 per annum plus £1 p&p
Single Issue: £3.50 plus p&p
Back Issue: £1.25 plus p&p
Overseas: US $13 payable in Dollars
Payable to: Josephine Austin
Inserts accepted: Yes
Terms: £25 per 1000
Circulation approx: 1000
Payment terms to contributors: None
Accept/rejection approx times: 2 months

FLAMING ARROWS

Literary journal, contemporary styles of fiction and poetry. New writers sought with distinctive style; polished prose, coherent, lucid, direct and strong poetry. Contemplative metaphysical, mystical, spiritual themes are sought which are grounded in physical senses. Also interested in Earth/Gaia sensibility, sensitivity to sacred space in landscape. Where is the sacred in contemporary life, how is it identified and sustained? Submissions received from throughout the world on these themes cohere into each issue. Each issue is only published when sufficient material of quality has been selected. Potential contributors are advised to order previous issues to sense the style and focus of Flaming Arrows. Before a poem finds its place in an issue, it progresses through successive readings after initial selection until it finds its own page in the general selection. The written work of each contributor creates the dynamic process of each issue's formation. Respect and gratitude to each contributor. Hope for each subscriber.

Address: Leo Regan, VEC, Riverside, Sligo, Ireland
Fax: +353 71 43093
Email: leoregan@eircom.net
Mag Frequency: Annual
Subscription: £2.65
Single Issue: £2.65
Back Issue: Issues 1, 2, 3 - £5; Issues 4, 5, 6 - £2.65
Payment in: Cheque or PO
Payable to: Flaming Arrows
Inserts accepted: No
Circulation approx: 500
Payment terms to contributors: One comp copy, copies at cost on request
Accept/rejection approx times: Initial selection - one week; final selection - six months

ℱ
FOCUS

Focus is the writers' magazine of the British Science Fiction Association. It publishes original fiction, poetry and artwork, together with articles written by professionals and fans on the creative processes of speculative fiction. Recent contributors have included authors Colin Greenland, Juliet McKenna, and Neal Asher, on topics as diverse as characterisation, rewriting, and dealing with editors.

Fiction submissions should be less than 5000 words, poetry less than 50 lines. SF, fantasy and psychological horror are accepted by post or email. Ideas for non-fiction articles should be queried with the editor. Artwork (black and white only, no originals) by post only, or put the work on the web and send the editor the URL. Full submission guidelines available on the BSFA website or from the editor. Focus is open to submissions from both members and non-members, who receive a contributor's copy as payment.

Editor Name(s): Simon Morden
Address: 13 Egremont Drive, Gateshead, Tyne & Wear NE9 5SE
Subs to: Paul Billinger, 1 Long Row Close, Everdon, Daventry, Northants NN11 3BE
Email: focus.editor@blueyonder.co.uk
Website: http://members.aol.com/tamaranth/
Mag Frequency: Twice yearly - May and November
Subscription: BSFA Membership £21 a year
Single Issue: £1.75
Back Issue: Some back issues available at 50p plus p&p
Overseas: Contact Membership secretary for details
Payment in: UK Sterling cheque/British PO/IMO
Payable to: UK BSFA Ltd, US Cy Chauvin (BSFA)
Inserts accepted: By negotiation with the BSFA
Advertising Rates: By negotiation with BSFA
Circulation approx: 600. British Science Fiction Association members also receive Vector (critical journal) and Matrix (news magazine) six times a year
Payment terms to contributors: Contributor's copy
Accept/rejection approx times: Should be less than 1 month

$\mathcal{F}$
THE FORTH NATURALIST AND HISTORIAN

This annual of the Forth Naturalist and Historian, University of Sterling, will this Nov 2001 be volume 24, was started in 1975 to promote studies and interest in the environment and heritage of the mid-Scotland area. Papers from it are fequently quoted as significant literature. Each issue has survey reports on the year's weather, and the birds; some 5 or 6 'naturalist' papers on environment and wildlife; similarly 5 or 6 'history' on heritage, society, arts archaeology...; and reviews/notes on books and articles of area interest.

Example contents of volume 23 included - 4 papers on Flanders Moss - geomorphology, vegetation, conservation, archaeology; the Weather of 1999; Forth area Bird report; Birds of Set-Aside; Forth Valley; Native woodlands of the Ochils; Biodiversity-conserving the variety of life; the Millenium canal wheel boat lift; Cowane's historic garden; St Mary's Church Aberfoyle; Music in Stirling; Early football at Callander; and Book reviews/notes - Bannockburn (2); Rothiemurchus; Root causes of biodiversity loss; Nigel Tranter - Scotland's storyteller; Shale voices; Kingdom of Kippen; Ardoch 2000; Theatrum Animlum - butterflies and moths; Red sky at night; Ancient trees; Stories behind Burns's songs.

Editor Name(s): Lindsay Corbett (Mrs), Neville Dix
Address: Hon Sec L. Corbett, Forth Naturalist and Heritage, University of Stirling, Stirling, FK9 4LA
Telephone: 01259 215091
Fax: 01786 464994
Email: lindsay.corbett@stw.ac.uk
Website: stw.ac.uk/departments/naturalsciences/Forth
Mag Frequency: Annual
Subscription: £6
Single Issue: £6
Back Issue: Various as list/catalogue
Overseas: $12
Payment in: any currency
Payable to: Forth Naturalist and Historian
Inserts accepted: No
Advertising Rates: None
Circulation approx: 300
Payment terms to contributors: None
Accept/rejection approx times: All papers refereed authoritively

F FORTNIGHT

An independent review of politics and the arts in Northern Ireland. Established in 1971 Fortnight has been an independent and non sectarian voice of reasoned debate and analysis. Publishes political articles, mainly on Irish issues, but also room for European/International. Also columns, book reviews, arts reviews, cultural analysis, commentary. 1-2 pages of poetry.

Editor Name(s): John O'Farrell, Mairtin Crawford
Address: 81 Botanic Avenue, Belfast, BT7 1
Telephone: 028 9032 4141 and 028 90 232353
Fax: 028 9023 2650
Email: mairtin@fortnitght.org, jofarrell@fortnight.org, rgoldsmith@fortnight.org
Website: www.fortnight.org
Mag Frequency: Monthly
Subscription: £28 per year, unwaged/students/prisoners deduct £5
Single Issue: £2.20
Back Issue: £2.40
Overseas: Europe £33, RoW £47, unwaged/students/prisoners deduct £5
Payment in: Sterling cheque, PO, bank draft
Payable to: Fortnight Publications
Inserts accepted: Yes
Terms: £45 per 1000
Advertising Rates: £85 plus VAT per quarter page
Circulation approx: 4500
Payment terms to contributors: On arrangement
Accept/rejection approx times: 1 month

FREEHAND

FreeHand is a magazine for writers who want to share their work with like-minded people. Under new editorship since October 1998, FreeHand maintains its A4 format and easygoing style. It has, over the course of 2001 attracted more talented writers. Each issue contains a mix of poetry and prose. There are articles and short stories with several subscribers regularly contributing to their own section. Submissions are invited in all these forms (short stories... up to 3500 words). Illustrators capable of producing good quality black and white line art are actively sought for front covers. Rather than becoming a competitive publication, FreeHand aims to remain a platform for mainstream writing and artwork and a vehicle for the promotion of those poets/ writers who have achieved publication in a small way either through self-publishing or acceptance of short-run publications. If you write, FreeHand wants to read it. Submissions preferably from subscribers only, but we are not a vanity press and will happily publish good work from non-subscribers. There is no payment for publication. FreeHand is fairly traditional in the work it publishes and 'off the wall' contemporary work is not required.

Editor Name(s): Jo Wood
Address: 15 Meols Drive, Hoylake, Wirral CH47 4AD
Telephone: 0151 632 1720 or 0777 5903462
Email: josephinewood@barcleys.net
Mag Frequency: Quarterly
Subscription: £12 pa
Single Issue: £3
Overseas: £16 pa/£4 single
Payment in: Cheque
Payable to: Footprints
Inserts accepted: Yes
Terms: On application or reciprocal
Advertising Rates: On request or reciprocal
Circulation approx: 250
Payment terms to contributors: None
Accept/rejection approx times: Getting better

F
FREELANCE MARKET NEWS

Established in 1968, Freelance Market News is a monthly newsletter giving news, views and advice about new publications - plus the trends and developments in established markets, at home and abroad. With feature articles, author profiles, book reviews, news of competitions, festivals and residential courses, professional advice and problem solving - writers can be sure they are kept up to date with what is happening on the writing scene.

Address: Sevendale House, 7 Dale Street, Manchester M1 1JB
Fax: 0161 228 3533
Email: fmn@writersbureau.com
Mag Frequency: Monthly (not published in July)
Subscription: £29 per year (11 issues) £17 (6 issues)
Back Issue: £2.50
Overseas: As UK
Payable to: Freelance Market News
Inserts accepted: Yes
Terms: £50 per 1000
Payment terms to contributors: £35 per 1000 words, guidelines available for SAE
Accept/rejection approx times: 2 weeks

THE FROGMORE PAPERS

The Frogmore Papers publish poetry and prose by new and established writers. Founded in 1983, the magazine has featured work by a wide variety of poets from Linda France, John Mole and Sophie Hannah to Elizabeth Garrett, Pauline Stainer and Katherine Pierpoint. The annual Frogmore Poetry Prize, founded in 1987, was won by Ann Alexander in 2000; previous winners include John Latham, Tobias Hill, Mario Petrucci and Ross Cogan.

Address: 18 Nevill Road, Lewes, East Sussex BN7 1PF
Subs to: The Frogmore Press, 42 Morehall Avenue, Folkestone, Kent CT19 4EF
Website: www.frogmorepress.co.uk
Mag Frequency: Bi-annual (March/September)
Subscription: £7 one year,£12 two years
Single Issue: £3.80 (inc p&p)
Back Issue: £2.50
Overseas: US $20, Europe £10
Payment in: US subs in bills only no US cheques
Payable to: The Frogmore Press
Inserts accepted: No
Circulation approx: 500
Payment terms to contributors: Complimentary copy
Accept/rejection approx times: 1-6 months

ℱ
FUGAZI.NET

We've been working with small press groups and have now set-up a secure server that allow us to display products and take credit card and debit card payments across the Internet. This site is dedicated to working with and linking small press ventures into a cohesive web presence. It is free to join and we only take commission on what's sold. Consider the much discussed ability the Net has of creating a level playing field for smaller enterprises to match major players and the explosive growth of e-commerce. This could mean small press ventures ditching the 'small' without ditching any control or independence. The Internet is growing at an almost exponential rate, but so is the number of business' stepping into e-commerce. Individually, a single publisher's website will not even make a splash. But link the vast number of small press publishers together and every reader, bit of publicity or conference one publisher can benefit every other publisher. Linked we could ensure our whole is greater than the sum of our parts. We specialise in horror, Sci-fi and Fantasy but will certainly consider anybody with enthusiasm for their products to join us. We have further unfolding plans to expand the numbers of people who browse our sites and promote our collective.

Email: For information: info@fugazi To join: join@fugazi
Website: http://www.fugazi.net

FURRY FABLES

A5 - minimum of 48 pages - Black and White. Contains all types of animal stories from new and established authors. Competition winners and short listed entries are also included. We only accept rhyming poetry. No surreal stories or ones that leave the reader guessing. No swear words or sex. 25p of each new subscription is given to a Cat/Animal charity. 10 copies are sent to charity to raise funds at-CPL-Rhyl, Basildon, Telford and we collect stamps for the National Illiostomy Society. New submission procedure with form, send 19p SSAE for free guidelines. No material held over.

Editor Name(s): Amanda Gillies
Address: PO Box 241, Oakengates TF2 9XZ
Telephone: 01952 277872
Email: Fables@writers.brew.clara. net
Website: http://www.writers.brew.clara.net/club/
Mag Frequency: Quarterly
Subscription: £10 per year or £13 RoW
Single Issue: £3.50 sterling or 11 IRC's
Overseas: US only $27 Dollars payable to - Dreamwalker Press and sent to PO Box 720862, Orlando, FL 32872-0862, USA (Please note, US cheques only to this address, no mss. All enquiries to the UK office with a minimum of 2 IRC's for a reply)
Payable to: Writers Brew Club
Inserts accepted: Yes
Terms: £10 per 100
Advertising Rates: £50 full page only - 2 adverts per magazine only
Circulation approx: Growing
Payment terms to contributors: Free copy
Accept/rejection approx times: 6 weeks, subscribers are given preference - but we publish at least 3 non-subscribers each magazine

ℱ
FUTURION

Futurion: Neo-sci-fi fanzine features the short stories, poetry, artwork and collages of Leigh Smith. After years of pumping out free artwork, collages, poetry and short stories Leigh Smith decided to create his own fanzine. Five issues exist so far, may mutate into a one-page A4 newsletter or explode and go weekly knocking 2000 AD off the shelves. Futurion has come to save sci fi ! Come to meet the dark inhabitants of Unicorn Park! No X piles or Star Tat fans need write. Futurion is best described as a mix of The Ghosts of Motley Hall/ Bladerunner/ Dune/ Spawn and Louise Clifford. They offer us no future thus we must create our own! Also home of geek star puppet video! Base Camp of Dreamsmith Productions Stop motion/ cartoon animations. The neo wave is here!

Address: 16 Bridge Street, South Quay, Maryport, Cumbria CA15 8AE
Email: futurion@hotmail.com
Mag Frequency: Every couple of months
Subscription: £5
Single Issue: £1
Overseas: Beware U-Boats
Payment in: Make it cash and fast
Payable to: Mr L J Smith
Inserts accepted: Yes
Terms: Free
Circulation approx: 200
Payment terms to contributors: Copy of fanzine
Accept/rejection approx times: 1-2 weeks

GAIJIN

g

The mid-1990s incarnation of Gaijin was a forum for anecdotal essays, revelatory memoirs (rarely more so than in its infamous 'Secret Fears, Private Pleasures' edition) and offbeat humour. Although its roots lay in the sub-culture of science fiction fanzines, Gaijin's branches extended well beyond - and its 21st century resurrection aims to be no different.

Editor Name(s): Steve Green
Address: 33 Scott Road, Olton, Solihull B92 7LQ
Email: ghostwords@yahoo.co.uk
Mag Frequency: We aim to appear twice a year, dependent upon the amount of material available to publish.
Subscription: We don't want subscribers - we want participants!
Single Issue: For a sample, send a trade copy of your own zine or a large envelope and three first-class stamps (UK only)
Back Issue: Back issues will be used as cavity filling.
Inserts accepted: No.
Circulation approx: 200-400, dependent upon how many stamps we can afford.
Payment terms to contributors: Beyond improving your karma, all we can offer is a complimentary copy and lots of copies of future issues. Even when you ask us to stop.
Accept/rejection approx times: A month, maybe two. Hey, this is meant to be a hobby. No poetry or fiction.

G GAIRM

A quarterly publication, in Scottish Gaelic, encompassing fiction, poetry, current affairs, articles on technical topics, folklore, song, reviews with some pictorial features. The periodical was founded in 1951-52. Gairm Publications also publish a wide range of books: dictionaries, grammars, novels, short stories, poetry, children's books, Gaelic music books etc. Only Scottish Gaelic contributions accepted.

Address: 29 Waterloo Street, Glasgow G2 6BZ
Mag Frequency: Quarterly
Subscription: £9 UK
Single Issue: £1.80
Back Issue: Variable; pack of 50 back issues £28 (£40 overseas)
Overseas: £11
Payable to: Gairm Publications
Inserts accepted: Yes
Terms: £30 per 1000
Circulation approx: 1000
Payment terms to contributors: Approx £10 per page
Accept/rejection approx times: 2-3 weeks

GENTLE READER

𝓰

'Gentle Reader' is a quarterly short story magazine aimed at the person who enjoys a good read. The subject matter is varied - crime, comedy, romance, sci-fi - and appeals to a broad range of readers. There are a few simple poems and a humorous anecdote on general topics. One of the main ideas for publishing this magazine is to give short story readers a bridge between popular magazines and literary ones. The other reason is to help quality writers to publish their work.

Editor Name(s): Lynne E Jones
Address: 8 Heol Pen-y-bryn, Penyrheol, Caerphilly, Mid Glamorgan CF83 2JX
Telephone: 029 2020886369
Email: lynne_jones@hotmail.com
Mag Frequency: 3 times per annum
Subscription: £8.50
Single Issue: £2.50
Back Issue: £2.00
Overseas: £11.50 subscription, £3.20 single copy, Europe £10.50, £3.00
Payment in: Sterling or S A Rands
Payable to: L E Jones
Inserts accepted: Yes
Terms: Reciprocal
Advertising Rates: Reciprocal for other writing magazines, free charity ads
Circulation approx: 80
Payment terms to contributors: Complimentary copy
Accept/rejection approx times: 2 months

G GLOBAL TAPESTRY JOURNAL SC

Global Tapestry Journal first manifested in the early sixties as Poetmeat magazine. It was then part of a network of alternative literary press and counter-culture imprint, who unsuccessfully attempted to bypass (and make obsolete) large commercial publishing houses. Its present incarnation is far less ambitious - but reverts back to anarchic roots and evolutionary utopian theoretic.

A manifestation of exciting creativity. Innovative prose writing and novel extracts. Bohemian, post-Beat and counter-culture orientation.

Our SC (Second Coming) resurrection is now unburdened by institution or private funding. It is now produced completely in-house.

Editor Name(s): Dave Cunliffe
Address: Spring Bank, Longsight Road, Copster Green, Blackburn, Lancs BB1 9EU
Telephone: 01254 249128 (messages only)
Mag Frequency: Quarterly
Subscription: £9, 4 issues postal
Single Issue: £2.40 single postal
Overseas: £10 postal
Payment in: Sterling or USA dollars equivalent
Payable to: D A & R Cunliffe
Inserts accepted: No
Circulation approx: 1,500 to 2,000 per issue
Payment terms to contributors: One issue of magazine only
Accept/rejection approx times: As soon as possible

GOOD STORIES

Quarterly magazine of original short stories of all kinds.

Editor Name(s): Andrew Jenns
Address: Oakwood Publications, 23 Mill Crescent, Kingsbury, Warwickshire B78 2LX
Telephone: 01827 873435
Mag Frequency: Quarterly
Subscription: £14 (4 issues) post free
Single Issue: £3.50 plus 50p postage
Back Issue: £2.50
Overseas: £20
Payment in: Sterling only
Payable to: Oakwood Publications
Inserts accepted: Yes
Terms: By negotiation
Advertising Rates: Media pack on request
Circulation approx: 3000
Payment terms to contributors: On publication
Accept/rejection approx times: 9 weeks

G GREVATT & GREVATT

Non-commercial publisher and bookseller specializing in poetry, in academic books on language and linguistics (especially chinese), on religion and philosophy (especially Indran). No unsolicited MSS; SAE with proposals. Small print runs, so royalties unlikely unless more than 500 printed and sold, but all books produced accurately and to a high standard, attacting good reviews. Prizes kept as low as possible, with special offers to students, unemployed and retired people.

Editor Name(s): Siew-Yue Killingley
Address: 9 Rectory Drive, Newcastle upon Tyne, NE3 1XT
Telephone: 0191 2858053
Email: siew-yue@fsmail.net
Website: http://grevatt-grevatt.freeservers.com/index.htm
Mag Frequency: one or two per year book
Subscription: Pre-publication subscription prices according to book price (10% - 20% off)
Single Issue: As low as possible of books
Back Issue: Books never remaindered. Some price rises apply
Overseas: Price of books: normally 30% of UK price
Payment in: Sterling; small amounts from overseas in cash accepted if registered
Payable to: GREVATT & GREVATT
Circulation approx: International
Payment terms to contributors: Nil unless 500+ copies printed and sold. In that case 10% of retail price
Accept/rejection approx times: Normally within 6 months, usually much sooner

HANDSHAKE

Handshake is a very specialised magazine, consisting of a single sheet of A4 devoted entirely to SF poetry. One side of the magazine consists of news and information about genre poetry - information submitted should be typed, single-spaced, ready for photocopying. Adverts are OK if small. Side two has now evolved into a 'poetry magazine' - but being only one side of a single sheet means I can take no epics! Short poems preferred, and as I always have more poems than information I prefer the latter. You are advised to see a copy before submitting. All rights revert to author on publication. All submissions must be accompanied by an SAE, and have not been published elsewhere.

Address: JF Haines, 5 Cross Farm, Station Road, Padgate, Warrington WA2 OQG
Mag Frequency: Irregular-Time sensitive items are difficult to handle
Subscription: SAE/IRC/Stamps/Trade
Single Issue: Same
Back Issue: Same - very few ever available
Overseas: SAE/IRC/Stamps/Trade
Inserts accepted: Yes - genre poetry related only
Circulation approx: 60 plus
Payment terms to contributors: Copy of newsletter
Accept/rejection approx times: Soon as I can and within a month if possible, though if you're close to an issue being printed it could be longer

ℋ
HEADLOCK PRESS

The magazine has folded due to lack of funds, but Headlock Press continues to publish collections of poetry by new and established writers. In the first instance, interested authors should send one poem with a letter of enquiry and return postage.

Editor Name(s): Tony Charles
Address: Tony Charles, Old Zion Chapel, The Triangle, Somerton, Somerset TA11 6QP
Telephone: 01458 272962

ℋ HEADPRESS

Since 1991, Headpress journal has been at the forefront of 'transgressive' publishing, with incisive and cutting-edge essays on films and film makers, religious manias, fanaticism, weird crime cases, sex queens, curious music, art, artists, pornography, trash and sleaze. (We do not publish poetry or fiction). With No. 13 Headpress went from magazine format to perfect-bound. With No. 19 the page count increased to 160 pages. All early editions, including No. 14 are sold out. Headpress also produces a mail-order catalogue for new and second-hand books, available for a 1st class stamp/ IRC. Some of the praise for Headpress: 'Particularly bizarre... disturbing and sometimes delightful' - Time Out. 'An entirely healthy interest in violent death and deviant sex' - i-D. 'This is the top dog, the main man and is unbeatable... Interesting, disturbing, fascinating and entertaining, Headpress is the zine for the Millennium' - The British Fantasy Society. Critical Vision is the book publishing side of Headpress, always on the look-out for interesting manuscripts of a non-fiction nature. Write to Headpress for further details.

Address: 40 Rossall Avenue, Radcliffe, Manchester M26 1JD
Fax: 0161 796 1935
Email: david.headpress@zen.co.uk
Website: http://www.headpress.com/
Mag Frequency: Two times a year
Subscription: £16 for two editions
Single Issue: £8.99
Back Issue: Sample copy £4.95 (edition number our discretion)
Overseas: £18 Europe, £20 USA and RoW (two editions) includes 10% discount off New Critical Vision books
Payment in: UK bankable cheque/Post Giro/IMO
Payable to: Headpress
Inserts accepted: No
Circulation approx: 2500
Payment terms to contributors: Complimentary copy plus small fee
Accept/rejection approx times: 3 to 4 weeks

♯
HJOKFINNIES SANGLINES

Poetry should play for high stakes and the internet is a good forum. A place for visionary verse is on the screen.

Our internet magazine is in 8 sections and at present has an editorial team of 3. The main concerns and connections are the fine art of poetry, the precision art of engineering, philosophy and politics.

We feel that the internet essay is new literary territory. If you'd like to write for HjfS, I suggest both registering (it's free) on the forum to post an introduction, and emailing the editor with a synopsis of the article.

Address: Electronic only till further notice
Email: yok@yfinnie.demon.co.uk
Website: http://www.yfinnie.demon.co.uk

ℋ HOLLYWOOD MUSICALS SOCIETY

Published over 10 years - articles on stars and backroom people in musicals of the Golden Age.

Editor Name(s): Patience Gent
Address: 1 Pond Meadow, Milford Haven, Pembs SA73 1HB Wales
Telephone: 01646 695920
Email: gentian@cwcom.net
Website: http://lucath.tripod.com/mags.html
Mag Frequency: 2 - 4 pa
Subscription: UK £5
Overseas: US $10
Payment in: UK cheques or dollar bills
Payable to: P Gent
Inserts accepted: No
Circulation approx: 250
Payment terms to contributors: None

ℋ
HQ POETRY MAGAZINE
(The Haiku Quarterly)

HQ (founded in 1990) is an international poetry magazine that publishes a broad range of work - from the highly experimental to the very traditional. The emphasis is on quality and originality. About one third of the magazine's space is given over to haiku and haikuesque poetry; the rest to mainstream poetry and reviews/articles. HQ encourages the publication of new work by established writers (Alvarez, Kirkup, Redgrove, Brownjohn, Middleton, Patten, Shuttle, Stryk, Lydiard etc in previous issues) and developmental/experimental work by new poets (Mike Hogan, Liz Newman, Gary Bills, James Morris etc). It should be noted that Howard Sargeant and Roland John at Outposts and Mike Shields at Orbis have been a strong influence on HQ's editor, and this is reflected in the magazine's style.

Editor Name(s): Kevin Bailey
Address: 39 Exmouth Street, Swindon, Wiltshire SN1 3PU
Telephone: 01793 523927
Mag Frequency: Variable
Subscription: £10 UK
Single Issue: £2.80
Overseas: £13
Payment in: Cheque, PO, UK/Cash, sterling cheques non-UK
Payable to: The Haiku Quarterly
Inserts accepted: Yes
Terms: By arrangement
Advertising Rates: By arrangement
Circulation approx: 500 (readership via libraries etc, 1000 plus)
Payment terms to contributors: Free copies of magazine - some financial assistance to contributors in need
Accept/rejection approx times: Up to 6 months depending upon workload

HU

The North of Ireland's premier literary magazine, celebrating 30 years of publishing the best poems, stories, interviews, articles and book reviews. Past contributors include Seamus Heaney, Paul Muldoon, Tony Harrison, Carol Rumens and many more. Get a back issue and see for yourself.

Editor Name(s): Tom Clyde
Address: HU Publications, PO Box 15, Holywood, Co Down BT18 9UP
Mag Frequency: 3 a year
Subscription: £12 UK and Ireland
Single Issue: £3
Back Issue: Varies
Overseas: £17
Payment in: Sterling
Payable to: HU Publications
Inserts accepted: Yes
Terms: On application
Circulation approx: 1000
Payment terms to contributors: Token and 2 copies
Accept/rejection approx times: 3 months

I

ILLUMINATIONS

Incorporating all arts 'Illuminations' seeks to deliver ideas and creativity. Each magazine contains fevered scribbling, poetry, stories, artwork, photography, collages, reviews (events, film, music, books), interviews and informed articles.

Illuminations arrives under the ideology that all arts are interrelated... so the approach is not narrow; all genres, all art forms, all subjects. We are always looking for unsolicited work of all kinds but please send an SAE and author's note with your contribution. Previous contributors include Jeremy Reed, Poppy Z Brite, Alisdair Gray and Patrick Jones.

Within Illuminations, past, present and future converge, truth, memory, knowledge and prediction, freedom of imagination, exploration, love, death, life, expression and style. Promoting creativity, seeking experience. Imagination and fiction play a large role in our real lives...

Editor Name(s): Anji Jain Prescott
Address: 17 Campbell Drive, Larbert, Stirlingshire FK5 4PP
Telephone: 0771 831 5649 (phone or text)
Email: illuminations@aprescott.fsnet.co.uk
Website: www.geocities.com/illuminationsxx/index.html and Yahoo! Club illuminationsxx
Mag Frequency: 4 times a year
Subscription: £7.50 per year
Single Issue: £2 per issue
Back Issue: £2.00
Overseas: £3 per issue, £12 per year
Payment in: Cheque or postal order, overseas: cash notes or international money coupon
Payable to: A J Prescott
Inserts accepted: No
Advertising Rates: £10 per half page, £20 per full page
Circulation approx: 150
Payment terms to contributors: Free copy of magazine
Accept/rejection approx times: 2-3 weeks

THE INTERPRETER'S HOUSE

We started as a Bedfordshire magazine, and our title comes from Pilgrim's Progress '...the house of the Interpreter, at whose door he should knock, and he will show him excellent things.' We now get submissions from all over the world, and I am looking for excellent poems and short stories (up to 2500 words), so please don't send me your second-best work. We welcome new and established writers, normally publish only one piece per person, and don't do reviews. We are associated with the Bedford Open Poetry Competition, and the winners are published each February.

Editor Name(s): Merryn Williams
Address: 10 Farrell Road, Wootton, Bedfordshire MK43 9DU
Subs to: Anne Chisholm, 38 Verne Drive, Ampthill, Bedfordshire MK45 2PS
Mag Frequency: Feb, June and Oct each year
Subscription: £10
Single Issue: £3 plus 50p postage
Overseas: At present the same
Payable to: The Interpreter's House
Inserts accepted: Yes
Circulation approx: 300
Payment terms to contributors: None
Accept/rejection approx times: Fast

I

INTERZONE

Interzone publishes science-fiction and fantasy short stories, plus reviews, interviews, etc. It does not publish verse. Perhaps the last monthly fiction magazine in Britain - in any genre!

Editor Name(s): David Pringle
Address: 217 Preston Drove, Brighton BN1 6FL
Telephone: 01273 504710
Email: interzone@cix.co.uk
Website: www.sfsite.com/interzone
Mag Frequency: Monthly
Subscription: £32 (inland)
Single Issue: £3
Overseas: £38 per annum
Payment in: Sterling or US $ - or by credit card
Payable to: Interzone
Inserts accepted: No
Advertising Rates: Email to enquire
Circulation approx: 8000
Payment terms to contributors: £30 per 1000 words (fiction only)
Accept/rejection approx times: 2 months

IOTA

Looking for well-crafted poetry with something to say and the ability to say it with economy and force. The longer the poem, the harder it is to fit it in, so shorter pieces have the edge and epics are definitely out. There is no limitation on style or subject; the magazine aims to include the complete range of poetry, so light verse, as well as more serious poetry, is always welcome. However, the editor claims no expertise (or facilities) for concrete poetry - apart from that, anything goes. The magazine also carries book reviews and a round-up of interesting magazines received.

Editor Name(s): David Holliday
Address: 67 Hady Crescent, Chesterfield, Derbyshire S41 0EB
Telephone: 01246 276532
Mag Frequency: Quarterly
Subscription: £10
Single Issue: £2.50
Back Issue: £1
Overseas: As above, or US $5 per issue/$20 per year (plus $10 if by cheque), or equivalent in other currencies
Payment in: Anything negotiable
Payable to: Iota or David Holliday
Inserts accepted: Yes
Terms: Free assuming space
Advertising Rates: No adverts - no space
Circulation approx: 500
Payment terms to contributors: 2 complimentary copies
Accept/rejection approx times: 2 weeks for first reaction (unless preparation of next issue takes precedence); final decision may take up to a year

I
ISLAND

A magazine of new poetry inspired by the natural world and the landscape of Britain, and the relationship between people and the land. Also features artwork.

Editor Name(s): Robert Ford
Address: 3 Kingsway, Balderton, Newark, Notts NG24 3DJ
Mag Frequency: Twice yearly
Subscription: £4 for 2 issues
Single Issue: £2
Payment in: Cheque or postal order
Payable to: Island
Inserts accepted: No
Circulation approx: 100
Payment terms to contributors: Complimentary copy
Accept/rejection approx times: 4 weeks

IVY PUBLICATIONS

Mend your English, by Ian Bruton-Simmonds, ISBN: 0 620 15019X

It is not a magazine but a book (150 pages). It is recently in bookshops throughout Britain. It is not a reference book, but a turner-on-of-lights. It lists good reference books.
Telephone: 0208 671 6872
Fax: 0208 671 3391
Single Issue: £9.99 in bookshops
Payment in: Sterling

J THE JOURNAL OF SILLY

The best in single panel cartooning, by the world's top professional cartoonists. See the gags even before they appear in the likes of Private Eye, The Times, The Observer, The Express, The Telegraph, Independent, Punch and the rest plus exclusives to JOS.

Address: PO Box 22903, London N10 2WW
Email: ham@dircon.co.uk
Website: www.ham.dircon.co.uk
Mag Frequency: Quarterly
Subscription: £6 one year/£16 three years
Single Issue: £1.50
Back Issue: £5
Overseas: £10 Europe/£24 RoW for one year
Payable to: The Journal Of Silly
Inserts accepted: Yes
Terms: £40 per 1000
Circulation approx: 1000
Payment terms to contributors: N/A
Accept/rejection approx times: 1-10 weeks

THE JOURNAL (once 'of Contemporary Anglo-Scandinavian Poetry')

Founded 1994, the aim of the original magazine was for it to be a showcase for Scandinavian poetry in translation alongside contemporary poetry written in English. Scandinavian contributions, however, arrived in fits and starts; consequently the magazine has had to become known simply as 'The Journal'. The Journal is bigger, and A4, with its extra pages carrying comment and reviews, as well as the usual 'happy concoction of contemporary poetry'. 'Good to see the reader challenged', one reviewer said of the new format.

Editor Name(s): Sam Smith
Address: 11 Heatherton Park, Bradford on Tone, Taunton, Somerset TA4 1EU
Telephone: 01823 461725
Email: smithsssj@aol.com
Website: http://members.aol.com/smithsssj/index.html
Mag Frequency: 3 times a year-depending on submissions
Subscription: £7
Single Issue: £2.50
Back Issue: £2
Overseas: £9 (USA £11)
Payment in: Cheque/IRCs/cash. No barter.
Payable to: Sam Smith
Inserts accepted: No
Circulation approx: 150
Payment terms to contributors: 1 complimentary copy
Accept/rejection approx times: Within 4 weeks

KICKIN' & SCREAMIN'

Kickin' & Screamin' want poetry that shouts emotion and leaves the reader gasping. Poems that liberate the spirit and help us find our place in space. Social and political comment that uplifts and inspires - no deep, bleak, dark despair. Poems that rise to the challenge, deal with the difficult and offer a creative alternative. Poetry in any style - rhymed, unrhymed, not too long - enclose SAE for return. See the world anew, strange and wonderful.

Address: 5 Canberra Close, Greenmeadow, Cwmbran NP44 3ET South Wales
Mag Frequency: Bi-monthly
Subscription: N/A
Single Issue: Free (send SAE)
Overseas: Free (with appropriate SAE)
Inserts accepted: No
Circulation approx: Increasing
Payment terms to contributors: Free copy
Accept/rejection approx times: 1-3 months, work returned only with SAE

KIMOTA

Kimota is a magazine which tries to bend the boundaries between the genres. Fantasy, sf, horror, slipstream, even crime and western themes if they are mixed with the first three. It is the natural home of the unclassifiable, but obviously 'genre' story. Physically it is perfect bound with card covers and contains approximately 80 pages. Kimota is an illustrated magazine and emphasises stylish stories, articles and production values. Submissions should be well written and contain original ideas. It is advisable to check out a copy before submitting.

Address: 52 Cadley Causeway, Fulwood, Preston, Lancs PR2 3RX
Email: editor@kimota.co.uk
Website: http://www.kimota.co.uk
Mag Frequency: Twice yearly
Subscription: £10 for 4 (free p&p in UK)
Single Issue: £2.99 (free p&p in UK)
Overseas: $10 cash or Sterling International Money Order
Payment in: Cheque or Postal Order (UK)
Payable to: Graeme Hurry
Inserts accepted: No
Circulation approx: Increasing
Payment terms to contributors: £2 per 1000 words and copy
Accept/rejection approx times: 6 weeks

𝒦
KONFLUENCE

Konfluence is a magazine with a West Country slant. Based in the Five Valleys converging on Stroud, Glos, the magazine aims to provide a platform for new and established voices. It also aims to showcase the work of talented minor poets who haven't won that competition/caught a commercial publisher's eye... but could with luck and in time. The Editor is also interested in poetry written by people whose main creative medium lies in related fields: musicians, sculptors, visual/conceptual and performance artists etc. No genre of poetic style is preferred but the poems must broach that intangible marriage of form and content that makes them 'zing'. Any length of poem, though ideal length is approximately 40-50 lines. Recent contributors have included:Geoff Stevens, Barry Tebb, Brenda Williams, Ian Caws, Steve Sneyed and Daisy Abey

Editor Name(s): Mark Floyer
Address: Bath House, Bath Road, Nailsworth, Glos GL6 0JB
Telephone: 01453 835896
Fax: 01453 835587
Email: Floherns@aol.com
Mag Frequency: 1 per 9 months
Single Issue: £3.50
Back Issue: Konfluence 1 = £1.50, Konfluence 2 = £3, Konfluence 3 = £3.50
Payment in: Cash/cheque/stamps/postal orders
Payable to: M A Floyer
Inserts accepted: Yes
Circulation approx: Approximately 100 copies
Payment terms to contributors: Free copy of magazine
Accept/rejection approx times: Fortnight turn-around

KRAX

A light-hearted poetry magazine - witty, amusing and whimsical, interspersed with descriptive narrative. Usually contains some short fiction, an interview with a writer of interest and illustrations. There's a chunky review section of books, tapes and magazines for added variety, too. Quite a large proportion of American contributors. Some of the content is unsuitable for children although we don't actively seek risqué material. There is currently a substantial backlog of items awaiting publication, although good quality illustrations are always welcome.

Editor Name(s): Andy Robson
Address: c/o 63 Dixon Lane, Leeds, Yorkshire LS12 4RR
Mag Frequency: Nine monthly approximately
Subscription: £10 for 3 subsequent issues
Single Issue: £3.50
Back Issue: Details on request
Overseas: $20 for 3 issues ($35 AUS/CAN)
Payment in: Overseas - currency notes or moneygram only
Payable to: A Robson
Inserts accepted: No
Circulation approx: 60% UK, 40% USA
Payment terms to contributors: Single copy of magazine (cover art payment on publication)
Accept/rejection approx times: Up to ten weeks overseas

ℒ
LATERAL MOVES

Lateral Moves is published by a voluntary arts organisation, on a non-profitmaking basis. Since 1994 we have been featuring high-quality humour, poetry, short stories, artwork, articles and occasional reviews/interviews. The magazine's contributor base contains a strong international element, perhaps because foreign subscriptions are charged at UK rates, but our team of specialised readers is careful to view each contribution on its own merit. For this reason, new writers will rub shoulders with the more experienced. And it is certainly true that contributors to the magazine can influence its direction. We request that all submissions of material are accompanied by a return SAE, and are pleased to receive stories/longer articles in plain text format on disk. Humour, especially pictorial, is especially in demand. Lateral Moves is looking to swap pages with any other magazine willing to participate in our experiment...

Editor Name(s): Alan White, Nick Britton
Address: c/o 5 Hamilton Street, Astley Bridge, Bolton BL1 6RJ
Telephone: 01204 596369
Mag Frequency: Bi-monthly
Subscription: £12/US $20 per annum
Single Issue: £2.85/US $5
Overseas: As UK subscription cost
Payment in: Sterling cheques/postal orders (US residents may send dollar bills to avoid bank charges)
Payable to: Lateral Moves
Inserts accepted: Yes
Terms: Exchange/free for partners and subscribers
Advertising Rates: Exchange/free for partners and subscribers
Circulation approx: 150
Payment terms to contributors: Complimentary copy
Accept/rejection approx times: Three to six months

THE LAYABOUT

Offbeat, richly illustrated humour magazine in the style of Douglas Adams, P G Wodehouse, Lewis Carroll, Mad Magazine, Monty Python, The Simpsons. The Layabout contains short stories, articles, cartoons and nonsense verse. In most cases, there is a 19th-century slant. Layabout regulars include the 'Auntie Layabout' advice column, the adventures of bungling Victorian scientific-detective Barrington Smythe, Layabout slack-jawed photographer Skip Possumstew, Slavic mafia-man Vratislav and the Baron Butcher cartoon series loosley based on the works of Edgar Allen Poe and J R R Tolkien. For submitters, stories can be up to 8000 words, though under 5000 is preferred. Characters and situations should be one or more of the following: vivid, eccentric, witty, offbeat, pompous, absurd. Please send photocopies only and indicate whether you wish them returned; if so, please include sufficient postage or coupons. Email submissions are acceptable. All art work should be unfolded and free of blemishes. Payment of one copy for stories and for multiple poetry and cartoon submissions will be answered within a month. If two months go by, please drop us a line to check if we received it. Please study an issue before submitting.

Editor Name(s): Viscount Rochfarte, Henry Ramsager
Address: 17 Alwyn Close, St Ives, PE27 3HL
Email: gnome-power@ntlworld.com
Website: In development
Mag Frequency: 3-4 times/year
Subscription: £6.50 for 3 issues
Single Issue: £2.25 or US $5.00
Back Issue: £2.00 (Also still have a few slightly damaged No. 2 issues, unsold returns from book shops, these can be bought for £1.75)
Overseas: US $13 for 3 issues
Payment in: £ or US $
Payable to: The Layabout
Terms: Write for further information
Circulation approx: 250-350
Payment terms to contributors: Copy of issue they appear in

$\mathcal{L}$
LEGEND - WORLDS OF POSSIBILITY

Legend is an A4, 60 page, B&W illustrated magazine that publishes fiction, non fiction, graphic stories and interviews connected with Arthurian Fantasy, Romantic Fantasy, Alternate History, Alternate Worlds, Myth and Magic. It will appeal to anyone who has an interest in mystery and magic, and the imagination to indulge in their infinite possibilities. Writers have included Hugh Cook, Marni Scofiodio Griffin, Rob Krijnen-Kemp, Margaret Walker, Paul Finch and Terry Gates-Grimwood. Illustrators include Russell Dickerson, GAK, Gerald Gaubert, Sarah Zama and Helen Field.

'I feel that in no time at all Legend will become the pre eminent fantasy magazine in Britain' - Michael Lohr
'A beautifully presented package stuffed with goodies! All in all, a great read!' - Ceri Jordan
'I must say I was extremely impressed with the quality of presentation and excellent artwork.' - Nichola Caines
'A lot more here to enjoy than not. Count me in for the ride.' - Peter Tennant
'Stunningly produced.' - A. C. Evans
'I am honoured to be part of this publication.' - Barbara Tarn
'Legend has a lot going for it. It feels like a magazine whose editor is bursting with things he wants to try.' - Neil Williamson (the FIX - Summer 2001)

Editor Name(s): Trevor Denyer
Address: 7 Mount View, Church Lane West, Aldershot, Hampshire, GU11 3LN
Telephone: 01252 664699
Email: tdenyer@ntlworld.com
Website: www.roadworksweb.free-online.co.uk
Mag Frequency: Quarterly
Subscription: £15
Single Issue: £4 ($8 US. £5.50 Europe. £6 ROW)
Back Issue: £3 ($8 US. £5 Europe. £6 ROW)
Overseas: $30 US. £20 Europe. £22 ROW
Payment in: Cash, cheque or money order
Payable to: T. Denyer
Inserts accepted: Yes
Terms: Exchange
Advertising Rates: Negotiable
Circulation approx: Approx 100
Payment terms to contributors: First British serial rights, contibutors copies
Accept/rejection approx times: 1 to 3 months

LEXIKON

This quarterly Ezine (also available on audio cassette and computer disc for just GBP1.25 per issue) profiles work by new and established writers and carries a wide-range of poetry, short fiction, news stories, special features, author interviews, book reviews, details of paying markets for writers and current literary competitions, etc. 'Our mission is to give writers of all abilities and disciplines maximum exposure and encouragement, as well as offering lots of friendly advice. We don't just see ourselves as a magazine publisher, but a place where you can contact us for help and information on anything connected with writing and publishing. Always feel free to telephone us during office hours or send e-mail enquiries. Already we have featured the likes of Phil Ford who now writes regularly for Coronation Street, the award winning poet Dr Philip Higson who has published no less than nine original coolections of poetry, et al.' Authors whose work has been accepted for publicaton will automatically be sent a complimentary copy of the magazine in a format of their choice: computer disc, PDF, (for which you'll require Acrobat Reader which can be download free from our website), Word.doc, plain text, by e-mail (in any of the aforementioned) and on audio cassette.

'by publishing online, writers increase their chances of reaching a far greater readership which can only result in them being spotted by agents and publishers who maybe interested in publishing collections of their work commercially.'

Lexikon publishing also produces a free fortnightly newsletter for writers, editors and publishers, which is sent to subscribers by e-mail. This free publication carries the latest literary news, regular announcements, special features, book news and reviews, plus details of literary competitions. Sign up now by sending a blank e-mail to lexikon-subscribe@topica.com

News items, features articles (literary only please), book reviews and announcements, are always welcomed. Mailto: newsletter@lexikon-publishing.co.uk or visit www.lexikon-publishing.co.uk/ where you'll be able to view and download back issues.

Subs to: Poetry: up to 60 lines max, Stories: up to 2000 words max, Book reviews: up to 500 words max, News items: up to 300 words max, Feature articles: up to 1000 words max
Telephone: +44 (0) 1782 205060
Email: submissions@lexikon-publishing.co.uk
Website: www.lexikon-publishing.co.uk/lexikon/index.htm
Mag Frequency: Quarterly (should be monthly)
Single Issue: GBP1.00 (secure online ordering using Master/Visa)
Terms: Work may be submitted wordprocessed on side of A4, on computer disc in: Word.doc; plain text; by e-mail in the same formats and in Braille.

L
LINKS

Publishes quality, unpublished poetry and reviews. Any subject or style, length up to 100 lines. Poems selected on merit. Attempts a balance of established writers with new poets who show promise. No poems accepted by email.

Editor Name(s): Bill Headdon
Address: Bude Haven 18 Frankfield Rise, Tunbridge Wells TN2 5LF
Email: billheaddon@supanet.com
Mag Frequency: Twice a year
Subscription: £4 per year, £7.50 2 years, state pensioners £1.50 and £5.50, overseas £6 and £10
Single Issue: £2
Overseas: £3 per issue
Payment in: Sterling cheques only
Payable to: Links
Inserts accepted: No
Circulation approx: 300
Payment terms to contributors: Complimentary copy of magazine
Accept/rejection approx times: 2 weeks

LITERARY REVIEW

Founded 1979. Monthly. Publishes book reviews (commissioned), features and articles on literary subjects. Prospective contributors are best advised to contact the Editor in writing. Unsolicited manuscripts not welcome. Runs a monthly poetry competition, the Literary Review Grand Poetry Competition, on a given theme. Open to subscribers only. Articles published in the magazine.

Address: 44 Lexington Street, London W1R 3LF
Subs to: Literary Review Subscriptions, 45-46 Poland Street, London W1E 5HU
Email: litrev@dircon.co.uk
Mag Frequency: Monthly
Subscription: £30 UK
Single Issue: £2.70
Overseas: £36 Europe/£36 (US $60) US and Canada Airspeed/£50 (US $84) RoW airmail
Payment in: Cheque/Mastercard/Visa/Amex
Payable to: The Literary Review
Inserts accepted: Yes
Terms: £34 (under 10gsm per 1000)
Circulation approx: 15000
Payment terms to contributors: Varies
Accept/rejection approx times: No unsolicited manuscripts

£

THE LITTLE RED BOOK

The International Guide to Pagan Resources. Lists of Pagan magazines, shops, services etc, with an events calender and local moots listing. Approximately 150 pages, A5 size paperback format with colour cover.
Also includes a magazine section - we consider fiction, poetry, cartoons and factual articles that are Pagan-oriented.

Editor Name(s): Brian P Dobson
Address: Oakleaf Circle, PO Box 513, Bamber Bridge, Preston PR5 6UZ
Telephone: 01772 499009
Fax: 01772 491581
Email: oakleafcircle@yahoo.co.uk
Website: http://uk.geocities.com/oakleafcircle
Mag Frequency: 4 times a year
Subscription: £14
Single Issue: £4 (UK), £5 Europe, $12 RoW
Payment in: Sterling/cash
Payable to: Oakleaf Circle
Inserts accepted: No
Advertising Rates: All-text ads free (must be Pagan-oriented)
Circulation approx: 500
Payment terms to contributors: Free copy
Accept/rejection approx times: 6 months

LONDON REVIEW OF BOOKS

The London Review of Books is the largest literary magazine in Europe. Founded in 1979, the LRB appears twice a month with essay-length reviews of recent books in the fields of literature, politics, history, philosophy, science and the arts. LRB uses around 200 contributors a year, including many of the leading non-fiction writers in the USA and UK. LRB publishes Frank Kermode, Alan Bennett, Edward Jaid, Jenny Diski, Hilary Mantel, Marina Warner, Ian Hamilton, Colm Toibin and many other distinguished writers. It has been called the most 'radical literary magazine in Britain.

Editor Name(s): Mary-Kay Wilmers
Address: 28 Little Russell Street, London WC1A 2HN
Telephone: 020 7209 1141
Fax: 020 7209 1151
Email: edit@lrb.co.uk
Website: www.lrb.co.uk
Mag Frequency: 24 times a year
Subscription: £70.80 UK
Single Issue: £2.95
Back Issue: £3.50
Overseas: £78 Europe, £84 RoW
Payment in: £ Sterling
Payable to: LRB Ltd
Inserts accepted: Yes
Terms: £78 per 1000
Advertising Rates: Full page £2,277
Circulation approx: 37,778 (ABC)
Payment terms to contributors: £100 per 1000 words
Accept/rejection approx times: 1-2 months

ℒ

THE LONG POEM GROUP NEWSLETTER

A4pp well-printed newsletter devoted to debating the long poem in our time, and publishing: the transactions of the Long Poem Group; a checklist of long poems published in Britain in the last 30 years; and one or two reviews of newly-published long poems.

Editor Name(s): William Oxley and Sebastian Barker
Address: 6 The Mount, Furzeham, Brixham, South Devon TQ5 8QY
Email: pwoxley@aol.com.uk
Website: http://www.bath.ac.uk/-exxdgdc
Mag Frequency: Occasional
Subscription: Free - for SAE of 27p, A5 or larger envelope
Single Issue: Free - for SAE of 27p, A5 or larger envelope
Overseas: 2 x IRCs
Inserts accepted: No
Circulation approx: 400 - 500
Payment terms to contributors: None
Accept/rejection approx times: N/A

MAELSTROM

Maelstrom is a genre fiction magazine, publishing short stories up to 10,000 words in length. We publish mainly science fiction, fantasy, horror and mystery stories, plus a few poems of a similar nature. We also publish a few book reviews and letters, as well as artwork illustrating the stories.

Address: 24 Fowler Close, Southchurch, Southend-on-Sea, Essex SS1 2RD
Email: solmag@solpubs.freeserve.co.uk
Website: www.solpubs.freeserve.co.uk
Mag Frequency: Twice yearly
Subscription: 2 for £3.50; 4 for £6.50
Single Issue: £1.80
Back Issue: Numbers 1-5 £1/Numbers 6 and 7 £1.80
Overseas: US 2 for $10, 4 for $20
Payment in: Equivalent in cash - no foreign cheques
Payable to: Sol Publications
Inserts accepted: Yes
Terms: 35p per 100g
Circulation approx: 250
Payment terms to contributors: £4 per 1000 words/£5 per 1000 words if supplied on disc
Accept/rejection approx times: 3 months

M
THE MAGAZINE

A publication of the Creative Writing Programme of Open Studies, Warwick University. Publishes poems and short stories. Poets submit 2-4 poems, up to 50 lines. Stories up to 1500 words. Subjects eclectic. Submissions must be accompanied by stamped, self-addressed envelope for return or acknowledgement. We do not review or otherwise publicise poetry or short story collections. The Magazine is available by mail order or in local (Warwick area) bookstores.

Editor Name(s): Gillian Bailey, Jenny Dodge
Address: c/o Open Studies Dept of Continuing Education, University of Warwick, Coventry CV4 7AL
Mag Frequency: Twice a year
Subscription: N/A
Single Issue: £3.50 mailed/£3 in local shops
Back Issue: £4
Overseas: £1 extra postage
Payment in: Sterling cheques
Payable to: Warwick University, Open Studies
Inserts accepted: No
Terms: Unknown
Circulation approx: 250
Payment terms to contributors: 1 free copy
Accept/rejection approx times: variable - up to six months

MAGMA

Founded in 1994 and published by the Stukeley Press. Each issue is edited by a different member of the Press within a common editorial approach. Poems in the mainstream-modernist range. Interest in new poets and experimental work. Recent interviews with Mark Doty, Kate Clanchy, Ruth Padel, Don Paterson, Vicki Feaver, Billy Collins. Reviews/articles. Images black and white also welcome, whether accompanying poems or freestanding.

Address: David Boll, Editorial Secretary, 43 Keslake Road, London NW6 6DH
Email: magmapoems@aol.com
Website: www.champignon.net/magma
Mag Frequency: 3 times yearly
Subscription: £11 plus postage outside UK: DRL copy £1.15 Europe, £2.10 Pacific Rim, £2.00 USA etc.)
Single Issue: £4 plus postage if outside UK
Back Issue: £2
Payment in: IMO/Sterling cheque
Payable to: Magma
Inserts accepted: Yes
Circulation approx: 300 print, c. 10,000 web
Payment terms to contributors: Free copy of magazine
Accept/rejection approx times: Usually within 2 months

ℳ
MAGNOLIAWORLD FRIENDS GAZETTE

A friendly magazine for those wishing to correspond with penpals worldwide on a large variety of subjects. Long list of pals, some just want a friendly word, others may have a collection, eg dolls, teddies, spoons, bookmarks etc. Each issue includes one or more craft idea and pattern, gardening page, story or poem, puzzle, recipes, list of other penpal clubs, tips and other useful information. Also VC Round Robin and Letter RR. Please send 1 viewcard to join. Send magazine fee or SAE/IRC or sorry no reply.

Editor Name(s): Mrs B Jones
Address: 69 Pinhoe Road, Exeter EX4 7HS
Mag Frequency: Every 3 months
Subscription: UK - 4 issues £3.75 includes p&p
Single Issue: £1 includes p&p
Overseas: All countries 4 IRCs for single copy
Payment in: Overseas: $ & IRCs
Payable to: B Jones
Circulation approx: 100 plus
Payment terms to contributors: None. Penpal names listed free and other clubs listed free

THE MAGPIE'S NEST

Welcomes poetry and short fiction of an unusual theme. Not keen on material of a romantic nature.

Editor Name(s): Bal Saini
Address: 176 Stoney Lane, Sparkhill, Birmingham B12 8AN
Email: bal.saini@virgin.net
Mag Frequency: Quarterly
Subscription: £6 per annum
Single Issue: £1.50
Overseas: £8 per annum
Payment in: Cheque
Payable to: The Magpie's Nest
Inserts accepted: No
Advertising Rates: £10 per half page
Circulation approx: 400
Accept/rejection approx times: 8-10 weeks

𝓜
MALFUNCTION PRESS

Poetry must have a science fiction or fantasy slant. Works with an Italian connection regarded with interest. Castle and fortification studies also considered for Postern Magazine.

Address: Malfunction Press (PE Presford), Rose Cottage, 3 Tram Lane, Buckley, Flintshire CH7 3JB Wales
Subs to: Postern only £1.25 per issue
Email: rosecot@presford.freeserve.co.uk
Mag Frequency: Not fixed
Subscription: 1st class SAE only
Single Issue: Same
Payable to: PE Presford
Inserts accepted: No
Circulation approx: To demand

MANIFOLD

M

Manifold publishes original high-quality poetry in any traditional or innovative style, in any variant of English, and also major European languages (French, German, Italian, Spanish, Latin); likewise translations of poetry from less-known languages. Our major requirement is that poems be good of their kind. Most themes are acceptable - but poets submitting works on political, 'protest' or religious themes should make sure their offerings have some genuine poetic quality. (Manifold is a poetry magazine, not a pulpit or soapbox!) Manifold runs a series of on-going competitions for specified themes or forms. Prizes are modest, but there are no entry fees. In addition to poetry, Manifold also publishes book, theatre and art reviews, and also the 'Roundabout' gossip column of the poetry scene. Manifold is strongly opposed to any form of censorship - hence it accepts no grants or subsides of any kind (knowing that these all too often come with invisable 'strings'). Its pages are open to the works of subscribers and non-scribers alike, though there are certain incentives and fringe benefits for subscribers.

Editor Name(s): Vera Rich
Address: Manifold, 99 Vera Avenue, London N21 1RP
Telephone: 020 8360 3202
Fax: Same as phone
Email: verarich@clara.co.uk
Website: http://members.xoom.com/manifoldpoet
Mag Frequency: Quarterly
Subscription: £8 (UK)
Single Issue: £2.50
Back Issue: £2
Overseas: £10 per year if paid in Sterling. Otherwise US $25 per year, $35 for two years (because of conversion charges)
Payment in: Payment accepted in any convertible currency (but see subscription rates above). Special arrangements are available for subscribers in Central-Eastern Europe, the Baltic States and the CIS. (Please write for details)
Payable to: Manifold
Inserts accepted: No
Advertising Rates: At present Manifold does not carry advertising
Circulation approx: Manifold has only recently been relaunched
Payment terms to contributors: None at present, save for the normal complimentary copy, and modest prizes for competition winners
Accept/rejection approx times: At least three months

M
MARKINGS

Now in its 7th year and established as one of Scotland's leading arts and literary magazines that has integrated itself into its local community as well as reaching major cultural centres nationwide. Markings is funded from various sources including local businesses and the Scottish Arts Council and it thereby maintains independence by being reliant on no one single body. Hence Markings is not afraid of controversy and is committed to providing a platform for new talent. It also publishes extensive, often serialised, articles and criticism and is always on the lookout for good line drawings and encourages the art of translation.

Editor Name(s): John Hudson
Address: 77 High Street, Kirkcudbright, Dumfries & Galloway DG6 4JW Scotland
Telephone: 01557 331557
Fax: Same as phone
Email: markings@btinternet.com
Website: http://www.j.hudson.btinternet.co.uk/markings
Mag Frequency: 3 per year
Subscription: £5
Single Issue: £3
Back Issue: Same
Overseas: Same
Payment in: Sterling
Payable to: Markings
Inserts accepted: Yes
Terms: Free to good causes
Advertising Rates: £80 full page, £45 half page, £25 quarter page
Circulation approx: 1000
Payment terms to contributors: Pay for commissioned/requested articles/poems
Accept/rejection approx times: 8 weeks

MARQUIS

M

The fetish fantasy magazine. Stylish full colour magazine featuring the best fetishistic photographs, illustrations, stories and fetish scene news. Only fetish erotica stories published, which are illustrated by the publishers. Published in 3 language editions - English/German/French.

Editor Name(s): Peter W Czernich (Germany)/Neal Mather (UK)
Address: Marquis, PO Box 1426, Shepton Mallet, Somerset BA4 6HZ
Telephone: 01749 831 397
Fax: 01749 831 380
Email: neal.v@ukonline.co.uk
Mag Frequency: Quarterly
Subscription: £55 (6 issues) £28 (3 issues)
Single Issue: £10
Overseas: USA $125 (6 issues) $65 (3 issues)
Payment in: Cheque/credit card/Switch/PO/cash
Payable to: Marquis
Inserts accepted: No
Advertising Rates: Full page £1000/smaller ad space and lineage available
Circulation approx: 40,000 (total 3 editions)
Payment terms to contributors: Upon publication, up to £50 per printed page (rates vary)
Accept/rejection approx times: 3 months

𝓜
MAYPOLE EDITIONS BIENNUAL ANTHOLOGY

Publisher of plays and poetry in the main. Two to three titles a year. Titles: Snorting Mustard One; Snorting Mustard Two; Metallum Damnantorum; Love Sonnets; Chocolate Rose Memoriam. Neon Lily Tiger; A Crusty Tome; Black Ribbons; Fusing Tulips. Novels: X and the Glawkoid Party; Memento Mori, Cock Robin; No Bodyguard (a director's cut version) Fulvia; Plays: Laurel Trireme; Frog; Battle Beach; Piraeus Pelican; Camillus; Medea Two; Tarquinia; Tarquinia Two; Procne; Cinderfield; Egretta and Lucretia; Henry 11; Zukov. Next year's plays: Aella; Jugertha; Cwendreda. Unsolicited manuscripts always welcome, provided return postage included. Poetry is always welcome for collected anthologies, and should be approximately thirty lines of tight verse, broadly covering social concerns, ethnic minority issues, feminist issues, romance generally, travel brogues and lyric rhyming verse. No politics, except evenly comparative. The bi-annual collected anthology is designed as a small press platform for first-time poets who might not otherwise get into print, and a permanent showcase for those already published who want to break into the mainstream via a junior vehicle. Catalogue £1, plus A5 SAE. Please be patient when submitting because of the huge volume of submissions. Exempt charity status.

Address: 22 Mayfair Avenue, Ilford, Essex IG1 3DL
Mag Frequency: Once every two years
Single Issue: £7.95
Payable to: Barry Taylor

M

MEMORY LANE

Memory Lane is a lively magazine covering popular music of the 1920s through to the 1950s. Our particular areas of interest are dance bands, vocalists, instrumentalists, big bands, jazz, personalities, music hall and variety. The accent is placed firmly on the British scene, although we do make the occasional excursions across the Atlantic. (We do not cover rock 'n' roll, pop music, rock, folk, country, classical music or opera.) Our readers come from all walks of life and span all age groups. In particular, Memory Lane has become a focal point for collectors of 'popular' 78 rpm records. Each quarterly issue contains articles and features by our team of top writers and journalists. We include biographical features, reviews of CD and cassette re-issues, book reviews, discographical information, obituaries and picture pages. We also have a very spirited readers' letters section and encourage well-researched articles from new writers. We also publish advertisements. It is all presented in a relaxed and informal style which makes Memory Lane both an informative and enjoyable read. Associated with Memory Lane is a cassette club through which registered subscribers are able to borrow especially made pre-recorded cassettes free of charge. Memory Lane also incorporates the Al Bowlly Circle for Admirers of Britain's Greatest Singer of the '78 RPM Era'. Visit our web site for further details.

Editor Name(s): Ray Pallett
Address: PO Box 1939, Leigh-on-Sea, SS9 3UH
Email: editor@memorylane.org.uk
Website: www.memorylane.org.uk
Mag Frequency: Quarterly (Feb, May, Aug, Nov)
Subscription: £10 (UK) £14 (Overseas surface mail)
Single Issue: £2.50 (UK) £3.50 (Overseas surface mail)
Payment in: UK: cheque/PO/cash, Overseas: draft in sterling drawn on bank in UK
Payable to: Memory Lane
Inserts accepted: Yes
Terms: £75 per 1000
Advertising Rates: From £5 (mini display) to £75 (full page display)
Circulation approx: 2000
Payment terms to contributors: Individually negotiated
Accept/rejection approx times: 3 weeks

M
MENARD PRESS

Menard Press, founded in 1969, specialises in literary translation, mainly of poetry. In addition to literary texts, it has published essays on the nuclear issue and a number of testimonies by survivors of Nazism. Menard's worldwide trade distributors are Central Books, apart from North America, where SPD Inc (Berkeley) represents it. Menard Press has a new seperate imprint, Menard Medames, for the publication of erotic texts. The first one was published in 2001: Anthony Howell's poems Spending, with illustrations by Dilys Bidewell.

Editor Name(s): Anthony Rudolf
Address: Menard Press, 8 The Oaks, Woodside Avenue, London, N12 8AR
Telephone: 020 8446 5571
Fax: 01770 8446 5571
Terms: Imprints: Menard Press, Menard Medames. No unsolicited Mss

M

MERMAID TURBULENCE

Founded in 1993, Mermaid Turbulence publishes a handful of books every year along with hand made and artists books. Areas of intrest are: Essays, architecture, art, fiction, food, photography, poetry and children's books. Complete catalogue available upon request.

Editor Name(s): Mari-aymone Djeribi
Address: Annaghmaconway, Cloone, Leitim, Ireland
Telephone: 00 353 78 36134
Fax: 00 353 78 36134
Accept/rejection approx times: Three weeks, 1 month

M
MODERN DANCE

Music review magazine that reviews all types of music - mainly CDs (albums), occasional music-related videos and books. Pop, rock, jazz, classical, metal, blues and opera - indeed, everything! Also Modern Dance would be interested in Music-related articles for publication in either the magazine or on the website.

Address: 12 Blakestones Road, Slaithwaite, Huddersfield HD7 5UQ
Fax: 01484 842324
Email: moderndance@btinternet.com
Website: www.madasafish.com/~moderndance
Mag Frequency: 2-3-4 months
Subscription: Free with SAEs (maximum of five)
Single Issue: Free with SAE
Back Issue: No back issues
Overseas: Not available
Payable to: N/A although donations welcome D Hughes
Inserts accepted: Yes
Terms: £10
Circulation approx: 4000
Payment terms to contributors: N/A
Accept/rejection approx times: N/A

M
MODERN POETRY IN TRANSLATION

MPT, an international journal founded by Daniel Weissbort and Ted Hughes in the 60s, has been relaunched by King's College London under Daniel Weissbort's editorship. Published twice a year, the journal is dedicated to new translations into English of poems from all over the world, with no restrictions on period and no ideological bias. MPT also publishes articles on translation (with the emphasis on practice rather than theory), reviews of new translations and occasional features on individual translators. There is generally a substantial 'themed' section: issues 1 to 17 have featured Yves Bonnefoy, Franz Baermann Steiner (a bi-lingual edition with previously unpublished poems and Michael Hamburger's translations), Anna Kamienska and other Polish and East European poets, the Jerusalem International Poetry Festival, Galician-Portuguese troubadours, Brazil, Wales, France, Filipino and Pacific Rim, Russian poetry, Peru, Dutch/Flemish poets, modern Greek poetry, Palestinian and Israeli poets, contemporary Italian poets, German and French poetry, and Non-English language poetry in England. Most issues of the New Series have run to over 248 pages; MPT is effectively a well-designed paperback book. Forthcoming issues will include 'Iraqi poetry' and 'European Voices'. Recent editions include 'Mother Tongues'.

Address: Professor Norma Rinsler, MPT, School of Humanities, King's College London, Strand, London WC2R 2LS
Fax: 020 7848 2415
Website: www.kcl.ac.uk/mpt
Mag Frequency: Twice yearly
Subscription: £20 annually
Single Issue: £10
Back Issue: £7.50
Overseas: £24 or $36 (US dollars)
Payment in: Sterling/IMO/AMEX money order
Payable to: King's College London (MPT)
Inserts accepted: No
Advertising Rates: £90 full page/£45 half page
Circulation approx: 400 plus
Payment terms to contributors: £12 per poem or £15 per page as appropriate
Accept/rejection approx times: Usually 4-6 weeks

ℳ
MONAS HIEROGLYPHICA

Monas Hieroglyphica was founded in 1994 and is looking for articles on: Magick, Paganism, Literature, Horror, History and Archaeology. Fiction should be no longer than 2,000 words, or by arrangement by the editor for longer pieces, and be of the above subjects. Artwork must be of the highest standard, be in black and white and be of powerful themes.

Fast becoming recognised as a publication of literary integrity, has featured interviews with authors Storm Constantine, Freda Warrington, Joi Brozek, Caitlin R Kiernan and forthcoming interviews with Poppy Z Brite and many more.

Monas Hieroglyphica also has featured interviews with alternative bands Children On Stun, All Living and Faithful Dawn.

'... the artwork... is quite remarkable. Clearly there is a lot of commitment from the writers of this 'zine'.' - Chronicles Magazine.

'MH comes across as the thinking Goth's fanzine.' - The Bloody Quill.

'This is a fascinating literary zine... a serious journal... Along with some very striking artwork, this is an interesting package.' - New Hope International.

'I strongly advise every single Zine Zone reader to get a copy.' - Zine Zone.

'Buy it!' - Tombraver Magazine.

Editor Name(s): Jamie W Spracklen - Editor, Sandra Scholes - Assistant Editor
Address: 58 Seymour Road, Hadleigh, Benfleet, Essex SS7 2HL
Email: monas_hieroglyphica@postmaster.co.uk
Website: http://www.geocities.com/SoHo/Museum/9668
Mag Frequency: 4 issues a year
Subscription: £6
Single Issue: £1.50
Back Issue: By arrangement
Overseas: £12
Payment in: Sterling
Payable to: Jamie Spracklen
Inserts accepted: Yes
Terms: Free
Advertising Rates: Free in most cases
Circulation approx: 100
Payment terms to contributors: Copy of magazine
Accept/rejection approx times: 2 weeks

M

MONDO

Mondo is not your usual angst-ridden, sixth form navel-gazing title. Instead, it's the only comic which is like a bloody good night out - but minus the hangover! It's got top comic strips, pin-ups, articles, text stories and an attitude too! We're always looking for new contributors... drop us a line... and bring a bottle!

Editor Name(s): Lee Davis
Address: 140 Amersham Avenue, Edmonton, London N18 1DY
Mag Frequency: Monthly, summer special and special editions
Subscription: £12 per 12 issues/£6 per 6
Single Issue: £1
Back Issue: £1.50
Overseas: Write for details
Payment in: Pounds Sterling
Payable to: Lee Davis
Inserts accepted: Yes
Terms: Write for details
Circulation approx: 50-200
Payment terms to contributors: N/A
Accept/rejection approx times: 2-3 weeks or less

M
MOONSTONE

Moonstone, founded in 1979 features pantheistic/ecological poetry of all descriptions. Regular contributors include Steve Sneyd, Patricia Prime and Kenneth C Steven. Notes on contributors, short reviews and exchange listings are included. Occasionally black and white artwork is accepted. Opinions given by contributors are not necessarily those of the editors. Previously unpublished work, clearly typed with SAE, should be sent to the address below. Study the magazine before submitting mss is advised.

Editor Name(s): Talitha Clare and Robin Brooks
Address: Talitha Clare, 'Moonstones' SOS, The Old Station Yard, Settle, North Yorkshire BD24 9RP
Email: Talitha.clare@virgin.net
Mag Frequency: Quarterly at the Festivals
Subscription: £7 pa
Single Issue: £2
Back Issue: £2.50
Overseas: $24 pa USA/Canada/Australia/Europe
Payment in: Notes/bills only. No cheques except in sterling
Payable to: Talitha Clare
Inserts accepted: Yes
Terms: By arrangement
Advertising Rates: By arrangement
Circulation approx: Increasing
Payment terms to contributors: Free copy of magazine - contributors retain their copyright, by request
Accept/rejection approx times: All contributions of a pantheistic/ecological nature considered within 6-8 weeks; SAE essential

MOTHER EARTH MAGAZINE

M

A women's magazine with a difference, covering personal development, lifestyle and spirituality, psychology, alternative therapies, global and environmental issues, animal welfare, creativity and inspiration, life changes, fascinating history, tradition and folklore, personal experiences and empowerment.

Editor Name(s): Jane Reid
Address: 5 Grosvenor Close, Great Sankey, Warrington, Cheshire, WA5 1XQ
Email: motherearth@themutual.net
Website: Coming shortly
Mag Frequency: Six - monthly
Subscription: £5 per year, £10 for two years, payment in sterling
Single Issue: £2.50
Back Issue: Last issue only - £2.50 each
Overseas: Outside EC include £1.50 extra per copy
Payable to: Jane Reid
Inserts accepted: No
Terms: Free advertising in exchange for articles, poetry or artwork accepted. Free advertising for selected charities and causes.
Advertising Rates: Magazine is A4 size: 1/6 page £15, 1/4 page £20, 1/2 page £30, whole page £50.
Circulation approx: 500 and growing
Accept/rejection approx times: Within 1 month

M
MSLEXIA: FOR WOMEN WHO WRITE

Mslexia is for women who write, who want to write, who teach creative writing, or who have a special interest in womens literature. Mslexia combines features and advice about writing with some of the most striking new fiction and poetry by women. Myslexia gives the insider's view of women's writing: What editors are looking for (and what puts them off); the psychology of creativity; professional advice on presenting work; reviews of the best new books by women; consumer reports on writing guides, correspondence courses; websites and more.

Myslexia's readers say the magazine has changed their lives. Some have received letters from literary agents or radio producers who scan the magazine for fresh talent. Fay Weldon called Mslexia 'Diverse and brilliant' while Jo Shapcott said that it 'Deserves to go flying into people's hands'. Contributors to the magazine include Wendy Cope, Anne Fine, Maggie Gee, Jackie Kay, Al Kennedy, Michele Roberts, Fay Weldon and many more.

Submissions are welcome from poets, prose-writers and journalists. Please request contributors guidelines in the first instance.

Editor Name(s): Debbie Taylor
Address: 5 Charlotte Square, Newcastle Upon Tyne NE1 4XF
Telephone: 0191 2616656
Fax: 0191 2616636
Email: postbag@mslexia.demon.co.uk
Website: www.mslexia.co.uk
Mag Frequency: Quarterly
Subscription: £18.75
Single Issue: £4.75
Overseas: £24 Europe/£30 RoW
Payment in: Sterling, Euro Cheque or drawn on the UK
Payable to: Mslexia Publications Ltd
Inserts accepted: Yes
Terms: £100 per 1,000
Advertising Rates: Upon request
Circulation approx: 7000, readership of 12,000
Payment terms to contributors: £25 per poem or 1000 words of prose
Accept/rejection approx times: 3 months after closing date

MULTI-STOREY

M

An innovative new literary magazine featuring short stories, poetry, interviews, book reviews and art, presented in a book format with colour cover. We are eager to publish new-comers as well as those already established. Each issue is themed: the first issue out in June 2000 has a glamour theme. Potential contributors should contact us for guidelines prior to submitting their work. Always enclose a SAE.

We run short story competitions every issue in association with BBC GMR. The winner will hear their story on the radio and see it published in Multi-Storey. Contact us for competition guidelines.

Editor Name(s): Gary Parkinson, Bill Jones, Finella Davenport
Address: PO Box 62, Levenshulme, Manchester M19 1TH
Mag Frequency: 2 per year
Subscription: £7 a year (incl p&p)
Single Issue: £3.95 (incl p&p)
Overseas: £10 per year (incl p&p)
Payment in: Cheque
Payable to: Multi-Storey editors
Advertising Rates: contact the editors
Circulation approx: 500 for the first issue: this number will be increasing
Payment terms to contributors: a complimentary copy
Accept/rejection approx times: 4 weeks to 4 months

N.PARADOXA

n.paradoxa is the only international feminist art journal in the world. n.paradoxa publishes in depth scholarly articles on the work of contemporary women artists which discuss issues in feminist theory. Contributors are women artists, curators, academics and art critics, worldwide. Two seperate editions are published: print is bi-annual and thematic (96 pages), (ISSN 1461 - 0434); online is quarterly (ISSN 1462 - 0426). Different issues/volumes have different contents. Articles are both commissioned. Book reviews and web-site reviews are also published. Print version began in 1998.

Editor Name(s): Katy Deepwell
Address: KT Press, 38 Bellot St, London, SE10 0AQ
Telephone: +44 (0) 208858 3331
Fax: +44 (0) 208858 3331
Email: k.deepwell@ukonline.co.uk
Website: http://web.ukonline.co.uk/n.paradoxa/
Mag Frequency: Print: 2x, Jan/July. Online: Quarterly
Subscription: Print 2 Vols Annual, £18 Ind. UK/Europe, £32 Instituitions UK/Europe
Single Issue: £7.95/$12
Overseas: Print 2 vols annual, $38 Ind. ROW (outside europe) $72 Institutions ROW
Payment in: £ or $ as specified for postal area
Payable to: Available on request
Inserts accepted: Yes
Advertising Rates: Available on request
Circulation approx: 2500
Payment terms to contributors: By arrangement
Accept/rejection approx times: 3 months prior to publication

NATIONAL SMALL PRESS CENTRE

Founded in 1992 at Middlesex University, England, the National Small Press Centre provides a focus for small presses and independent self-publishers and actively promotes them by collecting and disseminating information, exhibitions, talks, courses, workshops, conferences and fairs. Publishes News From The Centre (bi-monthly) and Small Press Listings (quarterly). Joint annual subscription to these publications: £12. Small Press Fairs are held annually in Royal Festival Hall in London and the Centre's Handbook is available by mail order for £12 plus £1.50 postage. The Centre is twinned with the Mainz Mini-Press Archive in Mainz, Germany and the New York Small Press Center.

Editor Name(s): John Nicholson
Address: BM Bozo, London WC1N 3XX
Advertising Rates: On request

N
NETWORK NEWS

Sinister Beasts, Earth Mysteries, The Occult Shenanigens of the Royal Family, The Occult Symbolism of British Currency, Time Travelling Punk Rockers, Nocturnal Emissions Merchandising and much much more in this occasional journal of guerrilla ontology.

Editor Name(s): Nigel Ayers
Address: Earthly Delights, PO Box 2, Lostwithiel, Cornwall PL22 0YY
Email: nigel.ayers@virgin.net
Website: www.earthlydelights.co.uk
Mag Frequency: 4 issues per Imaginary Time year
Subscription: £5
Single Issue: £1.50
Overseas: £10
Payment in: Cash
Payable to: N Ayers
Inserts accepted: No
Advertising Rates: £1000 per page
Circulation approx: 50,000
Payment terms to contributors: Negotiable
Accept/rejection approx times: 30 Days

NEW FICTION

New Fiction publishes short stories by new and established writers. We decided that the art form was sadly neglected and that authors had little scope for seeing their work in print.* 30 stories are chosen per volume and published in perfect bound books.

*so we decided to recitfy this dire situation.

Editor Name(s): Heather Killingray
Address: Remus House, Coltsfoot Drive, Woodston, Peterborough, PE2 9JX
Telephone: 01733 890099
Fax: 01733 313524
Inserts accepted: No
Accept/rejection approx times: 3 months

NEW HOPE INTERNATIONAL REVIEW

Books, magazines, cassettes, CDs, PC-software, videos. A unique guide to items you probably won't find in your local shop. Reviews run from a few paragraphs to a few pages or more and reviewers are afraid neither to praise nor to damn. Though its first love is poetry, it covers world and local affairs, literature, music, art, history, religion, science, computers, health and much more. Essential reading for writers, librarians and all lovers of words. NHI does not publish unsolicited reviews. If you would like to be a reviewer for us, write to the editor, stating any areas of special interest/ expertise. The last printed edition Vol.20 #3, includes poetry by Christopher Allan, Kaye Axon, Rick Doble, David A Groulx, Gordon Hassall, Bill Headdon, Santiago Montobbio, Colin Nixon, Trish O'Brien, Michael J Rcith, Nathalie Thomas, Robert Truett, Lawrence Upton, Lloyd Vancil, and Gordon Wardman, as well as hundreds of reviews. ISSN 0260-7958. Price £3.75 (£5 - ex UK). All reviews are now published only on the Internet at http://www.nhi.clara.net/online.htm

Editor Name(s): Gerald England
Address: Gerald England, Editor, New Hope International Review, 20 Werneth Avenue, Gee Cross, Hyde SK14 5NL
Reviews to: Gerald England
Email: newhope@iname.com
Website: http://www.nhi.clara.net/online.htm
Payable to: G England

NEW VISION
(Formally Science Of Thought Review)

Based on the teaching of English Christian mystic Henry Thomas Hamblin, the Review has been in existence since 1921. It is devoted to the spiritual life and applied right thinking. First-hand experiences are popular that give a positive note to the reader looking for uplift, inspiration and solace. We cover meditation, complementary medicine and self development - but no more poetry please. As we are a charity, an SAE would be appreciated.

Address: Elizabeth Medlerl, New Vision, Bosham House, Bosham, Chichester, West Sussex PO18 8PJ
Fax: also phone:01243 572109
Email: scienceofthought@mistral.co.uk
Mag Frequency: Bi-monthly
Subscription: £7 annually (minimum)
Single Issue: £1.25
Back Issue: 70p (including postage)
Overseas: £9 Australia/New Zealand; $26 USA $24 Canada (Airmail extra)
Payment in: Cheque; Visa/Delta/Mastercard
Payable to: Science of Thought Press
Inserts accepted: On consideration
Circulation approx: 1500 (including 200 abroad)
Payment terms to contributors: Copy of magazine
Accept/rejection approx times: 2-4 weeks

NEW WELSH REVIEW

Wales's leading literary quarterly in English, New Welsh Review provides a literary/ cultural platform for critical articles, poems, short stories and reviews of interest primarily, but by no means exclusively, to a Welsh audience and all with an interest in Wales. It is a place where the best of Welsh writing in English, past and present, is celebrated, discussed and debated but, interpreting its brief very widely, it also takes a keen interest in resonant literary and cultural developments in other parts of the British Isles and much further afield. New Welsh Review is mainly concerned with books but it also covers developments in theatre in Wales (there is a special section), film and broadcasting, as a natural extension of its literary/cultural brief.

Editor Name(s): Victor Golightly
Address: New Welsh Review, Chapter Arts Centre, Market Road, Cardiff CF5 1QE Wales
Fax: 029 2066 5529
Email: nwr@welshnet.co.uk
Mag Frequency: Quarterly
Subscription: £18 pa (£38 two years)
Single Issue: £5.40
Back Issue: £4
Overseas: Subscription cost plus £2 surface, £6 airmail
Payment in: Sterling cheque/PO/Visa
Payable to: New Welsh Review Ltd
Inserts accepted: Yes
Terms: £80 per 1000
Advertising Rates: Full page £50/half page £30/quarter page £20/eighth page £10
Circulation approx: 900
Payment terms to contributors: Articles £20 per 1000 words/Short stories £50
Accept/rejection approx times: 3 months

THE NEW WRITER

The New Writer is a contemporary writing magazine which publishes the best in fact, fiction and poetry. It's different and it's aimed at writers with a serious intent; everyone who wants to develop their writing to meet the high expectations of today's editors. The team at The New Writer are committed to working with their readers to increase the chances of publication. That's why masses of useful market information and plenty of feedback is provided. More than that, we bring you the best in contemporary fiction and cutting-edge poetry backed up by searching articles and in-depth features in every issue. This is a forward-looking magazine with a range of contributors expert in their subjects. Whether you've just started to write or you're a more experienced writer wanting to explore new ideas and techniques, this is essential reading. Also, book reviews, competitions update, news and readers' views.

Editor Name(s): Editor: Suzanne Ruthven, Publisher: Merric Davidson
Address: PO Box 60, Cranbrook, Kent TN17 2ZR
Telephone: 01580 212626
Fax: 01580 212041
Email: editor@thenewwriter.com
Website: www.thenewwriter.com
Mag Frequency: 10 per annum
Subscription: £32.50
Single Issue: £3.50
Back Issue: Free
Overseas: £39.50 (Europe)/£45.50 (RoW) - airmail
Payment in: Sterling/Master Card, Visa, Eurocard, Switch
Payable to: The New Writer
Inserts accepted: Yes
Terms: £60 per 1000
Advertising Rates: Full page £95/Quarter £40/Back cover £195
Circulation approx: 2000
Payment terms to contributors: £20 per 1000 words non-fiction/£10 per story/£3 per poem
Accept/rejection approx times: 1 month

NEW WRITING SCOTLAND

Submissions to the 2001 volume of New Writing Scotland will be taken from 1st October 2001 until 31st January 2002.

New Writing Scotland publishes poetry and short fiction by writers resident in Scotland or Scots by birth or upbringing. The work must be neither previously published nor accepted for publication and may be in any of the languages of Scotland.

Submissions should be typed, double-spaced, on one side of the paper only and the sheets secured at the top-left corner. Prose pieces should carry an approximate word-count. You should provide a covering letter, clearly marked with your name and address. Please do not put your name or other details on the individual works. Submissions should be accompanied by two stamped addressed envelopes, with sufficient postage (one for a receipt, the other for return of the mss) and sent by 31st January 2002.

Please be aware that we have limited space in each addition, and therefore shorter pieces are more suitable - although longer items of exceptional quality may still be included. A maximum length of 3,500 words is suggested. Please send no more than two short stories and no more than six poems.

Editor Name(s): Duncan Jones (Managing Editor)
Address: ASLS, c/o Dept of Scottish History, 9 University Gardens, University of Glasgow, Glasgow G12 8QH
Telephone: 0141 330 5309
Fax: Same as phone
Email: d.jones@scothist-arts.gla.ac.uk
Website: www.asls.org.uk
Mag Frequency: Annual
Single Issue: £8.95
Overseas: £8.95 plus p&p
Payment in: Sterling
Payable to: ASLS
Inserts accepted: Yes
Terms: Single sheet, folded to A5 or smaller
Advertising Rates: Inserts only - £75
Circulation approx: 800
Payment terms to contributors: £10 per printed page
Accept/rejection approx times: 9 months

NEWSWIRE - GLOBAL MARKETS NEWSLETTER

Whether you are just starting or already winning Newswire is the essential tool for all writers, artists and photographers looking to sell their work worldwide. Why make one sale when you can make 10? Newswires unique mix of features, exclusive market news and tips from editors and other writers has helped thousands turn their hobby into a profession.

Editor Name(s): John Dunne
Address: 14 Honour Avenue, Goldthorn Park, Wolverhampton WV4 5HH
Telephone: 01902 652999
Fax: 01902 652999
Email: voyagemag@zyworld.com
Website: http://members.fortunecity.com/regentbooks/Newswire.html
Mag Frequency: Bi-monthly
Subscription: 6 issues £15, 12 issues £25
Single Issue: £3
Overseas: 6 issues £20 - Europe, £25 - ROW
Payment in: Sterling or Dollars
Payable to: JGD
Inserts accepted: Yes
Terms: £10 per 1000
Advertising Rates: £50 per page or prorata
Circulation approx: 1800
Payment terms to contributors: Up to £10 per 1000 words
Accept/rejection approx times: 1 Month

NIGHT DREAMS

Night Dreams (founded 1994) features poetry, short stories and articles concerning the weird, the frightening and the gruesome. It follows the style of the pulp magazines of the '30s and '40s.

Address: 52 Denman Lane, Huncote, Leicester LE9 3BS
Subs to: 47 Stephens Road, Walmley, Sutton Coldfield, West Midlands B76 2TS
Mag Frequency: Quarterly
Subscription: £10.50 pa
Single Issue: £2.80
Back Issue: £2.50
Overseas: £12.50 pa
Payment in: IMO/Cheque/PO
Payable to: Kirk S King
Inserts accepted: Yes
Terms: £10
Payment terms to contributors: £3 per 1000 words plus free copy

NIGHTMARE ABBEY

Nightmare Abbey, the Peterborough SF Club's gothic site, was started in 1997 to mark the Dracula Centenary. It exists to promote the local, (north Cambs, south Lincs, east Northants, west Norfolk), gothic scene, (such as it is). Rather than using fiction, poetry or music reviews, (except in certain circumstances - there are already plenty of venues for these), focuses on other aspects of Gothic Lifestyle. Check out the site and ask the site manager about submitting on either disk, down the wire or in hardcopy.

Editor Name(s): Bakul Patel
Address: c/o 58 Pennington, Orton Goldhay, Peterborough PE2 5RB
Website: www.btinternet.com/~bakul/Gothic.htm
Mag Frequency: Regularly updated
Payment terms to contributors: None
Accept/rejection approx times: Slower than it should be...

NOMAD

Nomad Magazine contains writing by people with mental health problems, survivors of abuse, addictions or disability. Our aim is to publish high quality, stimulating literary work for the general public. We aim to share insights gained from living at the margins of society, where discoveries are sometimes comic, often painful, never mundane. We publish work by both established and new writers.

Editor Name(s): Managing Editor: Gerry Loose, selecting editors change from issue to issue
Address: 4C4 Templeton Business Centre, 62 Templeton ST, Glasgow, G40 1BA
Telephone: 0141 5564554
Fax: 0141 4008442
Email: sps@spscot.co.uk
Website: www.spscot.co.uk
Mag Frequency: 3 times a year
Subscription: £6
Single Issue: £2.50
Back Issue: 1-6 £1.98
Overseas: £7.50
Payment in: IMO
Payable to: Survivors' Poetry Scotland
Inserts accepted: Yes
Terms: By negotiation
Advertising Rates: £90 ¼ page, £120 ½ page, £200 full page
Circulation approx: 500 - 1000
Payment terms to contributors: £20 per contributor
Accept/rejection approx times: 6-8 weeks

NORFOLK POETS AND WRITERS

'Spinning Webs' is emailed every month, with bulletin updates and reviews. Norfolk Poets and Writers is for anyone willing to admit they are still learning, whatever their level of experience. News, reviews, shared critique, website display and info on mini Competitions are all part of this eZine. Members can advertise thier new books free and selected poetry and short stories are published on the website.

Norfolk Poets runs an open competition, 'Disasters Comic Verse' and Tales? Books published of best entries-SAE for rules and deadlines.

Membership is free and anyone not on the internet may receive a free printout for the price of a stamp.

Editor Name(s): Wendy Webb
Address: PO Box 210, Taverham, Norwich NR8 6WX
Telephone: 0798 917 4076
Email: To subscribe: norfolk-poets-subscribe@egroups.com or enquiries: wwbuk@yahoo.co.uk
Website: www.webbw.freeserve.co.uk
Mag Frequency: Monthly plus updates and reviews
Subscription: Free. By post: 6 stamps for 6 issues
Single Issue: Free by email, or SAE
Overseas: Email only, free
Payment in: £ Sterling
Payable to: Wendy Webb Books
Inserts accepted: Occasionally
Terms: Reciprocal
Advertising Rates: £5 for line ad in eZine plus small box ad in printout copies. £20 for 6 months. Free advertising of members books, free ads for small press magazines, by submission
Circulation approx: members 50,mailing 200
Payment terms to contributors: Publication only, free ebook, discount print books.
Accept/rejection approx times: 1 week

𝒩
THE NORTH

The North magazine offers the best of contemporary poetry by new and established writers, as well as critical articles and reviews. Submissions are welcome (up to 6 poems; please enclose SAE).

Address: The Studio, Byram Arcade, Westgate, Huddersfield HD1 1ND
Telephone: 01484 434840
Fax: 01484 426566
Email: edit@poetrybusiness.co.uk (no submissions by email)
Website: www.poetrybusiness.co.uk
Mag Frequency: Twice a year
Subscription: £10
Single Issue: £5.50
Back Issue: £3
Overseas: £16 (sterling or credit card only)
Payment in: Cheque/PO/Cash in sterling/Visa/Mastercard
Payable to: The Poetry Business Ltd
Inserts accepted: Yes
Terms: Minimum charge £10
Circulation approx: 500
Payment terms to contributors: By arrangement
Accept/rejection approx times: 1 month

O

OASIS

Oasis aims to present a wide range of excellent writing, concentrating on originality of thought, expression and imagination. In doing this, it tends to veer towards the non-traditional, the experimental, in both poetry and prose. Translations are a strong feature of the magazine. Those intending to submit work should, ideally, purchase a copy or two first to discover the nature of the magazine. Less than about 1% of submissions are accepted.

Editor Name(s): Ian Robinson and Yann Lovelock
Address: 12 Stevenage Road, London SW6 6ES
Telephone: 020 77365059
Mag Frequency: 3 issues per year
Subscription: £6 for 4 issues
Single Issue: £2.50
Back Issue: £2.50
Overseas: $30 or sterling equivalent (dollar cheques should be made payable to Robert Vas Dias)
Payable to: Oasis Books
Inserts accepted: Yes - but occasionally only and then by negotiation
Advertising Rates: None
Circulation approx: 350
Payment terms to contributors: Copies
Accept/rejection approx times: 1 month maximum

0

OBSESSED WITH PIPEWORK

In sequins and silver lycra you look superhuman, supernatural. A shaman, you seem to know how to fly. Candy floss is dropped forgotten among the straw and sawdust as the punters crane and peer to make you out appearing and disappearing up there in the strong lights and shadows under the striped canvas. They gasp and share your joy at transcending danger and the laws of gravity and entropy. That's what I mean when I say Obsessed With Pipework deals in high-wire poems that amaze and delight. Submissions of around six poems - any length, any style - are welcome, but remember the stamped addressed envelope, unless you submit via fax or email. Nothing predictable, obvious or merely clever, please - let us see your good stuff. The Obsessed criteria are originality, authenticity, creative risk and that 'aha!' feeling. OWP is one of those parties where you don't need breath freshener on the way, and you don't have to leave as the sun comes up on Monday morning. Wear makeup by all means, but as self-expression not concealment. The editor offers suggestions when appropriate.

Editor Name(s): Charles Johnson
Address: Flarestack Publishing, At Redditch Library, 15 Market Place, Redditch B98 8AR
Telephone: 01527 63291(daytime) 0121 445 2110 (evening)
Fax: 01527 68571
Email: flare.stack@virgin.net
Mag Frequency: Quarterly
Subscription: £12
Single Issue: £3.50
Back Issue: All sold out so far!
Overseas: By arrangement
Payment in: Sterling - cheque/cash/PO
Payable to: Flarestack Publishing
Inserts accepted: Yes
Terms: By agreement
Advertising Rates: By arrangement
Circulation approx: 100 plus
Payment terms to contributors: 1 free copy
Accept/rejection approx times: 6 weeks maximum

O

OCULAR

Eclectic magazine - Surreal/macabre fantasy/ horror; gothic, pagan/occult/philosophy...
articles, short stories, poems. Music/performance/art/books. Lavishly illustrated.
Not just a magazine... but a hymn - dedicated to the old gods and dwellers of dreams.
Unsolicited ms, batches of poetry, ink drawing may be sent (incl SAE) and are welcome.
Most music genres reviewed (but nothing 'mainstream' or 'middle-of-the-road'.

Editor Name(s): Lesley E Wilkinson
Address: Rosewood Cottage, Langtoft, Driffield, East Yorkshire YO25 3TQ
Telephone: 01377 267440
Mag Frequency: Twice yearly
Subscription: £4.50
Single Issue: £2.50
Overseas: £6.50 subscription, £3.50 single issue
Payment in: UK Currency/Stamps/PO/Cheques
Payable to: Lesley E Wilkinson
Inserts accepted: No
Advertising Rates: In magazine
Circulation approx: 500 rising
Payment terms to contributors: Free copy
Accept/rejection approx times: 2-4 weeks maximum

0
OLD YORKSHIRE

An A5 format magazine printed on quality paper which can trace its origins back to 1881. We specialise in recording Yorkshire's past for future generations. Articles ranging from prehistoric times up to circa 1970 will be considered. The only criterion is that they must be solely about Yorkshire and its people, nothing else will be considered. Articles with accompanying photographs or artwork stand a greater chance of acceptance. Features on Yorkshire's industry, famous or just ordinary people, abbeys, castles, battles, living conditions, customs, are all welcome. The scope is enormous. There is much of interest for the family historian: if you wish to know how your grandparents lived and worked then this is the magazine for you. Preferred article length is between 800-2,500 words. Longer features may be considered for serialisation. We also accept interesting single photographs with captions of up to 300 words. But please no Yorkshire fiction; all material submitted must be factual. We would particularly like to hear from authors who are willing to write about the history of some of Yorkshire's smaller villages. A 'guidelines for contributors' leaflet is available on request. We also publish a free e-journal which will keep you up to date with the latest events in Yorkshire. To subscribe to this free service just send your email address to e.journal@oldyorkshire.co.uk

Address: Brian Barker, Production Editor, Old Yorkshire Publications, 111 Wrenbeck Drive, Otley, West Yorkshire LS21 2BP
Telephone: 01943 461211
Fax: 01943 464702
Email: brian@oldyorkshire.co.uk
Website: www.oldyorkshire.co.uk
Mag Frequency: 5 times per year
Subscription: £12 annual
Single Issue: £2.50
Back Issue: £2.25
Overseas: £16 overseas (airmail)
Payment in: Sterling Banker's Draft overseas; Cheque/PO - inland; Mastercard; Visa
Payable to: Old Yorkshire Publications
Inserts accepted: No
Advertising Rates: On request
Circulation approx: Growing quickly
Payment terms to contributors: £10 per 1000 words pro rata plus 1 year's free subscription. Paid on publication
Accept/rejection approx times: 4 weeks

0

OLEANDER PRESS

Leading British publisher on the Arabian Peninsula; 'Italian Key Words' uniform with basic wordlists for Arabic, French, German and Spanish; travel books on Albania, Bulgaria, Finland, India, Japan, Libya, Oman, Poland and Saudi Arabia, with 'Wight Magic', 'The Aeolian Islands' and 'Bahrain'; reference books: 'A Lifetime's Reading' and 'A Dictionary of Common Fallacies'; local history: 'Cambridge Town, Gown and County' series; humour: 'English IS a Foreign Language' and 'Father Gander's Nursery Rhymes'; manual and case histories: 'The Small Publisher'; biography: 'The Life and Murder of Henry Morshead', 'The Emperor's Guest', 'Minister in Oman'; sensational 'Shakespeare' discoveries in 'De Vere is Shakespeare'; the satyr play included in the Aeschylean 'Oresteia' adapted by Whallon; the plays of Carey Harrison in signed, limited editions; the Mexican novel 'Forgotten Games' by Philip Ward

Address: 17 Stansgate Avenue, Cambridge, CB2 2QZ
Telephone: 01223 244688
Payment in: UK £
Payable to: The Oleander Press
Inserts accepted: No
Accept/rejection approx times: No submissions accepted

0

OLS NEWS

A quarterly print newsletter covering all aspects of open, flexible and distance learning. Describes the use of educational technology in the classroom-principally further and higher education in the UK but takes information from around the world. Specialises in case studies and always includes contact details.

Editor Name(s): Dr David P Bosworth
Address: 11 Malford Grove, Gilwern, Abergavenny, Monmouthshire NP7 0RN
Telephone: 01873 830 872
Email: OLS-News@zoo.co.uk
Mag Frequency: Quarterly (March, June, September, December)
Subscription: £28 Sterling (UK)
Single Issue: £8 Sterling
Overseas: Rest of EU £34 Sterling, RoW £40 Sterling (when drawn on a UK bank). $64 US or $100 Aus (paid to Synergy Media, PO Box 637, Northbridge, Sydney, NSW 1560)
Payment in: Sterling or US Dollars to the UK Address (payable to OLS News), Australian dollars to the Sydney address (payable to Synergy Media)
Payable to: OLS News or Synergy Media (see payment in)
Inserts accepted: Yes
Terms: Basic rate £25 Sterling
Advertising Rates: By negotiation
Payment terms to contributors: By special agreement only (all contributors receive a voucher copy of OLS News)
Accept/rejection approx times: Initial response by return; detailed nearer publication

O

ORBIS

Orbis receives no grant-aid from any source, and is therefore totally independent in its attitude and its choice of material. Now in its 30th year, it continues to be the most reader-orientated magazine in Britain, with letter columns and 'Reader Award' prizes for contributors. It is primarily a poetry magazine, and though it does publish prose occasionally, not much is used in a year (maximum:1000 words, not formula fiction). Virtually every kind of poetry is considered, except the more extreme experimental type, or poetry in which the message occludes the language. Likely to accept work from new writers, but accepts less than 2% of what is received.

*Special Note: Orbis is about to change hands, and different publishing arrangements are in place for the interim period. In 2001, the last issue under Mike Shidds' editorship, No 120, will be the only one published. It will be available as a special one-off, price £10.00. In 2002, Orbis will be merged with another magazine, and the new publication will be edited by Carole Baldock.

Address: 27 Valley View, Primrose, Jarrow, Tyne & Wear NE32 5QT
Mag Frequency: Quarterly
Subscription: £15
Single Issue: £4
Back Issue: £2
Overseas: US $28
Payable to: Orbis magazine
Inserts accepted: Yes
Terms: £50 per 1000
Circulation approx: 1000
Payment terms to contributors: £5 per acceptance/£50 per issue prizes
Accept/rejection approx times: Return post/up to 6 weeks in some cases

O
OSTINATO

Ostinato publishes poems/articles/interviews/prose relating to jazz/improvised music. The emphasis is on work that enshrines jazz and its practitioners in context; be it spiritual, socio-political or musical. Production values are very high. Original artwork and photographs are used. Review section is lengthy but mostly in-house. Ostinato is currently in limbo due to financial difficulties associated with ill health. Sales of back issues would help kick-start. Details/press package from Editorial Address. SAE please.

Address: PO Box 522, London N8 7SZ
Mag Frequency: Irregular
Subscription: Not currently applicable
Single Issue: Varies usually £2.50
Payment in: Sterling cheques only
Payable to: Ostinato
Inserts accepted: Yes
Terms: Swop with other magazines
Circulation approx: Unknown but reaches a wide audience
Payment terms to contributors: Contributary copy
Accept/rejection approx times: When magazine is active: 2 weeks; longer at other times

O

OTHER POETRY

A thrice-yearly magazine of poems, plus reviews (by internally appointed writers) occasional interviews or other articles. All submissions are judged on merit by four experienced editors (themselves well published poets).

Editor Name(s): Michael Standen (Managing Editor), Richard Kell, Peter Bennet, James Roderick Burns
Address: 29 Western Hill, Durham DH1 4RL
Website: www.otherpoetry.com
Mag Frequency: 3 times a year
Subscription: (UK) £10 per annum
Single Issue: (UK) £3.50
Overseas: Airmail: £14 pa, Surface: £13 pa
Payment in: Sterling only, by Cheque or by Banker's Draft drawn on the UK
Payable to: Other Poetry
Inserts accepted: Yes
Terms: £20 for single sheet or exchange arrangement
Circulation approx: 200 - 300
Payment terms to contributors: Minimum of £5 per poem
Accept/rejection approx times: 6-12 weeks

0

OUTPOSTS POETRY QUARTERLY

For more than fifty years Outposts has published new poetry by both the established and the yet to be recognised. The magazine has never supported a dogma, nor a coterie: it has been our policy to publish the best from the unsolicited material we receive. Two issues each year are general issues of new poetry plus reviews, one of which will carry an essay on some aspect of poetry such as rhyme technique, or an extended review of an important book or poet. A third issue will look at the work of a contemporary poet, such as James Brockway, Peter Dale, Sylvia Kantaris, Derek Walcott. Our fourth is a larger anthology issue with a translation section. Outposts is one of the few magazines open to new translations. It has been said that Outposts is the place to find tomorrow's poets today. The magazine is part of the Hippopotamus Press, so it is not surprising that some who had their first poems printed in Outposts have gone on to have full collections from the Hippopotamus Press. Recent issues have included new poetry by Peter Abbs, Alan Brownjohn, Ian Caws, William Cookson, Peter Dale, Philip Gross, John Heath-Stubbs, Elizabeth Jennings, Lotte Kramer, Edward Lowbury, Christopher Pilling, Sally Purcell, Peter Russel, Vernon Scannell, Penelope Shuttle and prose from Peter Dale, Anna Martin, William Oxley, Glyn Pursglove, Eddie Wainwright.

Editor Name(s): Roland John
Address: Hippopotamus Press, 22 Whitewell Road, Frome, Somerset BA11 4EL
Telephone: 01373 466653
Fax: Same as phone
Mag Frequency: Quarterly
Subscription: £14 for 4/£26 for 8
Single Issue: £5
Back Issue: £3 except specials
Overseas: £16 for 4/£29 for 8
Payment in: Sterling or Visa/Master Card
Payable to: Hippopotamus Press
Inserts accepted: Yes
Terms: £90 full list/£60 UK only
Advertising Rates: £60 full page/£30 half page
Circulation approx: 1200
Payment terms to contributors: Small: £5 a page, more for commissioned articles
Accept/rejection approx times: 1 week

0

OXFORD POETRY

Since its revival in 1983 Oxford Poetry has attracted a sound readership and many favourable reviews. Tom Paulin has called it one of the best small poetry magazines in the country. The main purpose of the magazine is to be a forum for new poets' work (and we have a talent for spotting poets early!), but each issue also includes reviews, interviews, features, a translation competition and work by famous writers. In 1990 Seamus Heaney established the Richard Ellmann Prize for the best poem in each volume of the magazine.

Address: Robert Macfarlane, Oxford Poetry, Magdalen College, Oxford OX1 4AU
Mag Frequency: 3 times per year (irregular)
Subscription: £9
Single Issue: £3 plus p&p
Back Issue: £1 plus p&p
Overseas: £11
Payment in: Overseas payments by IMO
Payable to: Oxford Poetry
Inserts accepted: No
Circulation approx: 500
Payment terms to contributors: No payment
Accept/rejection approx times: 6 months max

P
PAINTED, SPOKEN

Modern poetry. Potential contributors must have read earlier issues before sending work.

Editor Name(s): Richard Price
Address: 8 Richmond Road, Staines, Middlesex, TW18 2AB
Mag Frequency: 2 p.a
Subscription: Free on receipt of sae (A5)
Single Issue: Free on receipt of sae
Overseas: Free on receipt of sae (sorry, no reply coupons)
Payment in: none
Inserts accepted: Yes
Terms: None
Circulation approx: 100 or less
Accept/rejection approx times: Within a month

PANDA

56 pages, coloured graphics on about ten to twelve pages, glossy cover with poem and photo of author on book cover.

Editor Name(s): Esmond Jones
Address: 46 First Avenue, Clase, Swansea, W Glamorgan, SA6 7LL
Telephone: 01792 414837
Fax: 01792 414837
Email: esmond.jones@nteworld.com
Website: http://members.theglobe.com/esmond3/pandapage.html
Mag Frequency: Quarterly
Subscription: £10 per annum, £3.00 single copy. Overseas $58/$15 respectively
Single Issue: £3.00 / $5.00
Overseas: $15.00
Payment in: Cheque/postal order - UK, Dollar bills - Overseas
Payable to: Esmond Jones
Inserts accepted: No
Circulation approx: 200 copies
Payment terms to contributors: None
Accept/rejection approx times: One week

PASSION

Poetry, Fiction, Arts, Criticism, Culture. * Each year Crescent Moon is publishing four collections of poetry, fiction, reviews, and essays on fine art, cinema, music, politics, philosophy, the media, feminism and many kinds of criticism drawn from the UK, Europe, Canada and North America. * Many writers are being published for the first time here, while others are established writers who are featured in publications throughout the world. * Well-known poets and artists such as Andrea Dworkin, Richard Long, VS Naipaul, Peter Redgrove, DJ Enright, Penelope Shuttle, Colin Wilson, Ronald Blythe, Edwin Mullins, Geoffrey Ashe, Alan Bold and Jeremy Reed featured in the first issues. * The work ranges from the passionate, erotic and spiritual, to the humorous, polemical and incisive but it is always entertaining.

Address: PO Box 393, Maidstone, Kent ME14 5XU
Mag Frequency: Quarterly
Subscription: £10 individual/£15 institution
Single Issue: £2.50
Overseas: $22 individual/$30 institution
Payment in: Sterling/US $
Payable to: Crescent Moon
Inserts accepted: Yes
Terms: £30
Circulation approx: 200
Payment terms to contributors: Negotiable
Accept/rejection approx times: 4 months

PATCHWORD

On-line writers' resource centre, founded 2000.
Pages include poetry anthology, articles about all aspects of writing, book reviews (all genres), humourous non-fiction, diary dates and small ads. There is also a monthly selection of quotes and an extensive time-out section with quizzes, games, trivia etc. Since there is currently no charge for contributions we are happy to accept reprints. Our contributors include previously published and unpublished writers. Full guidelines are available on the website. E-mail submissions are greatly preferred - please include text in the body of the e-mail unless previous arrangements have been made to send attatched files. The response times given below apply to e-mail submissions

Editor Name(s): Gwyneth Box
Address: Calle carlos Arniches, 7, 2D, Madrid, 28005, Spain
Email: editor@patchword.com
Website: www.patchword.com
Mag Frequency: Website updated monthly
Advertising Rates: Diary enties free, small adds currently free. Consult for banner advertising.
Payment terms to contributors: None. Biographical details and links included
Accept/rejection approx times: Usually within 2 weeks; frequently 48 hours

P
PEACE & FREEDOM

Peace & Freedom is a magazine of poetry, prose and art which focuses on humanitarian/ animal rights/environmental issues mainly, but not solely. We are not looking for work which supports the status quo, so pro royalist, conservative tweeness we avoid like the plague. We're looking for challenging, thought-provoking work which shows genuine compassion. Satirical stuff is okay, too. We also run poetry competitions and forms are available for an SAE/IRC. Peace & Freedom was established in 1985 and has issued a number of booklets and books under the Peace & Freedom Press banner. For full details of Peace & Freedom Press please send an SAE/IRC.

Address: 17 Farrow Road, Whaplode Drove, Spalding, Lincs PE12 OTS
Email: peaceandfreedom@lineone.net
Website: http://website.lineone.net/~peaceandfreedom/
Mag Frequency: Twice yearly
Subscription: £7.50 for 4 issues
Single Issue: £1.75
Back Issue: £1
Overseas: $16
Payment in: UK cheque or PO/Overseas IMO or cash
Payable to: Peace & Freedom
Inserts accepted: Yes
Terms: £20/$50. Free to magazines who are willing to exchange circs
Circulation approx: 500
Payment terms to contributors: Free issue when work is published
Accept/rejection approx times: Less than 3 months

PEEP SHOW

Exploring the darker side of human sexual behaviour, Peep Show aims to bring you the best erotic horror fiction and artwork available. Published biannually as a high quality trade paperback with a full colour cover, the emphasis throughout the whole magazine is quality. High quality fiction, artwork and magazine appearance.

Submissions are always welcome. Story submissions can contain lots of sex, or they can have a more subtle erotic theme to them. The horror theme can be very strong and violent, or it can be more subtle. Please don't submit anything with sex involving children. Also, don't send anything containing incest or any other subjects like that. The artwork is usually commisioned, but samples are very welcome by email or regular snail-mail.

The only way the small press can survive is with your support. So if you can, please purchase a copy or subscribe to Peep Show and help me keep it alive. Thank you

Editor Name(s): Paul Fry
Address: 15 North Roundhay, Stechford, Birmingham, B33 9PE
Email: editor@peepshowmagazine.co.uk
Website: http://peepshowmagazine.co.uk
Mag Frequency: Biannually
Subscription: £8.50 post paid
Single Issue: £4.50 post paid
Overseas: $15 US, £9.50 Europe, £10.50 ROW post paid
Payment in: UK £ sterling cheques, US $ cheques, UK/US/Europe/ROW online credit card payments in US $
Payable to: MR P Fry
Advertising Rates: Mini Ad: £5 ($7). Half Page Ad: £10 ($14). Full Page Ad: £20 ($28) Colour Back Cover Ad: £50 ($70).
Payment terms to contributors: Fiction one complimentary copy. Artwork two complimentary copies
Accept/rejection approx times: Speedy (read subs on day received, reply straight away)

P PEER POETRY INTERNATIONAL

Have your own collection published free of charge. We publish (without charge to the two poets concerned) a collection of their poems, self-selected; by the poets voted by our readers and subscribers to be the best of those appearing in each issue of Peer Poetry. These are given to the poets concerned, to sell or give away. (not delivered freepost overseas)
To cater for long and short poems, providing space for a range of each poet's capabilities. To give outstanding writers a chance of publication. We provide two A4 pages for each qualifying poet (of 30+) to find out how their Peers compare their work with others in the magazine. To find and display poetry with fire and imagination, a feeling for the natural rhythms of language, having shape and plan, cherishing the sound and beauty of words and ideas. Work that if written in prose, will sound as poetry. Haiku (sequences preferably) Senryu and similar forms welcome, as are traditional and modern verse forms. For details send an SAE allowing for 40g.

Editor Name(s): Paul Amphlett
Address: 26 (WB) Arlington House, Bath Street, Bath, N.E Somerset BA1 1QN
Telephone: 01225 445298
Mag Frequency: Bi-annual
Subscription: £12 per annum plus £2 p&p (including free submissions)
Single Issue: £5.50 plus £1.50 p&p
Back Issue: £4 inclusive Oct '96 only
Overseas: As above: paid in dollar notes or sterling or IRC's, allow 400 grams for postage cost ex UK
Payment in: Sterling cheque, PO/IRC coupons acceptable @ 40p each or as 'Overseas'
Payable to: Peer Poetry
Inserts accepted: Depends on content
Circulation approx: 350
Payment terms to contributors: Nil - but an opportunity to have a collection of poems printed without charge
Accept/rejection approx times: 2/4 weeks - only if accompanied by 2 A5 SAEs or IRCs (state whether constructive criticism is appreciated) Telephone numbers please

PENDRAGON

The Pendragon Society was founded in 1959, and more than forty years on it is still investigating all aspects of the Arthurian story - the factual basis from archaeology and history, the narrative strand from legend, myth and folklore, and the creative impulse shown in literature, the arts and popular culture.

Pendragon is the journal of the Society and continues to have a wide readership in Britain and around the world. Each illustrated A5 issue is usually based on an appropiate Athurian theme and includes not only articles but also news, reviews, letters and - occasionally - some poetry and fiction. A typical edition might include contributions on Dark Age history, medieval romance, reviews of fantasy or science fiction using Arthurian motifs, and notices of films, plays or TV programmes based on the Matter of Britain. For new contributors, publication guidelines are available on receipt of a stamped self-addressed envelope.

Members include ordinary Arthurian enthusiasts (are enthusiasts ever ordinary?) as well as published authors, artists, poets, musicians and academics. Membership of the society is extended to annual subscribers who are given priority contribution acceptance and reduced price advertising rates.

Editor Name(s): Christopher Lovegrove
Address: Fred Stedman-Jones, Smithy House, Kingsley Road, Newton by Frodsham, Cheshire, WA6 6SX
Subs to: Pendragon, Smithy House, Newton by Frodsham, Cheshire WA6 6SX
Mag Frequency: 3 per annum
Subscription: £7.50
Single Issue: £2.50
Overseas: £10 Europe, £12.50 RoW
Payment in: Sterling cheque/PO/IMO/Travellers cheque
Payable to: The Pendragon Society
Inserts accepted: Yes
Terms: Please enquire
Advertising Rates: £20 per page and pro rata
Circulation approx: 500
Payment terms to contributors: Free copy
Accept/rejection approx times: 2-3 weeks (if postage included)

P
PENINSULAR

We are currently running a regular short story competition. Each issue will feature the 3 finalists (anonymously) and the readers will vote for 1st, 2nd and 3rd (£350 prize money up for grabs). plus 7 or 8 fabulous short stories, the odd article, readers letters. A good read! A5, perfect bound, at least 80 pages.

Editor Name(s): Shelagh Nugent
Address: Cherrybite Publications, Linden Cottage, 45 Burton Road, Little Neston, Cheshire CH64 4AE
Telephone: 0151 353 0967
Fax: 0870 165 6282
Email: helicon@globalnet.co.uk
Website: www.cherrybite.co.uk
Mag Frequency: Quarterly
Single Issue: £3.50
Back Issue: £2
Overseas: £4 Europe, £5 RoW
Payment in: Sterling or dollar bills
Payable to: Cherrybite Publications
Inserts accepted: Yes
Terms: Reciprocal
Advertising Rates: £50 per full page
Circulation approx: 400
Payment terms to contributors: £5 per 1000 words, payable on publication
Accept/rejection approx times: about 6 weeks

THE PENNILESS PRESS

Penniless Press publishes poetry, fiction, philosophy, comment, criticism, translations and reviews. Prose writers should try to limit their pieces to approx 3000 words. The magazine is eclectic in nature and has published work on Odysseus Elytis, jazz, modern painting, Carol Ann Duffy, Paul Durcan, Barry McSweeney, Jean Rhys, Walter Lowenfels, Maxwell Bodenheim, Peter Reading, Isacc Rosenfeld, crime writing, modern Greek poetry, Henry Roth, Ogden Nash, James Hanley, Kenneth Patchen, WS Graham, Alfred Kazin, Irving Howe. It has featured work by Jim Burns, Fred Voss, Adrian Mitchell, Geoff Hattersley, Gael Turnbull, Patricia Pogson, Geoffrey Holloway, Philip Callow, John Lucas, Joan Jobe Smith, Stephanie Norgate, Nazim Hikmet, Gordon Wardman, David Craig, Nick Toczek, Victor Serge, David Caddy, Andy Croft, Jose Watanabe, Pablo Neruda, Alexis Lykiard, Ortega y Gasset, Jose Cerna, Dave Tipton, Ken Clay, Sid Thomas, Steven Waling, John Manson, John Dunton, Martin Hayes, Tom Argles, Tulio Mora, Philip Sidney Jennings and more.

Address: 100 Waterloo Road, Ashton, Preston PR2 1EP
Mag Frequency: Quarterly
Subscription: £8.50
Single Issue: £2.50
Back Issue: £2
Overseas: £8.50
Payment in: Sterling cheque/PO
Payable to: Penniless Press
Inserts accepted: Yes
Terms: Will exchange inserts
Circulation approx: 250
Payment terms to contributors: Complimentary copy
Accept/rejection approx times: 2 weeks

℘
PENNINE INK

Pennine Ink was founded in the 1983 by Pennine Ink Writers' Workshop. It is administered by members and published annually. We have had favourable reviews from respected magazines and also on various websites. This is because we are very selective and publish only what we consider to be material of the highest quality. As a result, we have an international, as well as a local, readership. Poems should be no longer than 40 lines. Prose no longer than 1000 words. Please enclose an SAE. Thank you.

Editor Name(s): Laura Sheridan
Address: Pennine Ink c/o Mid Pennine Arts, Yorke Street, Burnley, Lancs BB11 1HD
Telephone: 01282 703657
Email: sheridans@casanostra.P3online.net
Mag Frequency: Annually
Subscription: not applicable as only published annually
Single Issue: £3 post free
Back Issue: £2
Overseas: not applicable as only published annually
Payment in: cheques
Payable to: Pennine Ink Writers Workshop
Inserts accepted: Yes
Circulation approx: 400
Payment terms to contributors: Free copy of magazine
Accept/rejection approx times: 2 months

PENNINE PLATFORM

We publish 'the pick of poetry from the Pennines and beyond', with some reviews, usually by the editor or commissioned. Please submit up to six poems, with name and address on every sheet and on SAE. Let us know if you'd like us to include your email address (with your name, beneath your poem).

Editor Name(s): Dr Ed Reiss
Address: IHS Dept. University of Bradford, Bradford, BD7 1DP
Email: a.e.reiss@bradford.ac.uk
Mag Frequency: Twice a year
Subscription: £8.50 incl p&p
Single Issue: £4.50 incl p&p
Overseas: £12 sterling or £17 in currency or £25 non-sterling cheque
Payable to: Pennine Platform
Inserts accepted: No
Circulation approx: 200
Payment terms to contributors: 1 free copy
Accept/rejection approx times: 3 months

℘
PHOENIX NEW LIFE POETRY

An international Journal for engaged poets, artists and writers of the New Millenium with a positive, eutopian, spiritual and wholistic vision for humanity and the planetary creation of which we are part, as its trustees and custodians, in the spirit of Percy Bysshe Shelley, William Blake and Allen Ginsberg, with links to poets and artists in North America, Africa, India, Greece as well as the UK and Ireland. Also available, online, as an email attatchment, in request.

More than a magazine, The Phoenix is also a friendship network for creators who are co-creative in a 'New Life-Style & Culture' New Rennaissance World-Wide as envisioned by its support association The Universal Alliance.

Positive-spirited poetry, dramatic sketches, meaningful short stories or philosophical writings or anthologies to review are welcomed, as are colour paintings (18 by 12 cms) as candidates for the the cover-picture.

Also available from The Phoenix are Special Phoenix Poets Publications, the first of these being Songs From & For The Spirit, A Personal Spiritual Journey in verse of a Vision Quester, some selected poems, songs, chants, prayers and meditations in chronological order from 1963 to the year 2000, by David Allen Sringer. £5 including p&p.

Phoenix Poets promote live poetry and music events so to promote both the poetry of the individuals involved and the movement for a wholistic culture.

Editor Name(s): David Allen Stringer
Address: Four Turnings Bungalow, Newtown, Fowey, Cornwall,PL23 1JU
Telephone: 00 44 01726 832196
Email: UK £12, Europe £14 (22 Euros), Beyond £16 ($24 US) etc.
Single Issue: A quarter of the above
Back Issue: A quarter of the above
Payment in: Sterling/Euros or US $ (currency notes)
Payable to: Universal Alliance
Inserts accepted: Subject to editorial approval - send sample with SAE
Advertising Rates: Negotiable according to the content
Payment terms to contributors: No payment - free copy of the issue in which one is included. The Phoenix is a strictly non-commercial co-operative.
Accept/rejection approx times: 1 to 2 months

PITCH

Sharp poetry, fiction, reflective criticism and illustrations. Established writers alongside previously unpublished.

Editor Name(s): Susan Tranter
Address: Bookcase, 17 Castle Street, Carlisle, CA3 8TP
Telephone: 01228 544560
Email: bookcasecarlisle@aol.com
Mag Frequency: Qaurterly
Subscription: £14 (inc p&p)
Single Issue: £4
Payment in: Cheque or credit card (sterling)
Payable to: 'Bookcase'
Inserts accepted: Yes
Terms: £50 for 300
Advertising Rates: £50 per A5 page
Payment terms to contributors: In transition
Accept/rejection approx times: 2 months

P
PLANET - THE WELSH INTERNATIONALIST

A bi-monthly magazine of the arts and current affairs, centred on Wales but in a broader context of Europe and the world beyond. Areas of special interest: poetry, fiction, politics, the environment, science, visual art. Recent contributors include, from Wales: Emyr Humphreys, Jan Morris, Gillian Clarke, Robert Minhinnick, Peter Finch; from abroad: Les Murray, Guy Vanderhaeghe, Jaan Kaplinski, Ian McDonald, Tabish Khair.

Editor Name(s): John Barnie
Address: Planet, PO Box 44, Aberystwyth, Ceredigion SY23 3ZZ Wales
Telephone: 01970 611255
Fax: 01970 611197
Email: planet.enquiries@planetmagazine.org.uk
Website: www.planetmagazine.org.uk
Mag Frequency: 6 pa
Subscription: £15
Single Issue: £3.25
Back Issue: Varies
Overseas: £16 surface (US $30)/£23 air (US $42)
Payment in: Sterling
Payable to: Planet
Inserts accepted: Yes
Terms: £30
Advertising Rates: Full page £75/half page £35/quarter page £20
Circulation approx: 1500
Payment terms to contributors: £40 per 1000 words prose/£25 minimum per poem, payment on publication
Accept/rejection approx times: 4 weeks

PN REVIEW

Six times a year. Reports, articles, poems, translations and reviews compete for space in Britain's most independent literary magazine. Committed to the traditional and the experimental in poetry, PN Review has remained above contemporary trends in theory and criticism. The emphasis is always on poems before poets, content over personality. From its pugnacious beginnings in the early seventies, to its present distinction as a place of discovery and appraisal, PN Review has been at the cutting edge of intellectual debate. Well away from the London-Oxbridge axis, PN Review has carved out a unique niche in the precarious world of literary magazines. In an age of post-modern relativism and uncertainty, it has taken its bearings from Modernism in the crucial foundation of the twentieth century canon. Contributors include: Eavan Boland, C H Sisson, Mark Doty, John Ashbery, David Constantine and Sujata Bhatt.

Editor Name(s): Michael Schmidt
Address: PN Review, 4th Floor, Conavon Court, 12-16 Blackfriars Street, Manchester M3 5BQ
Telephone: 0161 834 8730
Fax: 0161 832 0084
Email: pnr@carcanet.u-net.com
Website: www.carcanet.co.uk
Mag Frequency: 6 times a year
Subscription: 1 year: £29.50 personal/£35 institution 2 years: £56.50 personal/£68 institution
Single Issue: Specimen copy £5.50 or $10
Overseas: 1 year: $55 personal/$68 institution (add £12 or $25 for airmail) 2 years: $105 personal/$129 institution (add £24 or $50 for airmail)
Payment in: Sterling Cheque/Access/Visa
Payable to: PN Review
Inserts accepted: Yes
Terms: Price per 1000 - £380
Advertising Rates: Apply for details
Circulation approx: 1500
Payment terms to contributors: Dependent on length of article
Accept/rejection approx times: 6-8 weeks to hear

℘
POET TREE

The Poet Tree magazine is a general poetry and short story magazine, with the most diverse in writing styles and subjects. Here there are no rules. The Poet Tree is a bi-annual magazine alternating with A Bard Hair Day magazine.

Editor Name(s): Ian Deal
Address: 289 Elmwood Avenue, Feltham, Middlesex TW13 7QB
Email: partners_writing_group@hotmail.com
Website: www.homestead.com/partners_writing_group
Mag Frequency: Bi-annual - July 30th and January 30th
Subscription: England £5 sterling, Europe £6 or $10, International £8 or $12
Single Issue: England £2.50 sterling, Europe £3 or $5, International £4 or $6
Payment in: Sterling
Payable to: I Deal
Inserts accepted: Yes
Terms: £50 per 1000 or reciprocal advertising
Advertising Rates: £50 full page, £25 half page, £10 quarter page
Payment terms to contributors: None
Accept/rejection approx times: Within 2 weeks

THE POETIC CIRCLE OF FRIENDSHIP

Join our friendly poets and contribute to our anthologies. Your poems will be published for £3 each. You will receive a free book per issue. Help worthy charities. For further information contact Sandra Lunnon.

Editor Name(s): Sandra Lunnon
Address: 50 Flansham Park, Bognor Regis, Sussex PO22 6QN
Telephone: 01243 587761
Mag Frequency: 6 per year, 2 monthly
Subscription: £3.00 per poem, 1st book free
Single Issue: £2.50
Back Issue: £2
Overseas: By arrangement with poet
Payment in: Cheques or Postal Orders
Payable to: Sandra Lunnon
Inserts accepted: Yes
Terms: free to members
Advertising Rates: Free
Circulation approx: 125 members
Payment terms to contributors: none
Accept/rejection approx times: Reply within 7 days

P
POETIC HOURS

Poetic Hours (founded 1993) consists of a mixture of articles on famous poetry/ poets and readers' poetry. Poets are not paid but all the profits of the magazine are donated to major charities with each issue carrying reports of how money has been spent. This policy generates a positive attitude within the contributors which results in a wide range of diverse material from writers with a real enthusiasm for all aspects of poetry. Poetic Hours welcomes all types of work and subscribers are talented 'amateurs' of all ages from the UK and beyond. The magazine tends to reflect the interests poets have in reading the work of others like themselves; so regular features like 'My Xanadu' - where a subscriber examines his favourite poem - and a 'featured poet' allow people to read about the lives and influences of others. Poetic Hours is not for anyone who takes themselves too seriously, but should be of interest to all those who love poetry and are keen to learn and write their own.

Editor Name(s): Nick Clark
Address: 43 Willow Road, Carlton, Notts NG4 3BH
Email: erranpublishing@hotmail.com
Website: www.poetichours.homestead.com
Mag Frequency: Bi-annual
Subscription: £5 pa
Single Issue: £3
Back Issue: £3 plus SAE
Overseas: £7 pa sterling outside EU or $20 US
Payment in: Sterling, cheque (UK/EU only), US dollars cash only
Payable to: Erran Publishing
Inserts accepted: No, unless relating to non-profitmaking organisations
Circulation approx: Increasing
Payment terms to contributors: None

POETIC LICENCE

Poetic Licence publishes new poetry and line drawings. Based in Croydon, Surrey, most of its contributors and readership come from the Croydon/South London area - but good new poetry and line drawing is welcomed from anyone, anywhere. There are three editors for each issue of Poetic Licence, rotating through the varied membership of Poets Anonymous. There is therefore no particular 'house style'.

Editor Name(s): Rotates - contact is Peter Evans
Address: 70 Aveling Close, Purley, Surrey CR8 4DW
Telephone: 020 8645 9956
Email: poets@poetsanon.org.uk
Mag Frequency: 3 per year
Subscription: £7 pa
Single Issue: £2.50
Overseas: As UK
Payment in: Sterling cheques
Payable to: Poetic Licence
Inserts accepted: No
Circulation approx: 100
Payment terms to contributors: No payment
Accept/rejection approx times: Up to 3 months

ℙ
POETRY AND AUDIENCE

We do not discriminate against any form of poetry but our own interests bend towards, on the one hand, a more lyrical style, and on the other, language-based experimentation. Having said this, we publish purely on the basis of merit, and obscurity is welcomed. Previous contributors include Carol Ann Duffy, Geoffrey Hill and Tony Harrison, part of an established tradition which provides a forum for unpublished poets to see their work alongside the better known practitioners.

Address: c/o School of English, University of Leeds LS2 9JT
Fax: 0113 233 4774
Email: engwg@english.novell.leeds.ac.uk
Mag Frequency: 2 times a year
Subscription: £4 pa
Single Issue: £2
Back Issue: £1.50
Overseas: £6
Payment in: Cheque/PO payable as above
Payable to: The University of Leeds
Inserts accepted: Yes
Circulation approx: 200
Payment terms to contributors: Free copy of issue
Accept/rejection approx times: 10 weeks at most

THE POETRY CHURCH

The Poetry Church is an Anglo-American Christian poetry quarterly with a church music supplement. It publishes subscribers' poetry privately in the Feather Books Poetry Series and also members' hymns/music. Each year it compiles over 400 pages of new poetry and prayer in seasonal anthologies. Many of our poets are nationally known; others newcomers; some handicapped. We publish any Christian poetry we feel comes from the heart. Our poets range from academics to prisoners writing from condemned cells on death row. We feel we are encouragers of new Christian writers, as well as experienced ones. Not only does The Poetry Church encourage poets, it supports art and music with Christian themes. This year our magazine sponsored various music recitals and poetry readings throughout Britain and the States. The Poetry Church is used as a resource in preaching/teaching, and is increasingly bought by parishes as a supplement to the parish magazine.

Editor Name(s): Rev John Waddington-Feather/sub-editors Paul Evans, David Grundy, Tony Reavill
Address: Fair View, Old Coppice, Lyth Bank, Shrewsbury SY3 0BW
Telephone: 01743 872177
Fax: Same as phone
Email: john@waddysweb.freeuk.com
Website: www.waddysweb.com
Mag Frequency: Quarterly
Subscription: £7
Single Issue: £4
Overseas: $15
Payment in: Cheque/PO, Overseas US dollar bills or sterling cheque
Payable to: Feather Books
Inserts accepted: No
Advertising Rates: Negotiable
Circulation approx: 1000
Payment terms to contributors: None
Accept/rejection approx times: 1 week

ℐ
POETRY IRELAND REVIEW

The defacto journal of record in contemporary Irish poetry, we welcome submissions in English and Irish from poets living in Ireland and overseas. Please send an SAE with your contribution.

Editor Name(s): Maurice Harmon (Editor changes every 4 issues), Managing Editor: Joseph Woods
Address: Poetry Ireland Review, Bermingham Tower, Dublin Castle, Dublin 2 Ireland
Telephone: 00 3531 6714632
Fax: 003531 6714634
Email: poetry@iol.ie
Website: www.poetryireland.ie
Mag Frequency: Quarterly
Subscription: IR £24 surface/IR £40 airmail
Single Issue: IR £5.99/£7.61
Overseas: IR £24 (UK) Euro £30.50 IR £40 (airmail overseas) Euro £50.83
Payment in: Cheques/POs/Credit Cards
Payable to: Poetry Ireland Ltd
Inserts accepted: Yes
Terms: IR £150 (Euro £127.06) per 1000
Advertising Rates: No advertising - inserts only
Circulation approx: 1250
Payment terms to contributors: IR £25 per contribution (Euro £12.71) or 1 years sub
Accept/rejection approx times: 3-4 months

THE POETRY KIT

Internet-based resource for poets, specialising in listings of competitions, courses, events, magazines, publishers, workshops, and poetry organisations. Also carries high quality poetry and interviews with leading poets.

Editor Name(s): Ted Slade
Address: 36 Kings Avenue, New Malden, Surrey KT3 4DT
Telephone: 020 8949 0650
Email: tedslade@poetrykit.org
Website: www.poetrykit.org
Mag Frequency: On-going
Inserts accepted: No
Advertising Rates: See site
Payment terms to contributors: None
Accept/rejection approx times: 1 week

P
POETRY LIFE

Since Poetry Life first began in 1994 we have developed a hard won reputation for publishing the best of modern poetry and our aim has always been to new and talented poets to a wider audience. It is our intention to maintain this tradition by publishing both individual poems and through selected collections of work from new poets in the Poetry Life Recommendations. So far our recommendations have included work from: Kate Clanchy, Mario Petrucci, Keith Bennett, Christopher North and Robert Seatter.

All this and the Poetry Life Open Poetry Competitions with large cash prizes and the winners published in Poetry Life magazine and on the internet.

Editor Name(s): Adrian Bishop
Address: 1 Blue Ball Corner, Water Lane, Winchester, Hampshire SO23 0ER
Email: adrian.abishop@virgin.net
Website: http://freespace.virgin.net/poetry.life/
Mag Frequency: 3 issues a year
Subscription: £3 per mag
Single Issue: £3
Payable to: Poetry Life
Inserts accepted: Yes
Advertising Rates: Ask for rates
Circulation approx: 500 plus
Payment terms to contributors: We only pay for articles
Accept/rejection approx times: 2 hours - 2 months

POETRY LONDON

A leading international magazine, where new poets share pages with Les Murray, Sujata Bhatt, Marilyn Hacker, Claire Malroux, David Constantine, Rith Padel, Jo Shapcott and Jaan Kaplinski. Each issue is launched with contributors reading at prominent venues.

We also run an annual competition with a first prize of £1000, and publish the winning poems. Our reviews are incisive, our articles provocative. Recent reviewers include: Cirian Casson, Kate Kellaway, Bernard O' Donoghue, D M Black. Our listings section provides you with a comprehensive guide to poetry events and resources.

Editor Name(s): Poetry: Pascale Petit, Reviews: Scott Verner
Address: 1a Jewel Road, Walthamstow, London E17 4QU. Poems to: 26 Clacton Road, London E17 8AR
Telephone: 020 8521 0776
Email: editors@plondon.demon.co.uk
Website: www.poetrylondon.co.uk
Mag Frequency: 3 times a year
Subscription: £11 pa
Single Issue: £4
Back Issue: £1
Overseas: Europe £14.50 pa outside Europe £17.50 airmail, £14.50 surface
Payment in: Cash/Cheques
Payable to: Poetry London
Inserts accepted: Yes
Terms: Up to 10gms: £60 for 600
Advertising Rates: Quarter page £50/ crc £40; half page horizontal £100/ crc £80; half page vertical £100/ crc £80; full page £200/ crc £180 (crc = camera-ready copy)
Circulation approx: 1200
Payment terms to contributors: £20 first poem or page, subsequent £10
Accept/rejection approx times: 1 week to 2½ months

℘
POETRY MONTHLY

Established in April 1996, the key features of Poetry Monthly are that new and experienced poets share the same platform with critical feedback, praise or comment on the contents by fellow poets. A monthly magazine means that ongoing discussions can be more easily accommodated. Poetry Monthly also gives news of forthcoming reading, festivals and other poetry related events. There are also current poetry competitions listings and publishing opportunity announcements and book/magazine reviews.

The editor looks for poems in traditional, free verse or experimental form usuing dynamic, fresh and individual language allied with subtle use of poetic techniques. Stamped and self addressed envelopes or two International Reply Coupons must accompany all submissions and correspondence that require answers. Email submissions may be made, but not with file attachments.

Editor Name(s): Martin Holroyd
Address: 39 Cavendish Road, Long Eaton, Nottingham NG10 4HY
Telephone: 0115 9461267
Email: martinholroyd@compuserve. com
Website: http://ourworld.compuserve.com/homepages/martinholroyd
Mag Frequency: Monthly
Subscription: £14 per year or £9 per six months UK/EU
Single Issue: £2.00
Overseas: £24 sterling
Payable to: Poetry Monthly
Inserts accepted: Yes: £2 per 100
Payment terms to contributors: 1 copy of Poetry Monthly in which an author's work appears

POETRY NOTTINGHAM INTERNATIONAL

56 pages - Poems, reviews, features, short articles and letters. Well written poetry in free style rather than set form. Unpublished poetry only. Light verse also very welcome if it is witty and sharp. Subscribers competition every quarter.

Editor Name(s): Julie Lumsden
Address: P.O Box 6740, Nottingham, NG5 1QG
Mag Frequency: Quarterly
Subscription: £10 per annum
Single Issue: £2.75 plus 40p p&p
Back Issue: £1.50 incl p&p
Overseas: £17 sterling
Payment in: Cheques
Payable to: Poetry Nottingham International
Inserts accepted: Yes
Terms: £30 or will exchange with other magazines
Circulation approx: 300 approx
Payment terms to contributors: Complimentary copy
Accept/rejection approx times: 2 months maximum - often sooner

℘ POETRY NOW MAGAZINE

Poetry Now Magazine tries to publish a selection of poetry covering the broadest range of poetry the magazine's readers are writing. We aim to give enjoyment to, and answer the needs of, our readers. Every letter, poem and article that comes into the office makes a difference to the shape and direction of the magazine. This is the reason why it continues to change and grow. We hope that you will become a part of the driving force. Sections include: * Poems on a theme * Competition news, views and events * Poetry workshop * Articles of interest to poets * Featured, Book/Internet reviews and much more.

Editor Name(s): Rebecca Mee
Address: Remus House, Coltsfoot Drive, Peterborough PE2 9JX
Telephone: 01733 898101
Fax: 01733 313524
Email: pnmag@forwardpress.co.uk
Website: www.forwardpress.co.uk
Mag Frequency: Quarterly
Subscription: UK £15
Single Issue: £3.50
Back Issue: £2.50
Overseas: £18, $21 (U.S)
Payment in: PO/Cheque/Credit Card
Payable to: Forward Press Ltd
Inserts accepted: Yes
Terms: Reciprocal
Circulation approx: 2,000 - 3,000
Payment terms to contributors: Themed poems - £5, Editor's Choice poems - £10, Articles £5 per 500 words. Other payments negotiated
Accept/rejection approx times: 2 - 16 weeks

POETRY REVIEW

Britain's best-selling poetry magazine, published quarterly, features new poets, classic poems, new work by major writers and reviews of the latest poetry books.

Editor Name(s): Peter Forbes
Address: The Poetry Society, 22 Betterton Street, London WC2H 9BU
Telephone: 020 7420 9880
Fax: 020 7240 4818
Email: poetryreview@poetrysoc.com
Website: www.poetrysoc.com
Mag Frequency: Quarterly
Subscription: £27
Single Issue: £6.95
Back Issue: £9.95
Overseas: £42
Payment in: Credit card, Sterling cheque, cash
Payable to: The Poetry Society
Inserts accepted: Yes
Terms: Contact Lisa Roberts on 020 7420 9895
Advertising Rates: Contact Lisa Roberts on 020 7420 9895
Circulation approx: 5000

P
POETRY SCOTLAND

Poetry Scotland is a broadsheet quarterly dedicated entirely to new poetry. Subtitled Forty Poems By Twenty Poets, it includes Scottish and international writing in English, Scots and Gaelic. Available in over 100 outlets Scotland-wide, or post free from the publishers. Its quick response time makes it a favourite with the poets, and its generous educational discount and open format make it ideal for schools. Good trade terms to booksellers etc.

Editor Name(s): Sally Evans
Address: Diehard Publishers, 91-93 Main Street, Callander, Scotland FK17 8BQ and 3 Spittal Street, Edinburgh EH3 9DY
Telephone: 0131 2297252
Mag Frequency: Quarterly
Subscription: £5 for 5 issues
Single Issue: £1 post free
Overseas: £5 for 5 post free worldwide
Payment in: Sterling/sterling cheques
Payable to: Diehard Publishers
Inserts accepted: No
Advertising Rates: None
Circulation approx: 1200
Payment terms to contributors: 8 copies of publication, and payment for some solicited work
Accept/rejection approx times: 1 - 2 weeks

POETRY WALES

International quarterly, publishing best of welsh poets, plus other poets in english or english translation from round the world. Issues launched in New York, Winnipeg, Vancouver, Amsterdam, London, Hay.

Editor Name(s): Robert Minhinnick
Address: 38-40 Nolton Street, Bridgend CF31
Telephone: 01656 663018
Fax: 01656 663018
Email: pw@seren.force9.co.uk
Website: www.seren-books.com
Mag Frequency: Quarterly
Subscription: £12 a year
Single Issue: £3
Overseas: £4
Payment in: Sterling
Payable to: Poetry Wales
Inserts accepted: Yes
Terms: Variable
Advertising Rates: Negotiable
Circulation approx: 1000
Payment terms to contributors: £25 first poem, subsequent £10, prose - negotiable
Accept/rejection approx times: 1 month - 2 months

PQR (Poetry Quarterly Review)

PQR was launched in Autumn 1995. It is a broadsheet (A4) magazine providing in-depth reviews of both mainstream and small press poetry publishing. Features include: * Reviews of poetry books and collections * Work from a Featured Poet in each issue * Articles and essays on related topics * Listings: analysis of current poetry magazines * Editorial comment on the poetry scene * New Voices: promising list collections * Front Page: major new books. Invaluable guide for those wishing to find a magazine to place their work.

Editor Name(s): Derrick Woolf, Reviews Editor: Tilla Brading
Address: Coleridge Cottage, Nether Stowey, Somerset TA5 1NQ
Telephone: 01278 732662
Email: pqrrev@aol.com
Mag Frequency: 4 times a year
Subscription: £6
Single Issue: £2
Back Issue: £1.50
Overseas: Europe £8, USA £10 (airmail)
Payment in: Sterling only
Payable to: Odyssey Poets
Inserts accepted: Yes
Terms: Exchange basis
Advertising Rates: £7.50 - £60
Circulation approx: 500
Payment terms to contributors: Free copy to reviewers/agreed fee to Feature Poet
Accept/rejection approx times: 4 weeks

PRESENCE

Presence is a haiku magazine publishing haiku, senryu, tanka, renga and related forms in English. Other short poetry is accepted, if compatible. We also use artwork for black and white copying. Books for review and announcements of publications or events of haiku interest are welcome. We publish articles on all aspects of haiku, whether relating to the Japanese tradition or contemporary practice in English.

Editor Name(s): Martin Lucas
Address: 12 Grovehall Avenue, Leeds LS11 7EX
Website: http://members.netscapeonline.co.uk/haikupresence
Mag Frequency: 3 issues per year
Subscription: £10 for 4 issues
Single Issue: £3
Overseas: £10 or $20 (US) per 4 issues Surface Mail or £3 or $6 (US) per single issue Air Mail
Payment in: Cash or cheque/overseas cash only
Payable to: Haiku Presence
Inserts accepted: Yes
Circulation approx: 150 +
Payment terms to contributors: Free issue of magazine for first-time contributors. Also £20 best of issue award based on readers' poll
Accept/rejection approx times: Within 1 month

P PRETEXT

Pretext is a new literary magazine from the university of East Anglia which offers a small pocket of resistance to conglomerate publishing. It is a statement of independence and part of a new wave of community-based publications which offer a fresh perspective on the writers and writing that are important at the start of the 21st century. Volume 3 includes Tim Parks on Writerley Rancour, Toby Litt on Perversity and Dave Haslam on the North/South divide. Plus oodles of new fiction and poetry. Sorted.

Editor Name(s): Julia Bell, Anna Garry, Esther Morgan, Vic Sage, Ashley Stokes, Sara Wingate - Gray
Address: Pen & Inc, English and American Studies, University of East Anglia, Norwich NR4 7TJ
Telephone: 01603 592783
Fax: 01603 507728
Email: infoepenandinc.co.uk
Website: www.penandinc.co.uk
Mag Frequency: Twice a year
Subscription: £14 a year (UK)
Single Issue: £7.99
Back Issue: £7.99
Overseas: £16 European, £17 ROW (yearly)
Payment in: Sterling/credit card
Payable to: University of East Anglia
Inserts accepted: Yes
Terms: £50 per 1000
Advertising Rates: £40 per page
Circulation approx: 2,000
Payment terms to contributors: £50 plcontrib (fee soon to be introduced)
Accept/rejection approx times: 1 - 3 months

PROP

Prop publishes new poetry and short fiction, plus related essays, interviews and reviews. The magazine has previously published Tom Paulin, Charles Simic, Sophie Hannah, Nina Cassian, David Constantine, Jim Burns, Mark Kermode, Bill Naughton, John Kinsella, Julia Copus, Jane Holland, William Oxley and Ra Page. We are open to all styles of poetry and fiction, from the 'traditional' to the 'experimental'. It is suggested that those with ideas for essays/features contact the editors with a proposal first.

Editor Name(s): Steven Blyth and Chris Hart
Address: 31 Central Avenue, Farnworth, Bolton BL4 0AU
Telephone: 01204 707 428
Mag Frequency: Twice a year
Subscription: £10 for 4 issues
Single Issue: £3
Overseas: $15 for 4 issues
Payment in: International Money Order for overseas and Cheque/PO for mainland
Payable to: Prop
Inserts accepted: Yes
Terms: Reciprocal arrangements
Advertising Rates: By arrangement
Circulation approx: 300
Payment terms to contributors: Free copy of magazine
Accept/rejection approx times: 1-2 months

_P_
PULSAR POETRY MAGAZINE

Pulsar ISSN 1361-2336 - and Ligden Poetry Society (LPS) - were formed by Ligden Publishers in December 1994 with the aim of encouraging the writing of poetry for pleasure and possible publication in Pulsar (published quarterly). We seek interesting and stimulating work - thoughts, comments and observations; genial or sharp. Emphasis is on message, meaning and form, not keen on deeply religious poems. All poems submitted must be unpublished. LPS is non-profitmaking; funds received help cover the cost of printing, distribution etc. LPS/Pulsar are run by poetry enthusiasts for poetry enthusiasts - are not a business or corporate concern. Please subscribe - to keep the press turning. Published poets include Gerald England, Lewis Hosegood, Li Min Hua, A C Evans, Merryn Williams, Peter Wyton... For further information send A5 addressed return envelope containing 19p postage to the Editor.

Address: David Pike, 34 Lineacre, Grange Park, Swindon, Wiltshire SN5 6DA
Email: david.pike@virgin.net
Website: www.btinternet.com/pulsarpoetry
Mag Frequency: Quarterly
Subscription: £12
Single Issue: £3
Overseas: Europe £12 equivalent/USA $30
Payment in: By cheque - £ sterling preferred
Payable to: Ligden Poetry Society
Inserts accepted: Yes
Terms: 200/£15
Circulation approx: 300
Payment terms to contributors: Free copy of magazine
Accept/rejection approx times: Up to 4 weeks

PURPLE PATCH

Established in 1976, Purple Patch has a home-produced feel, yet maintains a high standard of poetry. Its gossip column laughs at and along with current news and trends in the poetry world (and cries a little sometimes). Short prose fiction and essays are welcome but their acceptance is limited by space. Following our 100th edition and 25 years of publication in 2001 we would like to make some changes. Alternate editions will remain as for previous policy but in between we'd like to see more daring poetical work, though quality must not be sacrificed.

Editor Name(s): Geoff Stevens
Address: 25 Griffiths Road, West Bromwich B71 2EH
Telephone: 07950 591455
Mag Frequency: 3 times a year
Subscription: £2.80 for 2 issues, 100th issue price to be fixed
Single Issue: £1.40
Overseas: £5 sterling cheques or $15 cash per 2 magazines
Payable to: Purple Patch
Inserts accepted: Yes
Terms: By negotiation
Advertising Rates: By negotiation
Circulation approx: 200
Payment terms to contributors: UK contributors - 1 copy
Accept/rejection approx times: 1 month

Q

QUANTUM LEAP

Poetry of all types, including rhyme. Plus, letters page and competitions (SAE or IRC with all submissions please). We want Quantum Leap to be a 'user friendly' magazine which encourages its contributors and readers, and gives opportunities for publication to both established poets and those yet to find their way into print (we remember what that feels like!). Will have a 'Five by...' feature in each issue showcasing the work of a particular poet. (Write with stamped addressed envelope, or IRC for guidelines and competition details).

Editor Name(s): Alan Carter
Address: Alan Carter, Editor, York House, 15 Argyle Terrace, Rothesay, Isle of Bute, PA20 0BD
Mag Frequency: Quarterly
Subscription: £12 (UK and EU); £14 (rest of Europe); £16/$32 (RoW)
Single Issue: £3.50 (UK and EU); £4 (rest of Europe); £4.50/$9 (RoW)
Back Issue: £3/$8 US
Overseas: See above
Payment in: PO/cheque
Payable to: A Carter
Inserts accepted: Yes - also reciprocal advertising
Terms: Ask!
Circulation approx: 180 and growing!
Payment terms to contributors: £2 per poem
Accept/rejection approx times: 2-4 weeks (Quantum Leap is getting very popular and publication may not be in the next issue but a later one, with an indication given at the time which issue is likely)

THE QUARTERLY MUSE AND MUSERS' CIRCLE

Quarterly Muse is an e-mail magazine and group. Established initially as a paper magazine in 1995.

Membership of The Musers' Circle:

To join the group, submit two sample pieces of work initially, (on any subject), by e-mail. The editor will let you know if you have been accepted for membership. The Muser's Circle is an e-mail only creative writing and poetry group. We each write up to two poems or one short story and one poem. Short stories may be up to/ approximately 1 A4 page (in 11 point). Each season we vote on the best work and the winner chooses the next topic to write about. The 'topic' can be a word, a sentence or part of a sentence or even a picture. The winner of best work for each issue also receives a signed certificate from the editor and a mystery book prize.

Membership is a great way to have fun while developing your writing skills, to make friends and contacts and get valuable feedback on your work. Members can include their biographies or submit articles and information on poetry or writing. Advertising on writing, poetry or anything related is free to members. All written submissions must be typed or pasted into an e-mail document (no attachments please). The editor reserves the right to refuse work which is below a certain standard or considered unsuitable for publication. All writing must be of good quality. Copywright remains with the authors. Accepted members receive an e-mail copy of the Quarterly Muse by or on the given dates.

Editor Name(s): Jane Reid
Address: 5 Grosvenor Close, Great Sankey, Warrington, Cheshire, WA5 1XQ
Subs to: Jane Reid, deadlines 1 month before publication
Telephone: 01925 574476
Email: QM@themutual.net
Mag Frequency: Quarterly, March 15th, June 15th, September 15th, December 15th
Single Issue: £8 per year
Payment in: Sterling
Payable to: Jane Reid

QWF

QWF aims to provide a platform for new women writers and to present a showcase of first class fiction for the discerning reader. A5 magazine around 80-90 pages with a glossy cover publishes about 12 short stories per issue plus articles and a lively readers' letter page and editorial. Looking for original short stories which are vibrant, whacky, off-beat or address women's issues. A thought-provoking read is essential. Accepts stories of less than 4000 words with covering letter. Stories must be previously unpublished. Runs an annual short story competition, open to all (including male writers). Cash prizes (£200 for winner). Winners published in QWF Magazine. Closes 21st August 2001.

Editor Name(s): Jo Good
Address: PO Box 1768, Rugby CV21 4ZA
Telephone: 01788 334302
Fax: 01788 334702
Email: jo@qwfmagazine.co.uk
Website: www.qwfmagazine.co.uk
Mag Frequency: Bi-monthly
Subscription: £23 for 6 issues
Single Issue: £3.95
Back Issue: £2
Overseas: £26 Europe/£33 RoW - subscription
£4.50 Europe/£5 RoW - single issue £2.75 Europe/£3 RoW - back issue
Payment in: Cheque or Postal Orders
Payable to: J M Good
Inserts accepted: Yes
Terms: Prefer a swap, or £30
Circulation approx: 300 subscribers and rising (2500 copies sold per year)
Payment terms to contributors: £10 short story/£5 article
Accept/rejection approx times: 1 month - potential contributors must send 3 x 1st class stamps for guidelines first

RAVEN NEWS

A4 Magazine printed in A5 format. Pagan/wiccan orientated with news of events, dates for your diary, advice, humorous letters, reviews, poems. We always include information on spell-working or magical practice. The tone is generally light, but we will tackle serious subjects such as the harrassment of witches by the press. Raven is also a mail order company, supplying weird and wonderful magical stuff, and folks who order from us will get a year's subscription to the magazine free! Send 2 first class stamps for catalogue.

Address: Raven, 17 Melton Fields, Brickyard Lane, North Ferriby, East Yorkshire HU14 3HE
Fax: 01482 631 496
Mag Frequency: 5 times a year
Subscription: £2
Single Issue: 50p
Overseas: £5
Payment in: Sterling only
Payable to: Raven
Inserts accepted: Yes
Terms: £5
Circulation approx: 1200
Payment terms to contributors: Our love and kisses

$\mathcal{R}$
RAW EDGE MAGAZINE

Raw Edge Magazine seeks to publish the best new writing from the West Midlands, plus news and comment of use to readers and writers in the area. Work from both established and new writers is considered on its own merits. Contributions are welcomed from all sections of the community, in any style of writing and on any subject. If you feel that you are not being represented by the writing, or cannot identify with it, send your own writing, or encourage those whose writing you do identify with to submit their work. Manuscripts received will normally be considered for the issue that is currently under preparation. Only in exceptional circumstances will any be carried over to future issues. Copies of the magazine will be reserved for all persons published in that issue. The Editor's decision is final. Raw Edge Magazine is published by The Moving Finger and is funded by West Midland Arts.

Editor Name(s): Dave Reeves
Address: PO Box 48567, Birmingham B3 3HD
Mag Frequency: Twice a year
Subscription: £2 pa
Back Issue: £1
Overseas: No overseas subscription
Payable to: Raw Edge TMF
Inserts accepted: No
Circulation approx: 16500
Payment terms to contributors: Only pay commissioned articles - negotiable
Accept/rejection approx times: Up to 6 months

REACH POETRY MAGAZINE

Monthly Poetry Magazine. A5, card cover, 48 pages. Poetry, letters, reviews. £50 readers' vote prize each month. In the event of a tie, the money is shared. Essential to read guidelines before submitting work.

Editor Name(s): Shelagh Nugent
Address: Linden Cottage, 45 Burton Road, Little Neston, Cheshire CH64 4AE
Telephone: 0151 353 0967
Fax: 0870 165 6282
Email: helicon@globalnet.co.uk
Website: www.cherrybite.co.uk
Mag Frequency: Monthly
Single Issue: £2.50
Back Issue: 4x first class stamps
Overseas: £3 Europe, £3.50 RoW
Payment in: Sterling or dollar bills
Payable to: Cherrybite Publications
Inserts accepted: Yes
Terms: Reciprocal
Advertising Rates: £20 per full page
Circulation approx: 400
Payment terms to contributors: No payment except a chance to win £50
Accept/rejection approx times: About 2 weeks

ℛ
THE REATER

Started in winter 1997 The Reater brings together exciting new British writing along with the best of Southern California. Produced in a high-quality paperback format, it features established poets, Simon Armitage, Ken Smith, Roddy Lumsden, Clare Pollard, Greg Delanty, Sean O'Brien, alongside excellent newcomers. Interleaved amongst the poetry and prose are interviews, reviews, and striking illustrations. The Reater is also the best outlet in the UK for new and reprinted material by the great names of LA/Long Beach literature: Charles Bukowski, Gerard Locklin, Fred Voss, Joan Jobe Smith, and others. Strictly no flowers just blunt chiselled poetry. The Reater can't be ignored.

Editor Name(s): Shane Rhodes
Address: 9 Westgate, North Cave, Brough, East Yorkshire HU15 2NG
Email: editor@wreckingballpress.com
Website: www.wreckingballpress.com
Mag Frequency: Twice yearly
Subscription: £15 per 2 issues
Single Issue: £7.95
Overseas: $28 per 2 issues
Payment in: Cheque
Payable to: Wrecking Ball Press
Inserts accepted: Possibly
Terms: Contact editor
Circulation approx: 1,000 - 1,500
Payment terms to contributors: Free copy, £15 per contributor
Accept/rejection approx times: 1-4 months

RED HERRING

Red Herring is a folded poetry sheet and welcomes new poetry of all kinds. It is distributed free through Northumberland Libraries thereby getting into the hands of a wide readership, much of which would not otherwise encounter new poetry.

Editor Name(s): Nicholas Baumfield, Jean Baker and Kathleen Hawkins
Address: Red Herring, MidNAG, East View, Stakeford, Choppington, Northumberland NE62 5TR
Telephone: 01670 844240
Fax: 01670 844298
Mag Frequency: 2-3 times a year
Subscription: £1 per issue
Single Issue: £1
Overseas: £1
Payment in: IMO/PO/sterling cheque
Payable to: Mid Northumberland Arts Group
Inserts accepted: No
Circulation approx: 3000
Payment terms to contributors: 6 copies
Accept/rejection approx times: 6 months

RED LAMP

A semi-annual journal which features poetry, cartoons, black and white photos, articles and reviews with socialist, realist and humanitarian themes. If you're submitting poetry, please ensure poems are direct, comprehensible and legible. Along with your submission, please include a biographical detail and/or your opinions associated with your writings for feedback. Email submissions are also accepted at present. Please enquire: evans_baj@hotmail.com. A SAE will be required if you wish to have your submission returned. Unfortunately, owing to budget limitations, writers who have their work published will not be given any cash payments. One copy of the journal, however, will be given or posted for acceptances. Subscribers make your cheques out to Brad Evans (Editor).

Editor Name(s): Brad Evans
Address: Red Lamp, 61 Glenmere Close, Cherry Hinton, Cambs CB1 8EF
Email: evans_baj@hotmail.com
Website: http:// www.geocities.com/red_lamp
Mag Frequency: Bi-annually
Single Issue: £2
Overseas: $5 (Australia) $4 (US)
Payable to: Brad Evans
Inserts accepted: No
Circulation approx: 100 (at present)
Payment terms to contributors: 1 Complimentary copy
Accept/rejection approx times: 2 - 3 weeks (if submission from UK), simultaneous submissions are accepted

THE RED WHEELBARROW

A magazine of poetry and opinion, which welcomes subscribers and submissions (of no more than 4 poems and SAE). Contributors to past issues have included Edwin Morgan, Janice Galloway, Douglas Dunn, Tracey Herd, W N Herbert, Ruth Padel, Robert Crawford, Jo Shappcott, Don Paterson, among others. The magazine is run voluntarily and not for profit.

Editor Name(s): Hugh Martin, Lilias Fraser and Kirsti Wishart
Address: The School of English, Castle House, The Scores, St Andrews, Fife, KY16 9AL
Telephone: 01334 462666
Fax: 01334 462655
Email: redwheelbarrow@se-andrews.ac.uk
Website: www.se-andrews.ac.uk/~www_se/pg/rw.html
Mag Frequency: Approx Biannually
Single Issue: £3.50 - £3.75
Back Issue: £2.50
Overseas: Details on request
Payment in: Sterling
Payable to: University of St Andrews
Inserts accepted: Yes
Terms: Details on request

ℛ
REFLECTIONS

Mainly poetry, some short pieces of prose, regular black and white photography and art work. Reflections provides an outlet for those interested in using the creative arts to share positive ideas and emotions. Many contributors choose to do this by offering appreciations of beauty, work which has a healing influence, or communicates aspects of their spiritual life, in the broadest sense of this term. Much of the poetry in Reflections adopts a traditional stance towards rhyme, rhythm and melody, although the editorial team welcomes both formal verse and free verse. Potential contributors should keep in mind that whatever its merits, work which focuses on the mundane, or has an overall negative tone is likely to fall outside of Reflections' remit. Reflections is not aligned to any political, social or religious movements. Work can only be returned if accompanied by suitable SAE; work may be offered anonymously.

Address: PO Box 178, Sunderland, SR1 1DU
Mag Frequency: Quarterly
Subscription: £5 annually incl p&p
Single Issue: 95p plus 30p p&p
Back Issue: 50p plus 30p (subject to availability)
Overseas: Europe £6.20 incl p&p/other on application
Payment in: Sterling only
Payable to: Reflections
Inserts accepted: No
Circulation approx: 200
Payment terms to contributors: Free copy
Accept/rejection approx times: 4 to 6 weeks

RELAPSE

Currently on its kick-ass 10th issue, this little magazine is everything you could ever need - music, poetry, humour, and a twist of madness. Essential reading...

Editor Name(s): Krystian Taylor
Address: 102 Old Church Road, Nailsea, Bristol BS48 4ND
Mag Frequency: Quarterly
Subscription: £4 incl p&p
Single Issue: £1
Back Issue: £1.50
Overseas: £7
Payment in: Cheque/PO/Cash
Payable to: Krystian Taylor
Inserts accepted: Yes
Terms: £25 for 1000/£15 for 500
Advertising Rates: £20 for full page A5
Circulation approx: 1000
Payment terms to contributors: Free copy

RESURGENCE

'The spiritual and artistic flagship of the green movement' - The Guardian.
Resurgence is a magazine of ecological and spiritual values with an international perspective.
Themes include: deep ecology, local economics, organic living, sustainable development, holistic science, biodiversity, spirituality and peace issues.

Editor Name(s): Satish Kumar
Address: Ford House, Hartland, Bideford, Devon EX39 6EE
Telephone: 01237 441 293
Fax: 01237 441 203
Email: ed@resurge.demon.co.uk
Website: www.resurgence.org
Mag Frequency: Every 2 months
Subscription: £23.50 (6 issues)
Single Issue: £3.95
Back Issue: £2.50
Overseas: Airmail: £35, Surface: £28
Payment in: £ or $ cheques/credit card
Payable to: Resurgence Ltd
Inserts accepted: Yes
Terms: £60 per thousand, either 10,000 (full print) or 6,500 (part print UK)
Advertising Rates: Single box (60mm x 66mm) £70, classified 70p per word
Circulation approx: 10,000
Payment terms to contributors: By arrangement only

RETORT

Retort publishes new work by established and emerging poets. Past contributors include Jon Silkin, Tobias Hill, Stephen Smith, William Oxley, Sean Street, Douglas Houston, Christine McNeill, Brendon McMahon, Sam Smith, Robert Hrdina, Vincent De Souza and Geoff Stevens, but we are also looking to encourage new poets with no track record of publication. The quality of the work is what matters. The magazine also includes articles and reviews and, when we get any, readers' letters. Articles and reviews are mostly commissioned. Retort runs a bi-annual poetry competition with substantial cash prizes. The prizewinning and five commended poems are published in the magazine. Retort is A5, perfect bound, 64 pages. Copyright is retained by the contributors. Submissions must be accompanied by adequate return postage.

Editor Name(s): John Lemmon
Address: Market Cross Publishing, PO Box 337, Redhill RH1 3YY
Mag Frequency: Twice a year
Subscription: £19 (for 4 issues)
Single Issue: £4.95
Overseas: Available on request
Payment in: Sterling cheques/drafts drawn on a UK bank/IMO/cash (at sender's risk)
Payable to: Market Cross Publishing
Inserts accepted: Yes
Terms: Negotiable
Advertising Rates: Varies, depends on whether or not graphics are included etc
Circulation approx: 400
Payment terms to contributors: Complimentary copies
Accept/rejection approx times: Up to 3 months

REVIEW OF SCOTTISH CULTURE

ROSC is the journal of the European Ethnological Research Centre and of the National Museums of Scotland. It covers all aspects of scottish material cultures especially traditional. It gives information on life and culture in Scotland as well as in neighbouring countries, providing well-researched source material at all local levels.

Editor Name(s): Alexander Fenton - Main Editor, with Hugh Cheape and Dr Rosalind Marshall
Address: European Ethnological Research Centre, c/o National Museums of Scotland, Chambers Street, Edinburgh EH1 1JF
Telephone: 0131 247 4086
Email: a.fenton@nms.ac.uk
Mag Frequency: Annual
Single Issue: £14
Back Issue: Vols 1 - 8: £3 each, Vols 9 - 11: £12 each
Payment in: Sterling
Payable to: EERC
Inserts accepted: No
Advertising Rates: £50 per quarter page
Circulation approx: 700

THE RIALTO

The Rialto strives to publish excellent poems by both new and established poets. Simon Armitage says it is 'The only Magazine that truly gives poetry the time and space it deserves': Carol Ann Duffy says 'The Rialto is simply the best.'

Editor Name(s): Michael Mackmin
Address: PO Box 309, Aylsham, Norwich, NR11 6LN
Subs to: £12
Website: www.therialto.co.uk
Mag Frequency: 3 issues a year
Single Issue: £4.25
Overseas: Europe £14, USA £18, Australia/Japan £19
Payment in: Sterling
Payable to: The Rialto
Inserts accepted: No
Circulation approx: 1500
Payment terms to contributors: £20 per person
Accept/rejection approx times: Up to 14 weeks

ℛ
ROADWORKS - TALES FROM THE HARD ROAD

Roadworks is an A5, 120 page, perfect bound magazine containing imaginative fiction, poetry, articles, interviews and illustrations. Writers have included Steve Harris, Stephen Baxter, Paul Pinn, Allen Ashley, Paul Finch, Nicholas Royle, Peter Tennant and Joel Lane. With YBF&H Honourable Mentions and nominations for the BFS Award for the BFS Award for Best Small Press magazine to its credit, Roadworks is synonymous with quality, entertainment and value.

'Excellent production values and lots of good reading' - Peter Tennant
'The production quality is superb' - Lauren Halkon
'I was impressed by the standard of writing and the quality names' - Andrew Hook
'Very impressive publication' - Karen Blicker

'Overall, Roadworks is an above average publication, and if editor Trevor Denyer keeps aiming high it has the potential to become one of the more dominant publications in the field' - Nick Di-Perna (reviewing Issue 2 in Zene # 18)

'Its main strength is its fiction, and it doesn't sell the reader short. This is a non-pretentious full-on story mag for lovers of dark fantasy and slipstream.' - Mike Thomas (the FIX - Summer 2001)

Editor Name(s): Trevor Denyer
Address: 7 Mountview, Church Lane West, Aldershot, Hampshire, GU11 3LN
Telephone: 01252 664699
Email: tdenyer@ntlworld.com
Website: www.roadworksweb.free-online.co.uk
Mag Frequency: Bi-annual (summer and winter)
Subscription: £9.50 ($15 US. £11.50 Europe. £12.50 ROW)
Single Issue: £5.00 ($8 US. £6 Europe. £6.50 ROW)
Back Issue: Very few available - Contact Editor
Overseas: $15 US. £11.50 Europe. £12.50 ROW
Payment in: Cash or Cheque or Order
Payable to: T. Denyer
Inserts accepted: Yes
Terms: Exchange
Advertising Rates: Negotiable
Circulation approx: Approx 150
Payment terms to contributors: First British Serial Rights, contributors copies
Accept/rejection approx times: 3 to 9 months

ROMANCE EROTICA

We are new, accepting novels in the romantic style. Send an SAE for details. Over 250,000 faithful followers! 191 authors published, no pornography. Advise you buy a book to see our style £6.25 each.

Editor Name(s): Neil Miller
Address: Romance Erotica, Black Cat Books, Mount Cott, Grange Road, St Michaels, Temterdem, Kent, TM30 6EE
Subscription: £6.25 per book
Back Issue: £6.25, £3 Travellers Tales
Payable to: Black Cat Books
Circulation approx: 250,000
Payment terms to contributors: 10 - 15% Royalties
Accept/rejection approx times: 2 Months, usually 1 week!

ℛ
ROUNDYHOUSE

Roundyhouse - 'The Poetry Magazine for the New Millennium' - was founded in 1999 with the express intention of being uncliquey and open to poetry of all kinds. Strict metre, free verse, modern, post-modern, rap, haiku, humour - anything goes, so long as it's good enough. We aim to be eclectic, non-partisan and above all witty and entertaining. We are definitely not ageist but to encourage young talent set a page or two aside for poets aged 19 or under (please enclose date of birth). Reviews are an integral part of Roundyhouse and we also publish prose articles on individual poets, living or dead, and on aspects of the poetry scene.

Although based in Wales, we welcome submissions from writers living elsewhere. Our annual poetry competition attracts entries from all parts of the UK and beyond. We are open to new ideas, publish letters and sell mainly by subscription (it's cheaper to buy that way too!).

Why Roundyhouse? It's the name of the pub in Cork where the founders thought up the idea of a new mag during a Wales-Ireland poetry exchange.

Editor Name(s): Sally Roberts Jones, Peter Read, Lloyd Rees, Brian Smith, Alexandra Trowbridge-Matthews, Herbert Williams
Address: 63 Bulch Road, Fairwater, Cardiff, CF5 3BX
Mag Frequency: Three times a year
Subscription: £9 annually
Single Issue: £3.50
Back Issue: £2
Overseas: £13
Payment in: Sterling cheque/IMO
Payable to: Roundyhouse
Inserts accepted: Yes
Terms: Negotiable
Advertising Rates: £40 full page, £25 half page, £15 quarter page
Circulation approx: Approx 200
Payment terms to contributors: Complimentary copy
Accept/rejection approx times: 8 weeks

ROUTE

Route is the hub of contemporary writing in the North of England. Packed full of stories, articles and poems from leading up and coming writers and performers, this magazine strives to bring the freshest, most exciting writers of this generation into the spotlight and promote contemporary writing to a new and wider audience. Route is a free magazine and offers the opportunity for anyone to have work published. Route represents the voice of now.

Editor Name(s): Ian Daley
Address: School Lane, Glass Houghton, Castleford, West Yorkshire, WF10 4QH
Telephone: 01977 603028
Fax: 01977 512819
Email: editor@route-online.com
Website: www.route-online.com
Mag Frequency: Bi - Monthly
Single Issue: Free
Back Issue: £1 (p&p)
Overseas: Available at £1 per issue (p&p)
Payment in: Cheque/Credit Card
Payable to: Yorkshire Art Circus
Inserts accepted: Yes
Circulation approx: 17,000 - 20,000
Payment terms to contributors: Negotiable

ℛ
RUBBERNECK

Rubberneck was founded in 1985 by its editor/publisher Chris Blackford and, after 30 paper format issues in 14 years, is now an e-zine. Its principal interest is international experimental music; in particular, improvised music, free jazz, and avant-garde rock. Contents consist of interviews, essays (usually written by leading musicians involved in experimental musics) and relevant CD and book reviews. Past issues have showcased the work of Simon H Fell, Hugh Davies, Biota, Michel Doneda, Max Eastley, Hans Reichel, Lol Coxhill, Pierre Favre, Peter Hammill, and many others. The large website also features film music and numerous reviews of arthouse videos, including silent cinema and animation. Occasionally, previously unpublished experimental fiction is published. Prospective contributors to Rubberneck are advised to check out the website before submitting their work by email, or by post accompanied by a SAE or IRC.

Editor Name(s): Chris Blackford
Address: Rubberneck, 21 Denham Drive, Basingstoke, Hampshire RG22 6LT
Email: rubberneck@btinternet.com
Website: http://www.btinternet.com/~rubberneck/
Mag Frequency: Updated monthly
Circulation approx: Global
Payment terms to contributors: None
Accept/rejection approx times: 2 weeks

THE RUE BELLA

The Rue Bella is a poetry and short story magazine that has gone from strength to strength, recently playing host to such figures as Patten, Zephaniah, Kinsella and Horovitz. For the most part the writing is fresh, unpretentious and worth reading through to the end. We welcome contributions on any subject from anywhere, no matter how many other magazines have given the thumbs down. All we ask of the writing sent to us is some small evidence of a little heart. As our second editorial says, 'we feel sure that some of the writers in this and future editions will lay down the lines with the power to rouse you from sleep, to take you outside and knock seven shades out of you, or simply, on occasion, to remind you of love and of feeling. This is why we are making the effort. We hope you will see the virtue in it'. 'May I, apropos of nothing... recommend The Rue Bella'. Roger McGough

Editor Name(s): Nigel Bird and Geoff Bird
Address: 16 Albion Terrace, Heptonstall Road, Hebden Bridge, West Yorkshire HX7 6BE, or 2F, 15 Warrender Park Terrace, Edinburgh EH9 1EG
Telephone: 01422 846 439 or 0131 229 3883
Website: www.ruebella.co.uk
Mag Frequency: 3 per year
Subscription: £9 for 4 issues, including postage
Single Issue: £3.00
Overseas: £12 for 4 issues, or £3 per copy
Payment in: Pounds Sterling
Payable to: Rue Bella
Inserts accepted: Yes
Terms: Reciprocation
Circulation approx: 500 - 700
Payment terms to contributors: Free copy
Accept/rejection approx times: 6-8 weeks

S
SALOPOET

Salopoet, founded in 1976, publishes poetry of members only. * Current membership is around 150. The magazine is published quarterly, the poems published being chosen by a panel of six committee members from poetry submitted by members. The Society runs two competitions per year - an open competition and one for members only. * The winning poems of the open competition are published each year in our Christmas Edition. Poetry reading evenings are held monthly at various members' homes.

Editor Name(s): Mr R A Hoult (Magazine Secretary)
Address: 5 Squires Close, The Fairways, Madeley, Shropshire TF7 5RU
Telephone: 01952 587487
Mag Frequency: Quarterly
Subscription: £10 pa
Single Issue: £2.50
Back Issue: £1
Overseas: £15
Payment in: Cheque or Postal Order
Payable to: Salopian Poetry Society
Inserts accepted: Yes
Circulation approx: 150
Payment terms to contributors: None
Accept/rejection approx times: 8 weeks

SAMHAIN

Britain's longest-running horror film magazine includes features, interviews, reviews etc, relating to the world of horror films and fiction. We are always on the lookout for new contributors, especially reviewers and feature writers based in Europe and the States.

Address: 77 Exeter Road, Topsham, Exeter, Devon EX3 OLX
Email: samhain@bta.com
Mag Frequency: Bi-monthly
Subscription: £9/$20 (5 issues)
Single Issue: £2.50 (cover price)
Back Issue: £2.50 each or full set (1-71) for £55
Overseas: £10 (Europe) $20 (US)
Payment in: US cash only - no US cheques
Payable to: Samhain
Inserts accepted: Yes
Circulation approx: Increasing
Payment terms to contributors: Free issues of the magazine

S
SCAR TISSUE

Scar Tissue publishes horror/dark-fantasy short fiction and poetry, sick-joke cartoons and weird illustration (artwork must be ink/black and white only), plus reviews of genre-related books, zines, films etc. Say anything in 500 words or less. We want sharply written prose and criticism. Mss must be single-spaced/camera-ready for Scar Tissue's no-budget, cheap 'n' cheerful, cut 'n' paste format. Advert swaps or contributors' guidelines from small press editors/independent publishers welcome. If in doubt send it anyway! NB: SAE/IRC essential for reply.

Editor Name(s): Tony Lee
Address: Pigasus Press, 13 Hazely Combe, Arreton, Isle of Wight PO30 3AJ
Telephone: 01983 865668
Mag Frequency: Irregular
Single Issue: Free for SAE/IRC
Overseas: 1 IRC per issue
Inserts accepted: Yes
Terms: Flyer swaps by arrangement
Advertising Rates: Adverts swaps welcome
Circulation approx: 200-300
Payment terms to contributors: Copy only
Accept/rejection approx times: 4-8 weeks

SCHEHERAZADE

Scheherazade is an A5 black and white illustrated magazine specialising in fantasy and science fiction with the emphasis on plot and character rather than technical effects. We also publish author interviews and other features. We do not publish poetry reviews. The magazine was originally started in response to the prevalence of 'cyberpunk' and other hard/masculine SF in most other British magazines. We wanted to provide an alternative for writers of short story fantasy and the 'softer' more human aspects of science fiction.

Address: 14 Queen's Park Rise, Brighton, East Sussex BN2 2ZF
Email: liz@shez.fsnet.co.uk
Website: www.shez.fsnet.co.uk
Mag Frequency: 2-3 times a year
Subscription: £9 (UK) £11.50 (overseas) - 4 issues
Single Issue: £2.80 (UK) £4.25 (overseas)
Back Issue: £2.50 (UK) £4.25 (overseas)
Overseas: £11.50 (sterling only)
Payment in: Sterling only. Cheques payable to Scheherazade.
Payable to: Scheherazade
Inserts accepted: No
Advertising Rates: Advert exchanges welcome
Circulation approx: 300
Payment terms to contributors: Small payment plus copy of magazine
Accept/rejection approx times: 3-4 months

S
SCI-WRITE

Sci-write is a new e-zine spawned from the print magazine Sci-Fright. Each monthly issue is sent to subscribers on the 1st of the month and includes SF/F/H markets, news, guidelines and articles/features for writers.
We regret that we cannot accept submissions from non-subscribers. All queries/info only available via email, do not contact the postal address.

Editor Name(s): Sian Ross-Martin
Address: Springbeach Press, 11 Vernon Close, Eastbourne, Sussex BN23 6AN
Email: sci-write2@carrotmail.com
Website: www.carrotwriter.com
Mag Frequency: Monthly
Subscription: Free to subscribers
Advertising Rates: via email

SCOTTISH STUDIES

Scottish Studies is the Journal of the School of Scottish Studies of the University of Edinburgh. It publishes research on Scottish traditional life and cultural history. Contributions are made by both the staff of the School and by other scholars in the field and take the form of full-scale articles, shorter notes and book reviews. Notes include first-hand reports of field work and research and transcriptions from the School's manuscripts and tape-recorded archives. Occasionally includes bibliographies.

Address: Dr John Shaw, School of Scottish Studies, 27 George Square, Edinburgh EH8 9LD
Subs to: Mrs R F Beckett at above address
Fax: 0131 650 4163
Mag Frequency: Annual
Subscription: £12
Single Issue: Current £10 (Vol 31)
Back Issue: £7
Overseas: US $25
Payable to: Scottish Studies
Inserts accepted: No
Circulation approx: 750

S
SCRIBBLE

Scribble is a quarterly magazine containing all kinds of short stories up to 3000 words. Although anything is considered, the more traditional type of story, containing a beginning, middle and satisfactory ending, is particularly welcome. The usual writers' guidelines apply, but full details can be obtained by sending a SAE to the editorial address. From spring 2002 a quarterly competition will be held with prizes of £50, £15 and £10. For all other published stories the payment will be a complimentary copy of the magazine. Annual subscribers will receive a credit voucher to the value of £4.00. These competitions are open to all and entry will be free to subscribers. Non-subscribers will pay an entry fee of £3 per story.

Editor Name(s): David Howarth
Address: Park Publications, 14 The Park, Stow on the Wold, Cheltenham, Glos GL54 1DX
Telephone: 01451 831 053
Email: parkpub14@hotmail.com
Website: ww.parkpublications.co.uk
Mag Frequency: Quarterly
Subscription: £10 (incl p&p)
Single Issue: £3 (incl p&p)
Back Issue: £2 (incl p&p)
Overseas: As above
Payment in: Sterling
Payable to: D Howarth
Inserts accepted: Yes
Advertising Rates: Negotiable
Circulation approx: 300 per quarter
Payment terms to contributors: cash prizes and copies
Accept/rejection approx times: Two weeks

SCRIBBLER!

Scribbler! promotes the use of English language and literature based on Key Stage 2 in the National Curriculum for children aged 8-12 years. The main features are encouraging children to write poetry and short stories, we have workshops and grammar pages to aid the children and encourage their creativity. We also feature articles, guest authors; in the past Jacqueline Wilson, Brian Jacques, Nick Arnold and Adeline Yen Mah; competitions, art gallery, book, film, game and music reviews are included to ensure learning stays fun.

Editor Name(s): Steve Twelvetree
Address: Scribbler!, Remus House, Coltsfoot Drive, Woodston, Peterborough PE2 9JX
Telephone: 01733 890066
Fax: 01733 313524
Email: youngwriters@forwardpress.co.uk
Website: www.youngwriters.co.uk
Mag Frequency: Quarterly
Subscription: £16.50
Single Issue: £4.15
Overseas: £19.50 for 4 issues
Payment in: Cheques, Postal Orders, Credit Card, Switch (Sterling)
Payable to: Forward Press Ltd
Inserts accepted: Yes
Terms: Available on request
Advertising Rates: N/A
Circulation approx: 7,000
Payment terms to contributors: Prizes
Accept/rejection approx times: 1 month after publication

S
SEAM

Lively new poetry from a wide range of writers, established and aspiring. Funded by Eastern Arts.

Editor Name(s): Maggie Freeman and Frank Dullaghan
Address: PO Box 3684, Danbury, Chelmsford, Essex CM3 4DJ
Mag Frequency: 2 yearly
Subscription: £6
Single Issue: £3
Overseas: £10
Payable to: Seam
Inserts accepted: Yes
Terms: Free, by reciprocal agreement
Advertising Rates: Please ask
Circulation approx: 250
Payment terms to contributors: 1 free copy
Accept/rejection approx times: 4 - 8 weeks

SEPIA

A small press magazine for poetry and prose (and some black and white artwork). No clichés - avoid genres - try to be original, try to be a little off the mainstream - don't use tricks of the trade - be original - be natural.

Editor Name(s): Colin Webb
Address: Kawabata Press, Knill Cross House, Knill Cross, Millbrook, Nr Torpoint, Cornwall PL10 1DX
Mag Frequency: 3 times a year
Subscription: £2
Single Issue: 75p
Back Issue: 75p
Overseas: £5 or $10
Payment in: UK bank cheques or currency (not overseas cheques)
Payable to: Kawabata Press
Inserts accepted: Yes
Terms: Swap inserts
Circulation approx: 100
Payment terms to contributors: Can't afford to pay - only a free copy of their issue
Accept/rejection approx times: Try to keep to 10 days but can be a month

𝒮
SEVENTH SENSE

Seventh Sense magazine is a bi-annual poetry magazine that addresses issues concerning the spirit.
'I want to know how God created this world. I am not interested in this or that phenomenon, in the spectrum of this or that element. I want to know his thoughts; the rest are details!' - Albert Einstein.

Editor Name(s): Ian Deal
Address: 289 Elmwood Avenue, Feltham, Middlesex TW13 7QB
Email: partners_writing_group@hotmail.com
Website: www.homestead.com/partners_writing_group
Mag Frequency: Bi-annual - July 30th and January 30th
Subscription: England £7 sterling, Europe £8 or $12, International £9 or $14
Single Issue: England £3.50 sterling, Europe £4 or $6, International £4.50 or $7
Overseas: £3.50 and return IRC's
Payment in: Sterling Cheques/PO
Payable to: I Deal
Inserts accepted: Yes
Terms: £50 per 1000 or reciprocal advertising
Advertising Rates: £50 full page, £25 half page, £10 quarter page
Payment terms to contributors: Free copy to contributors
Accept/rejection approx times: Within 2 weeks

S

SHAUN TYAS

I don't publish a magazine but I am a general intrest 'small press'. Subjects include medieval history, maritime, architectural history, place names, literary criticism. Until November I was in Stamford. I have two imprints SHAUN TYAS or PAUL WATKINS publishing

Editor Name(s): Shaun Tyas
Address: 1 High Street, Donington, Lincolnshire, PE11 4TA
Telephone: 01775 821542
Email: apwatkins@msn.com

S

SHEARSMAN

Shearsman is devoted to the publication of poetry - and occasionally reviews of new books - in the modernist tradition. Most work published tends to come from the UK, Ireland, the USA or Australia, but translations are also carried if copyright clearance is available. Unsolicited manuscripts are welcome, although it is suggested that potential contributors inspect the magazine first to see if their work might fit within its overall style - all too often it seems that contributors are more interested in scoring another acceptance than getting to know the journal or what it stands for.

Editor Name(s): Tony Frazer
Address: 58 Velwell Road, Exeter, EX4 4LD
Telephone: 01392 434511
Fax: Same as phone
Email: shearsman@appleonline.net
Website: www.shearsman.co.uk
Mag Frequency: Quarterly
Subscription: £6 pa
Single Issue: £2
Back Issue: £2
Overseas: £8 pa Europe, £12 pa RoW
Payment in: £ Sterling only
Payable to: Shearsman Books
Inserts accepted: No
Advertising Rates: Negotiable
Circulation approx: 200
Payment terms to contributors: 4 copies of the magazine
Accept/rejection approx times: 1 month

S

SHRIKE

Shrike publishes poets who do not take their environment and its tradition at face value but view its elements and realign them according to their own needs.

Address: 22 The Drive, Harrow, Middlesex HA2 7EN
Mag Frequency: Bi-annual
Subscription: £10 for 3 issues
Single Issue: £4
Back Issue: £2
Overseas: £15
Payment in: Cash/cheque
Payable to: Paul Wright or Jo Mariner
Inserts accepted: Yes
Circulation approx: 150
Payment terms to contributors: 1 copy

S
SILVER WHEEL

Silver Wheel is a pagan interest magazine published 4 times a year. We publish articles on Wicca, Paganism, Folklore, Shamanism, Druidry, traditional witchcraft and related subjects. We have an emphasis on practical matters with rituals, pathworking, recipes and personal experiences. No fiction or poetry.

Editor Name(s): Briony Robinson
Address: PO Box 12, Earl Shilton, Leics LE9 7ZZ
Email: Brionyrobinson@aol.com
Website: www.annafranklin.net
Mag Frequency: 4 pa
Subscription: £9 x 4
Single Issue: £2.50 x 1
Overseas: USA $5 or $20 x 4
Payment in: UK cheques and PO, US dollars overseas
Payable to: A Franklin
Inserts accepted: No
Circulation approx: 1000
Payment terms to contributors: Copy
Accept/rejection approx times: 21 days

SKALD

Skald is an old Norse word for a poet, but this magazine has featured all forms of creative writing. It is based in North Wales and aims to reflect that area to some extent. To that end, a proportion of the writing is in Welsh or from Wales, though fresh and original writing from elsewhere is always welcome. Artwork is also published if it is easily reproducible, and need not necessarily be illustration to accompany text.

Address: 2 Greenfield Terrace, Menai Bridge, Anglesey LL59 5AY North Wales
Mag Frequency: Every 6 months
Subscription: £3 for 2 issues (incl p&p)
Single Issue: £1.50 (incl p&p)
Back Issue: £1
Overseas: £6
Payment in: Cheque in sterling/PO
Payable to: Skald Community Magazine
Circulation approx: 300
Payment terms to contributors: Free copy of magazine
Accept/rejection approx times: 6 weeks

S

SKELETON GIRLS

Skeleton Girls is dedicated to real-life Gothic goddesses and contains poetry, prose, artwork and photography by the goddesses and similar work dedicated to them by their admirers. Details of other titles from the same address.

Address: Ty Fraen, The Park, Blaenavon, Torfaen NP4 9AG
Email: dolya@aol.com
Mag Frequency: Sporadic
Subscription: No subscription
Single Issue: £2 or $4
Payment in: Any currency
Payable to: Ms Lindsay Brewis
Inserts accepted: Yes
Circulation approx: 300 plus
Accept/rejection approx times: 2 weeks

S

SMITHS KNOLL

Founded in 1992 and named after the North Sea lightship, it aims at readability. Particularly attractive to would-be contributors are its two-week turnaround time for submissions and the editors' willingness to offer constructive criticism when they are interested in a poem. It showcases a wide range of poetry (previously unpublished in the UK) from different kinds of writers - established, up and coming, and complete first timers. It prints only poetry, well-presented and perfect bound.

Address: 49 Church Road, Little Glemham, Woodbridge, Suffolk, IP13 0BJ
Mag Frequency: 3 issues per year
Subscription: £12 for 3 issues
Single Issue: £4.50
Back Issue: £3-£4
Overseas: £14 for 3 issues, single issue £5
Payment in: Sterling only
Payable to: Smiths Knoll
Inserts accepted: Sometimes, by previous arrangement
Terms: Depends on postage cost
Circulation approx: 500
Payment terms to contributors: £20 plus complimentary copy
Accept/rejection approx times: Less than 2 weeks

S
SMOKE

New writing, poetry and graphics by some of the best established names, alongside new work from Merseyside, from all over the country and all over the world. Contributors have included Simon Armitage, David Constantine, Carol Anne Duffy, Douglas Dunn, Miroslav Holub, Jackie Kay, Roger McGough, Adrian Mitchell and Jo Shapcott.

Editor Name(s): Dave Calder and Dave Ward
Address: The Windows Project, First Floor, Liver House, 96 Bold Street, Liverpool L1 4HY
Telephone: 0151 709 3688
Mag Frequency: Twice yearly
Subscription: £3 for 4 issues
Single Issue: 50p plus postage
Overseas: £5 for 4 issues
Payable to: Windows Project
Inserts accepted: Yes
Terms: Exchange
Advertising Rates: N/A
Circulation approx: 1000
Payment terms to contributors: 1 copy
Accept/rejection approx times: 2 weeks

SNAPSHOTS

Snapshots is an internationally acclaimed haiku magazine featuring contemporary English-language haiku and senryu by both new and world-famous haiku poets. It is the only UK journal devoted exclusively to haiku and senryu. Contributors include Janice Bostok, Randy M. Brooks, David Cobb, Caroline Gourlay, Martin Lucas and Michael Dylan Welch. Snapshots is perfect-bound with a full-colour glossy card cover, and also features brief biographies of its contributors and a Best-Of-Issue Award as voted for by subscribers. Submissions of up to 20 individual haiku and/or senryu are welcome. These must be original, unpublished, not under consideration elsewhere and accompanied by a covering letter and an SAE (plus 2 IRCs internationally). Subscribers may also submit via email. Tanka may be submitted to our tanka journal Tangled Hair. Poems included in the magazine may also be published on the Snapshots website which also includes reviews and details of Snapshot Press books, etc. Snapshots also sponsors an annual competition for unpublished collections of haiku, senryu and/or tanka. In addition to a cash prize the winning author's collection is published by Snapshot Press. (Send SAE for details. Closing date 31 July.) ISSN 1461-0833.

Editor Name(s): John Barlow
Address: Snapshot Press, PO Box 35, Sefton Park, Liverpool L17 3EG
Email: jb@snapshotpress.freeserve.co.uk (subject line 'Snapshots')
Website: www.mccoy.co.uk/snapshots
Mag Frequency: Quarterly
Subscription: £18
Single Issue: £5
Back Issue: £4.50
Overseas: Subscription: £22 (US $36) Single Issue: £6 (US $10)
Payment in: Cheque/PO/IMO/Sterling Bank Drafts/US bills
Payable to: Snapshot Press
Inserts accepted: Yes
Terms: £10 or exchange. Must be haiku related
Advertising Rates: N/A
Circulation approx: 200
Payment terms to contributors: Best-Of-Issue Award
Accept/rejection approx times: Usually 1-4 weeks

S

SOL MAGAZINE

Published by Sol Publications, Sol is chiefly a poetry magazine, tied to no particular school of writing, preferring instead simply to publish the best poems that it receives from its contributors. Since it was established in 1969 it has published work by Roger McGough, David Halliwell, Thomas Land, Andrew Darlington, Frederic Vanson, Susan Fromberg Schaeffer, Margot K Juby, Michael Daugherty, David Jaffin, John Whitworth, Gavin Ewart, Ian McMillan, and many others. We also publish articles about literature and philosophy, short stories, up to 5000 words, and selective book reviews, plus a letter column. Artwork is also required.

Editor Name(s): Malcolm E Wright
Address: 24 Fowler Close, Southchurch, Southend-on-Sea, Essex SS1 2RD
Email: solmag@solpubs.freeserve.co.uk
Website: www.solpubs.freeserve.co.uk
Mag Frequency: Twice yearly
Subscription: 2 for £4.50, 4 for £8.00
Single Issue: £2.40
Back Issue: Enquire about availability
Overseas: US: 2 for $10, 4 for $20
Payment in: Equivalent in cash - no foreign cheques please
Payable to: Sol Publications
Inserts accepted: Yes
Terms: 35p per 100g
Advertising Rates: £10 per page; pro rata for fractions of a page
Circulation approx: 200
Payment terms to contributors: £1 per published page
Accept/rejection approx times: 3 months

THE SOLAR FLAME

THE SOLAR FLAME is a journal of the emerging Spiritual and cultural Renaissance. The finest spiritual/metaphsical poetry is invited.
REBIRTH offers a resurgence of poetry which aims to enrich life. Poetry invited in Classical, Romantic, Pastoral or Metaphsical vein.
The New Renaissance is an inclusive medium for the global revival of the human spirit through the world of ideas and the imagination, which seeks to put the heart and soul back into society. A high standard is sought. Submit up to 5 poems, not exceeding 30 lines, with sae/IRCs for reply. Previous publication details should be included. Copyright reverts to author on publication. Between poems of equal merit, subscribing contributors will be given preference, as it is they who help keep the magazine alive

Editor Name(s): Pamela Constantine
Address: Firebird Press, 104 Argyle Gardens, Upminster, Essex, RM14 3EU
Email: firebirdpress@hotmail.com
Website: www.homestead.com/firebirdpress
Mag Frequency: Quarterly in both cases
Subscription: £14. Non-sterling, US $35
Single Issue: £3.50. Non-sterling, US $10
Overseas: US $35
Payment in: Cheque/PO, British only; rest of world, US $ bills only
Payable to: P.Page
Inserts accepted: No
Circulation approx: The Solar Flame = Building, Rebirth = First Issue Autumn 2001
Payment terms to contributors: Complimentary copies

⑤
SOUTH

In July 1989 South was launched as a new poetry magazine. It is a merging of 'Doors', a poetry magazine concerned with the relationship between poetry in the country and the world beyond, and 'South', also an existing regional magazine, covering the southern counties of England. Poets from outside the region are welcome to contribute. Each issue contains poetry chosen from material submitted by poets, a poet profile, reviews, articles, and details of events and poetry competitions.

Poets published are invited to read at a celebration to launch each issue, giving poets an oppurtunity to hear each others' work and meet over a drink. Please send no more than 6 poems (with C5 sae). Poems should preferably be typed on A4 paper (one side only) with the poets's name and address clearly shown on the reverse side of each poem. We also welcome prose articles (about 800 words) on poets and topics of interest to readers and writers in the Southern counties. Details of poetry events taking place in the region would be gratefully received, along with letters and publications to be reviewed. SOUTH - primarily a poetry magazine for and from the southern counties of England - has a growing subscription base including many subscribers with affinities and intrests in the area, from Italy, Germany, France, Botswana and Switzerland.

Editor Name(s): Janet Peters
Address: Wanda Publications, (South Magazine), 75 West Borough, Wimborne, Dorset BH21 1LS
Telephone: 01202 889669
Fax: 01202 881061
Email: wanda@wordandaction.com
Mag Frequency: April and October each year
Subscription: £8 for one year (2 issues),£15 for two years (4 issues)
Single Issue: £4.50
Back Issue: Issues 1-14 £2, issues 15 onwards £3
Overseas: As UK plus p&p
Payment in: Cheque/PO
Payable to: Wanda Publications
Inserts accepted: No
Circulation approx: 400
Payment terms to contributors: 1 complimentary copy

S

SPANNER

A publication concerned with arts, music, poetry and performance with work by artists as the main contributors. Unsolicitied contributions are not required and are not read.

Editor Name(s): Allen Fisher
Address: 14 Hopton Road, Hereford, HR1 1BE
Email: kaa45@dial.pipex.com
Mag Frequency: Irregular
Subscription: £9 for 3 copies for individuals
Single Issue: £3
Back Issue: £3
Overseas: £3 sterling only
Payment in: Sterling only
Payable to: Spanner
Inserts accepted: No
Circulation approx: Mail order/subscription

5

THE SPICE-BOX

From July 2000 The Spice-Box is available free via the internet. Its main objective is to continue to provide a platform for new and lesser known writers to promote their work.

Editor Name(s): Malcolm Napier, Sally Roast
Address: Aramby Publishing, 1 Alanbrooke Close, Knaphill, Woking, Surrey GU21 2RU
Email: malcolmaramby@aol.com
Website: www.thespice-box.co.uk
Mag Frequency: Updated weekly
Single Issue: Free via internet
Overseas: Free via Internet
Payment in: Sterling
Payable to: Aramby Publishing (when appropriate)
Inserts accepted: No
Circulation approx: Unlimited
Payment terms to contributors: None
Accept/rejection approx times: 3 - 4 weeks

S

THE SPINSTER'S ALMANACK

The Spinster's Almanack, for textile enthusiasts, is published four times a year in January, April, July and October. It is edited by Rowena Edlin-White and Dee Duke who aim to produce a friendly but useful magazine with instructional articles, letters and reviews, Guild news, patterns and recipes. We research our material thoroughly but try not to take ourselves too seriously and we find that it is this approach which has made readers world-wide, in Great Britain, Eire, America, Australia, Canada and beyond and this makes for a good cross-fertilisation of ideas. New writers: we have a number of regular contributors but are always interested in new ones. If you would like to offer an article, send for our Guidelines for Contributors from the address below, enclosing a stamped addressed envelope, please.

Editor Name(s): Rowena Edlin-White and Dee Duke
Address: The Spinster's Almanack, Willow House, 11 Frederick Avenue, Carlton, Nottingham NG4 1HP
Subs to: Dee Duke, 23 Vaughan Avenue, Papplewick Lane, Hucknall, Nottingham, NG15 8BT Tel: 0115 9635538
Telephone: 0115 9873135
Email: ro.edlin-white@virgin.net
Mag Frequency: 4 times a year (Jan/April/July/October)
Subscription: £9
Single Issue: £1.90
Back Issue: Various - half price
Overseas: £10 surface/£12 airmail
Payment in: Sterling or US bills
Payable to: The Spinster's Almanack
Inserts accepted: Yes
Terms: For 250, £15
Circulation approx: 250 (subscriptions) but reaches many more through spinsters and weavers' guilds
Payment terms to contributors: £7.50 per article plus complimentary copy; we do not pay for reviews, recipes, letters
Accept/rejection approx times: 3 - 4 weeks

$\mathcal{S}$
SPLIZZ

Splizz was founded in 1993. It features poetry, prose and pictures alongside extensive reviews of contemporary music. Splizz started off as a bi-monthly publication, but now appears quarterly, and in the last few years has become extremely successful both in the UK and further afield. Our aim is to provide new writers with an opportunity for their work to be published alongside more established writers. We are always seeking a helping hand, and welcome your contributions at any time.

Editor Name(s): Amanda Morgan
Address: 4 St Mary's Rise, Burry Port, Carmarthenshire SA16 OSH
Email: amanda@stmarys4.freeserve.co.uk NB: for enquiries only. Submissions not to be made by email
Website: www.stmarys4.freeserve.co.uk/Splizz.htm
Mag Frequency: Quarterly
Subscription: £5
Single Issue: £1.30
Overseas: 5 IRCs per issue
Payment in: Sterling cheque/PO/IRC/cash
Payable to: Amanda Morgan
Inserts accepted: Yes
Terms: Negotiable
Advertising Rates: A5 ads-£3.50/centre pages or back cover-£5
Circulation approx: Worldwide, and still increasing
Payment terms to contributors: We are unable to offer any payment as we are a non profit making publication. However you do get the pleasure of seeing your work published, and read by readers throughout the world
Accept/rejection approx times: 3 - 4 weeks

SPRINGBOARD: WRITING TO SUCCEED

Founded 1990, Springboard is a quarterly magazine it is not a market for writers but a forum in which to find encouragement and help. Provides articles, news, market information, competition news directed at helping writers to achieve success. The magazine supports postal folios for groups of writers in various genres.

Editor Name(s): Sandra Lieberman
Address: 144 Alexandra Road, Great Wakering, Essex, SS3 0GW
Telephone: 01702 216247
Email: slieberman@tinyonline.co.uk
Mag Frequency: Quarterly
Subscription: £8 pa for existing members; £12 pa for new members & £15pa to join the Folio as well
Single Issue: £3
Back Issue: £2
Overseas: £8 plus £2 airmail
Payment in: Sterling
Payable to: Sandra Lieberman
Inserts accepted: No
Circulation approx: 200
Payment terms to contributors: Free issue to poets accepted for The Curate's Egg
Accept/rejection approx times: Reject 2-3 weeks but publication around 12 months

S

STAND MAGAZINE

'If you want the excitment of original literary achievement, of a passion for it, I recommend Stand.' Richard Holmes.

Stand is an independent quarterly publishing poetry, fiction and literary and cultural criticism. Founded in 1952 by the distinguished poet Jon Silkin, it has published Samual Beckett, Angela Carter, Peter Carey, Agustina Bessa-Luís, Lorna Tracy, BS Johnson, Geoffrey Hill, Tony Harrison, Paul Celan, Hans Magnus Enzensberger, Yves Bonnefoy, Pier Paolo Pasolini, Penelope Shuttle, Kathleen Raine, Michael Hamburger and many other. The New Series, edited by Michael Hulse and John Kinsella, is committed to taking the magazine into the forefront of literary debate. While tackling the concerns of literary communities worldwide, the magazine will also remain true to its traditional home base in the North of England. The editors' chief aim is always to publish the best writing they can find, whether by Nobel Prize winners or those new to publication.

Address: Worldwide Subscription Service, Unit 4, Gibbsreet Farm, Ticehurst, East Sussex, TN5 7HE
Subs to: Unit 4, Gibbs Reed Farm, Ticehurst, East Sussex TN5 7HE
Telephone: 01580 200 657
Fax: 01580 200 616
Email: stand@english.novell.leeds.ac.uk
Website: http:/saturn.vcu.edu/~dlatane/stand.html
Mag Frequency: Quarterly
Subscription: 1 year £25, 2 years £48
Single Issue: £7
Overseas: US/OS $49.50, AUS/NZ $72 for 1 year
Payment in: Cheque/Credit Card
Payable to: Stand Magazine Ltd
Inserts accepted: Yes
Terms: £150 UK only/£250 International
Advertising Rates: £62.50 (plus VAT) quarter page, £150 (plus VAT) half page, £250 (plus VAT) full page
Circulation approx: Variable
Payment terms to contributors: Payment and free copy
Accept/rejection approx times: 8 - 10 weeks

STAPLE

Staple - The magazine was established in 1982 and has steadily gained its reputation as a forum for good quality new writing. This year Staple is operating under new management: the new editors, Ann Atkinson and Elizabeth Barrett welcome submissions of original poetry and short stories which are assured and well crafted, and wish also to encourage writers who are innovative and prepared to take risks with style and form.

Editor Name(s): Ann Atkinson, Elizabeth Barrett
Address: Padley Rise, Nether Padley, Grindleford, Hope Valley, Derbyshire S32 2HE
Telephone: 01433 631949
Mag Frequency: 3 pa
Subscription: £10
Single Issue: £3.50
Back Issue: 2 for £4 + £1 p&p
Overseas: £15 Europe air, and surface RoW
Payment in: Sterling cheques or currency at sender's own risk (UK £ or US $ only)
Payable to: Staple
Inserts accepted: Yes
Terms: Exchange or payment
Circulation approx: Approx 500
Payment terms to contributors: £5 per poem, £10 per story
Accept/rejection approx times: Between 4 - 16 weeks - work not held over between issues

S

STARFISHMAN

Starfishman - 7 foot of sinew and muscle, crossing and recrossing the divide between the subconcious and ... whatever lies beyond.
Hero or villain? God or demon? You decide.
You are invited to contribute to the myths and legends that surround the Starfishman, he who, foreshadowed by the Hale-Bopp comet, left the ocean and came ashore at Whitby on May 13th 1997 (May 13th has now been designated World Starfishman Day).
This is an ongoing mail art project. Artwork, poetry, fiction and whatnot on the Starfishman welcome... you might find it a good idea to buy a copy first, though.

Address: c/o PO Box 77, Sunderland SR1 1EB
Mag Frequency: Variable
Single Issue: 3 x 1st class stamps
Payment in: UK postage stamps
Inserts accepted: Yes
Terms: On application
Circulation approx: Small but select
Payment terms to contributors: Free copy

S

STILL

still is an independent literary journal with a zen approach to haiku, tanka and short verse. It is a quarterly with international readership and the journal sponsors the bi-annual Haiku Award competitions (total prize money of £2000 annually) which attract global entrants. Each edition of still is 96 pages thick, has one poem to a page for maximum stillness, is thread sewn, perfect bound, A5 in size, with a full colour photograph on its cover on 275gsm artboard, and printed text on 100gsm paper. The journal is published by the empty press. Our website has had over 18000 visitors and include a large collection of haiku and new linked poems.

Editor Name(s): ai li
Address: 49 Englands Lane, London NW3 4YD
Email: still@info.demon.co.uk
Website: http://www.info.demon.co.uk
Mag Frequency: Quarterly
Subscription: £24 (inclusive of p&p)
Single Issue: £6.99 (inclusive of p&p)
Overseas: Subscription: Surface mail: £25, Air Mail: £30, Single issue: EC and Surface: £7.24, Air Mail: £8.49 (all inclusive of p&p)
Payment in: Cheques/PO/IMO/US Dollars
Payable to: still
Inserts accepted: Inserts by invitation only
Circulation approx: Press run 1000 - 2000 editions
Payment terms to contributors: None and no contributors copies
Accept/rejection approx times: Anything from 2 weeks to 3 months

S
STRIDE

After 33 issues as a poetry magazine, four issues as an 'occasional arts journal', and a few years gap Stride magazine welcomes you back to its new incarnation as a webzine. A gathering of new poetry, short prose, articles, news reviews and whatever takes our fancy. We don't intend to worry about producing Stride issue by issue, just keep updating what's on the site. Read on...

SUBMITTING TO STRIDE MAGAZINE: The editor, Rupert Loydell, welcomes submissions of 4 or 5 poems, short prose, reviews or articles. Please submit in the body of e-mails (not attachments) to submissions@stridemagazine.co.uk or by snailmail (with SAE for reply) to Stide Magazine, 11 Sylvan Road, Exeter, Devon, EX4 6EW. If in doubt about what you want to submit, ask first. E-mail to editor@stridemagazine.co.uk. Attatchments or snailmail without SAEs will not be considered or replied to.

Editor Name(s): Rupert Loydell
Address: STRIDE, 11 Sylvan Road, Exeter, Devon, EX4 6EW
Email: editor@stridemagazine.co.uk
Website: www.stridemagazine.co.uk
Mag Frequency: Updated/changed every 2 - 3 weeks
Inserts accepted: No
Circulation approx: 1000 readers per week
Accept/rejection approx times: 3 days

THE STUDENT MAGAZINE

An international publication for students of all ages. It has just been created (May 2000) 1st issue available on receiving the sterling amount of half of the cost of the subscription. It is essential to become a subscriber if you seek publication. All subjects accepted in poetry, prose, articles, illustrations, letters, points of view etc. Offensive subjects or bad language not accepted. A modern magazine for the keen student and outgoing person.

Editor Name(s): Jacqueline Gonzalez-Marina
Address: Fern Publications, 24 Frosty Hollow, East Hunsbury, Northants NN4 0SY
Fax: 01604 701730
Mag Frequency: Bi-annual
Subscription: £12 UK
Single Issue: £6 UK, £11 USA and overseas in general
Back Issue: £6 UK, £7 Europe, £11 USA and other countries
Overseas: £14 Europe, £22 RoW
Payment in: UK Sterling only
Payable to: Fern Publications
Inserts accepted: Yes
Terms: £8 per 100, £80 per 1000
Advertising Rates: It varies according to text or photos included. Request of an estimate is desirable
Circulation approx: About 1000
Payment terms to contributors: No payment given, just publicity and advice
Accept/rejection approx times: 2 weeks

S
SUMMER BULLETIN

32-page booklet with details of meetings, news of members, general information about the Yorkshire Dialect Society, prose and verse from members, new writers being encouraged to submit their work for consideration. We accept dialect from all corners of the vast, old county of Yorkshire.

Address: Summer Bulletin, 3 Northdale Mount, Bradford BD5 9AP
Subs to: Yorkshire Dialect Society 'Rambles' 61 Moor Lane, Carnaby, Bridlington YO16 4UT
Mag Frequency: Annually
Subscription: £7 for subscription to Summer Bulletin and Transactions of the Yorkshire Dialect Society, plus membership of the Society
Single Issue: £2
Back Issue: £1
Overseas: £7 Europe/£10 RoW
Payment in: Sterling UK £
Payable to: Yorkshire Dialect Society
Payment terms to contributors: None

SUNFLOWER POEMS OF CELEBRATION

'Sunflower Poems of Celebration' is a collection of upbeat and accessible poems by new and established writers, which aims to celebrate life (in all its aspects) experience, and joy in living. Acknowledging that poetry sometimes takes itself too seriously, it concentrates on what is largely pleasurable.

It is the last publication of SPG (Stafford Poetry Group) and represents twenty-five years' acquaintance with the small press poetry scene. It is a collection to enjoy.

Editor Name(s): Isabel Gillard
Address: St Lawrence Cottage, Sellman Street, Gnosall, Stafford ST20 0EP
Telephone: 01785 822343
Mag Frequency: One-off
Single Issue: £6.50 (incl p&p)
Payment in: Sterling
Payable to: Isabel Gillard
Circulation approx: Small - 300

$\mathcal{S}$
SUPERFLUITY

This high quality magazine is especially compiled to enhance and maximise the reading experience. Make the right choice, read your favourite poems from Superfluity. Internationally renowned.

Editor Name(s): Peter Larkin
Address: Scribbled Publications, PO Box 6234, Nottingham NG2 5EX
Telephone: 0115 9817196
Email: peter@larkin96.fsnet.co.uk
Mag Frequency: Quarterly
Subscription: £10 a year
Single Issue: £2.75
Overseas: £13 EU, £15 RoW
Payment in: Cheque/PO Sterling only
Payable to: Scribbled Publications
Inserts accepted: Yes
Terms: A5 or A6 flyers or order forms, £10 per 100
Advertising Rates: £10 half page, £15 full page
Circulation approx: 100 approx (1st issue)
Payment terms to contributors: Issue in which poet appears
Accept/rejection approx times: Within one month

SWAGMAG

The magazine of Swansea's writers and artists. Edited by Peter Thabit Jones, it publishes poetry, prose, features, interviews and reviews. Cartoons/photos/artwork. Includes work in the Welsh language too. Recent issues include interview with Adrian Mitchell, features on Paul Peter Piech, international artist, and anglo-welsh poet Harri Webb.

Editor Name(s): Peter Thabit Jones
Address: c/o Dan-y-bryn, 74 Cwm Level Road, Brynhyfryd, Swansea SA5 9DY Wales
Mag Frequency: Twice yearly
Subscription: £5 plus 50p postage
Single Issue: £2.50 plus postage
Back Issue: £1.50 plus postage
Overseas: On request
Payable to: SWAG, Swansea Writers' and Artists' Group
Inserts accepted: Yes
Terms: On request
Circulation approx: Increasing
Payment terms to contributors: Free copy of magazine
Accept/rejection approx times: 3 months

♪

THE SWEDENBORG SOCIETY MAGAZINE

The magazine publishes articles about or relating to the writings, life and thought of Emanuel Swedenborg.

Editor Name(s): Stephen McNeilly
Address: Swedenborg House, 20/21 Bloomsbury Way, London WC1A 2TH
Email: swed.soc@netmatters.co.uk
Website: www.swedenborg.org.uk
Mag Frequency: Once a year
Subscription: Free to members
Single Issue: Free to members, £1 to non-members
Back Issue: £1
Overseas: N/A
Payable to: The Swedenborg Society
Inserts accepted: No
Circulation approx: 1000
Payment terms to contributors: No payment

THE TABLA BOOK OF NEW VERSE

The Tabla Book Of New Verse is the successor to Tabla poetry magazine. Since its foundation in 1991, Tabla has pursued a policy of combining work commissioned from well-known poets with selected entries from a tie-in competition. Writers new to Tabla are requested to approach us through the competition in the first instance: please send an SAE. Those accepted for publication are then invited to offer work for future issues. A recognition that poets and poems, however accomplished, find their readers slowly has helped to shape Tabla's editorial policy; so, too, has the belief that it is preferable to publish too little than too much. Hence, only one slim volume of Tabla has appeared every twelve months since 1992. In that time, we have published new work by some of the most prominent names in contemporary verse, including Seamus Heaney, Carol Rumens, Peter Redgrove, Charles Simic, Paul Muldoon, Tobias Hill, Pauline Stainer, Charles Tomlinson, Anne Stevenson, John Burnside and Medbh McGuckian. Tabla has been widely praised in the poetry press for its contents and its elegant design. It has also twice enjoyed the distinction of publishing poems which have then been shortlisted for the Best Individual Poem Of The Year category of the Forward Poetry Awards. Selected poems from the 1999 book were reprinted in The Independent.

Editor Name(s): Stephen James
Address: Tabla, Dept of English, University of Bristol, 3-5 Woodland Road, Bristol BS8 1TB
Fax: 0117 928 8860
Email: stephen.james@bristol.ac.uk
Website: www.bristol.ac.uk/tabla
Mag Frequency: Annual
Subscription: N/A
Single Issue: £6
Back Issue: £2
Overseas: Add £1 (Europe), £2 (RoW)
Payment in: Sterling only
Payable to: Tabla
Inserts accepted: Yes
Terms: Exchange or by arrangement
Circulation approx: 600 plus
Payment terms to contributors: Competition prizes/complimentary copies
Accept/rejection approx times: 2 months from competition closing date

T
TAK TAK TAK

Formed in 1986 Tak Tak Tak is a publishing house and label dedicated to the experimental in writing, music and other media. Publications have taken various forms. We are not currently accepting unsolicited contributions.

Address: BCM Tak, London WC1N 3XX
Mag Frequency: Occasional
Subscription: Variable
Single Issue: Variable
Back Issue: Variable
Overseas: Variable
Payment in: Cheque/IMO/PO/registered cash
Payable to: Tak Tak Tak
Inserts accepted: No
Circulation approx: Variable
Payment terms to contributors: Copies or royalty by negotiation

TANGLED HAIR

Tangled Hair is the first journal published in the UK to be devoted exclusively to tanka. It features high quality contemporary English-language tanka by both new and internationally established poets. Contributors include Sanford Goldstein, Caroline Gourlay, Laura Maffei and Jane Reichhold. Tangled Hair is perfect-bound with a full-colour glossy card cover and each poem is printed on its own page for maximum effect. It also features brief biographies of its contributors and a Best-Of-Issue Award as voted for by subscribers. Submissions of up to 12 tanka are welcome. These must be original, unpublished, not under consideration elsewhere and accompanied by a covering letter and an SAE (plus 2 IRCs internationally). Subscribers may also submit via email. Haiku and senryu may be submitted to our haiku magazine Snapshots. Tanka featured in Tangled Hair may also be published on the Snapshots website. ISSN 1465-0363.

Editor Name(s): John Barlow
Address: Snapshot Press, PO Box 35, Sefton Park, Liverpool L17 3EG
Email: jb@snapshotpress.freeserve.co.uk (subject line 'Tangled Hair')
Website: www.mccoy.co.uk/snapshots
Mag Frequency: Quarterly
Subscription: £18
Single Issue: £5
Overseas: Subscription: £22 (US $36) Single Issue: £6 (US $10)
Payment in: Cheque/PO/IMO/Sterling Bank Draft/US bills
Payable to: Snapshot Press
Inserts accepted: Yes
Terms: £10 or exchange. Must be tanka or haiku related
Advertising Rates: N/A
Payment terms to contributors: Best-Of-Issue Award
Accept/rejection approx times: Usually 1-4 weeks

T
TEARS IN THE FENCE

An international literary magazine that combines new writing with criticism and reviews, Tears In The Fence is one of the leading poetry publishers in the UK. Recent contributors include Edward Field, Barry MacSweeney, Fred Voss, John Freeman, Ketaki Kushari Dyson, Mary Maher, KV Skene, David Hart, Jay Ramsay, Jeffery Skeate, Andrea Moorhead, KM Dersley, Martin Stannard, Peter Dent, Jim Burns, Jim Greenhalf, Sheila Hamilton et al.

Editor Name(s): David Caddy
Address: 38 Hod View, Stourpaine, Blandford Forum, Dorset DT11 8TN
Telephone: 01258 456803
Fax: 01258 454026
Website: www.wanderingdog.co.uk
Mag Frequency: 3 issues annually
Subscription: £12 for 3
Single Issue: £5
Overseas: $20 cash for 4, £17 for 3
Payment in: Sterling or US cash
Payable to: Tears In The Fence
Inserts accepted: Yes
Terms: £10 per 1000
Advertising Rates: Available upon request
Circulation approx: 1800
Payment terms to contributors: 1 copy of magazine
Accept/rejection approx times: 4 - 6 weeks
TEMS NEWS covers earth mysteries and related challenging issues: ancient sites, crop circles, dowsing, folklore, ghosts, healing, ley lines, old churches, sacred wells, UFOs, anomalous animals. Green Man Book and magazine reviews, cartoons, illustrated. (No poetry)

T

TEMS NEWS

TEMS NEWS is the newsletter of Travel & Earth Mysteries Society which is itself a Branch of ASSAP, the Association for the Scientific study of Anomalous Phenomena (a registested charity). TEMS holds monthly meetings and arranges field trips to places of historic and folklore significance.

Editor Name(s): Lionel Beer
Address: 115 Hollybush Lane, Hampton, Middlesex, TW12 2QY
Telephone: 020 8979 3148
Mag Frequency: Quarterly
Subscription: Magazine only £4.00, TEMS membership inc T N £8.00
Single Issue: £1.00 inc.post
Overseas: Add 15% for postage
Payment in: £s. or (US) $s bills
Payable to: Lionel Beer
Inserts accepted: Yes
Terms: Subject to negotiation
Advertising Rates: Sometimes free/subject to negotiation
Circulation approx: 150
Payment terms to contributors: Nil
Accept/rejection approx times: No fixed schedule

T
TERRIBLE BEAUTY

A Manic Street Preachers' fanzine exploring the fascinating subculture surrounding the band - intelligent, challenging, street spirit, preaching beauty and revolution of the mind. Features, articles, interviews, collages, poetry and reviews of events concerning the band as well as discussion on general popular culture. So, spill words - not blood! Political debate has always had a place in the fanzine and its name derived from a Manics lyric 'Beauty is such a terrible thing' and the Yeats poem 'Easter 1916' 'A terrible beauty is born' which refers to the uprising in Ireland in 1916. This literary/political link typifies the essence of the fanzine.

Editor Name(s): Mary O' Meara
Address: Flat 6, 11 Tring Avenue, Ealing Common, London W5 3QA
Email: mary_o_meara@hotmail.com
Mag Frequency: Twice a year
Subscription: £2.50 per issue
Single Issue: £2.50 per issue
Back Issue: £2.50
Overseas: £3 Europe, £3.50 RoW
Payment in: IRCs or International bank drafts in Sterling
Payable to: Mary O' Meara
Inserts accepted: Yes
Terms: Depends what it is. Free contacts/notices section
Advertising Rates: Negotiable - often free
Circulation approx: 500 plus
Payment terms to contributors: None (normally). Occasionally free copy of magazine or other item swapped
Accept/rejection approx times: About 3 weeks

TERRIBLE WORK

Poetry. Polemic. Reviews. Images. Heterogeneous Agitation. Particularly interested in publishing new and unknown writers whose work is independent and innovative.

Editor Name(s): Tim Allen, Steve Spence, Josephine Ebert
Address: 21 Overton Gardens, Mannamead, Plymouth Devon PL3 5BX
Email: tallentw@aol.uk (submissions in email body only)
Website: In preparation for 2001
Mag Frequency: Annual
Subscription: £8
Single Issue: £5
Back Issue: £3
Overseas: Europe £6, £4 subscription USA $9, $16 subscription
Payment in: Cheque/PO
Payable to: Terrible Work
Inserts accepted: No
Circulation approx: 350
Payment terms to contributors: Comp copies
Accept/rejection approx times: From return of post to 3 months

T
THE TEXT

The Text is a magazine for new and experimental writings of all kinds. Though it mostly publishes fiction and derivatives of fiction, it also publishes a long poems series. It does not publish individual short poems. The magazine comes unbound in an envelope, and occasionally features visual writing, and accepts submissions from all over the world. We will consider any form of writing, including scripts, polemics and adventurous essays, submitting work should not include CVs.

Editor Name(s): Keith Jafrate
Address: The Word Hoard, Kirklees Media Centre, 7 Northumberland Street, Huddersfield HD1 1RL
Telephone: 01484 452070
Fax: 01484 455049
Email: hoard@zoo.co.uk
Website: www.wordhoard.co.uk
Mag Frequency: Appears when sufficient quality submissions have arrived to fill an issue, usually 2 - 3 times per year
Subscription: £12 for 6 issues
Single Issue: £2.50
Back Issue: Single £2.50, or £6 for 3
Overseas: £12 for 6 issues
Payment in: Sterling
Payable to: The Word Hoard
Inserts accepted: No
Advertising Rates: On request
Circulation approx: 200 - 300
Payment terms to contributors: £50 plus 6 issues, subject to our finances remaining healthy
Accept/rejection approx times: Varies between 5 minutes and 9 months, depending on the workload

THE THIRD ALTERNATIVE

TTA is a multi-award-winning magazine of 68 matt art A4 pages and matt laminated colour cover which is heralded as one of the best, most innovative fiction magazines in the world. It publishes extraordinary new stories - these can be modern SF/fantasy/horror, or just as often not of any particular genre, blurring the borders between the outré and the mainstream. We publish many well-known authors but just as many newcomers, often giving writers their first ever credit. The magazine has an unrivalled record of honorable mentions and reprints in various anthologies, from The Year's Best Fantasy and Horror in the USA to The Time Out Book of New Writing. We also publish in-depth reviews, profiles and interviews, as well as regular provocative comment columns - all complemented by stunning artwork. Submissions are welcome as long as they follow standard ms format and are accompanied by SAE and covering letter. We also recommend Zene for continued updates and news. Please study issues of TTA before submitting - not a requirement, just a recommendation!

Editor Name(s): Andy Cox
Address: TTA Press, 5 Martins Lane, Witcham, Ely, Cambs CB6 2LB
Email: ttapress@aol.com
Website: www.tta-press.freewire.co.uk
Mag Frequency: Bi-monthly
Subscription: £18 (6 issues)
Single Issue: £3.25
Back Issue: £3.25
Overseas: Europe £3.75/£21, RoW £4.25/£24, USA $7/$36
Payment in: Cheque/PO etc. Foreign currency cheques acceptable
Payable to: TTA Press
Inserts accepted: Yes
Terms: Negotiable
Advertising Rates: Ad space available - contact publisher with SAE
Payment terms to contributors: £20 per 1,000 words plus copies
Accept/rejection approx times: 6 weeks

𝒯
THE THIRD HALF (LITERARY MAGAZINE)

The Third Half will, in future, vary per issue, but will showcase the work of 2 writers each time. Sets/mini-books of 24 pages need to be sent for appraisal (open subjects, but no obscenity wanted). A copy of the catalogue is available to writers for A5 sized envelope and 39p stamp (or 50p cheque to cover this). Recent editions have included the following poets:

(ISBN 0907759 327) Issue 29 Roy Iciffe and Gabriella Kraaiveld
(ISBN 0907759 378) Issue 30 Idris Caffrey and Khalid Khan
(ISBN 0907759 726) Issue 31 Andrew Detheridge and Tom Kelly
(ISBN 0907759 777) Issue 32 Margaret Pelling and Christine Billington
(ISBN 0907759 823) Issue 33 Jack Rickard and Helen Heslop
(ISBN 0907759 238) Issue 34 Hannah Welfare and Michael Newman

Editor Name(s): Kevin Troop
Address: 16 Fane Close, Stamford, Lincolnshire PE9 1HG
Telephone: 01780 754193
Mag Frequency: 2 or 3 months/quarterly
Subscription: £4
Single Issue: £4 incl p&p
Back Issue: £4
Overseas: $10
Payment in: by agreement
Payable to: KT Publications
Inserts accepted: No
Circulation approx: Worldwide
Payment terms to contributors: Individually agreed
Accept/rejection approx times: 1 week

T

THIS IS

Dare you risk reading This Is... the literary magazine dedicated to writing with a sharp cutting edge, writing that touches the wildness at the heart of life? It is the magazine for anyone who cares about modern literature. The angle of each issue differs encouraging distinctive, dangerous, trenchant, lyrical, idiosyncratic and exciting writing. The new venture contains prose, poetry, photography and black and white art. It is an A4 48 page publication, beautifully designed to last, printed on heavy quality paper. It is issued twice per year currently. This Is has been keenly received by readers, writers, literary agents, reviewers, bookshop buyers, in fact all who have read a copy. Don't resist, savour it, as soon as you can!

Editor Name(s): Carol Cornish
Address: Writing Space Publications, Box 16185, London NW1 8ZH
Telephone: 0171 586 0244
Fax: 0171 586 5666
Email: writingspace@bt.internet.com
Website: http://www.bt.internet.com/~writingspace/thisis/
Mag Frequency: Twice per year increasing in future
Subscription: 4 copies: £17.60 incl p&p
Single Issue: £3.50 plus p&p 90p
Overseas: 4 copies: £14 plus p&p £5.60 (£4.90 for 1, £19.60 for 4)
Payment in: Sterling or International Money Orders
Payable to: Writing Space Publications
Inserts accepted: Yes
Terms: By arrangement only
Advertising Rates: No advertising except reciprical arrangments
Circulation approx: 500 + and growing
Payment terms to contributors: None unfortunately
Accept/rejection approx times: Up to 6 months, frequently within 5 weeks

T
THOMAS HARDY JOURNAL

The Thomas Hardy Journal is published by the Thomas Hardy Society thrice yearly and has two main objects: to provide information about the Society's activities and to be a forum for the publication of letters, reviews and articles about Hardy's writings, his life and his background. Literary contributions are welcomed but will not be returned unless accompanied by the necessary postage. No payment is made for articles but writers have the satisfaction of publication in a periodical of authority and repute, and they will be given four complimentary copies of the issue in which their article appears. Articles should be typed in double spacing on one side of the paper only, and should be as brief as possible. Disks compatible with Word or Pagemaker, are welcome but not essential. 4,000 words should normally be regarded as the maximum. Please include a short entry (up to 10 lines) for the notes on contributors. The Editor reserves the right to shorten letters. Book reviews are usually invited but may be volunteered. They should normally be between 200 and 800 words. Any other items, such as relevant and reproducible illustrations, news cuttings, book excerpts and other miscellanea which might be of interest to our readers, will be gratefully received.

Address: 25 Hawthorn Grove, Heaton Moor, Stockport SK4 4HZ
Subs to: Thomas Hardy Society, PO Box 1438, Dorchester, Dorset DT1 1YH
Mag Frequency: 3 times a year
Subscription: £12
Single Issue: £4
Payable to: Thomas Hardy Society
Inserts accepted: Yes
Terms: £100
Advertising Rates: Full page £70/half page £35
Circulation approx: 1500
Payment terms to contributors: No payment, 4 copies

THUMBSCREW

Thumbscrew is an independent poetry journal publishing work by internationally renowned writers, alongside exciting new poets and critics. Important contributions include Ted Hughes on Sylvia Plath, recently-discovered stories by Louis MacNeice, and Charles Simic on the art of invective - as well as work from Paul Muldoon, Fleur Adcock, Craig Raine, Seamus Heaney, Anne Stevenson and others. Thumbscrew also sets out to provoke critical debate with a series of essays re-evaluating the reputations of several 'major' contemporary poets. Praising its 'sceptical stance' and 'independence of thought', Red Pepper recently concluded that Thumbscrew reads like 'Poetry Review's reckless younger sibling'. In other words, we have less money, but we're far more fun to be with.

Editor Name(s): Tim Kendall
Address: PO Box 657, Oxford OX1 3BE
Website: http://www.bristol.ac.uk/thumbscrew
Mag Frequency: 3 issues annually
Subscription: £10 pa
Single Issue: £3.50
Overseas: Europe £12.50/USA $28
Payment in: Cheque/PO
Payable to: Thumbscrew
Inserts accepted: Yes
Terms: £50 per 1000
Circulation approx: 580
Payment terms to contributors: 2 free copies
Accept/rejection approx times: 2 months

T
TIME BETWEEN TIMES

General interest, multi-path occult. A magazine for all Traditions. Contains news and views, history, stories, handicrafts and contacts. Available around the solstices and equinoxes. Article length up to 1000 words. Longer material by arrangement. Rapidly developing a 'cult' following - especially the magazines own cartoon strip 'Kingstone Henge'. Artwork black and white line drawings only please.

Editor Name(s): Llew
Address: Time Between Times, 41 Forest Road, Hinkley, Leics LE10 1HA
Email: tbt@oakapple.force9.net
Website: http:/www.oakapple.force9.co.uk
Mag Frequency: Quarterly
Subscription: £6 UK
Single Issue: £1.75
Back Issue: £2 incl p&p
Overseas: £7 Europe/$15 USA and Canada
Payment in: Cheque/crossed PO
Payable to: R Lapworth
Inserts accepted: Yes
Terms: Negotiable
Advertising Rates: On application
Circulation approx: 300
Payment terms to contributors: Free issue of magazine
Accept/rejection approx times: 6 weeks

TIME HAIKU

Time Haiku is a magazine (founded 1995) which publishes haiku, tanka and short poems in English. Short essays are published and there are articles on various aspects of haiku. The main intention of the magazine is to make haiku more accessible and popular and to provide a place where all types of haiku can be found. One of the aims is to have haiku accepted as a part of English Literature in the same way as the sonnet. Works by new writers are just as welcome as those of established haiku writers. The magazine is intended to appeal both to experts and those just curious about haiku. A newsletter is also published twice a year to give information about haiku and other poetry events. Past contributors have been Gavin Ewart, John Light, Chris Sykes, Dan Pugh and so on!

Editor Name(s): Dr Erica Facey
Address: Basho-an, Kings Head Hill, London E4 7JG
Mag Frequency: Twice yearly
Subscription: £6 annually
Single Issue: £2.75
Back Issue: £2.75
Overseas: £10 RoW
Payment in: Sterling cheques; foreign currency must allow for commission
Payable to: Time Haiku Group
Inserts accepted: Yes
Advertising Rates: £50 per page
Circulation approx: Increasing
Accept/rejection approx times: About 1 in 5 acceptances

T
TOCHER

Tocher - the name was chosen because of its fairly common use in both Scots and Gaelic, meaning dowry - contains some of the riches stored in the archives of the School of Scottish Studies. That archive now contains about 10000 tapes, as well as a large number of video recordings. Transcriptions of some of those have been issued in Tocher since 1971. There are stories and legends, songs, items on customs, children's rhymes, proverbs, riddles, the occasional recipe, and reminiscences of daily life from Shetland to the Borders. Items in Gaelic are translated into English, and glossaries are added to Scots items when that is thought appropriate. The production of the magazine is entirely done by the staff of the School of Scottish Studies, and it is printed in the University of Edinburgh. No 56, Summer 2000, contains a feature on Jimmy Williamson, a traveller with a story and songs of his own composition; a Gaelic song about a girl who masqueraded as a soldier, and a story from Shetland about an eagle stealing a baby.

Editor Name(s): Miss Morag MacLeod
Address: School of Scottish Studies, 27 George Square, Edinburgh EH8 9LD Scotland
Telephone: 0131 650 4150
Fax: 0131 650 4163
Email: Scottish.Studies@ed.ac.uk
Mag Frequency: Bi-annual
Subscription: £8 for 2 issues
Single Issue: £4.50
Back Issue: Issues 2-24 £1/26-43 £1.50/44-on £2
Overseas: $18 for 2
Payment in: £'s and US $'s
Payable to: Tocher
Inserts accepted: No
Advertising Rates: Full page £100/half page £50/quarter page £25 (A5)
Circulation approx: 800
Payment terms to contributors: N/A
Accept/rejection approx times: N/A

T

TRANSACTIONS OF THE YORKSHIRE DIALECT SOCIETY

Transactions reflects the work and interests of the Yorkshire Dialect Society, founded in 1897 to study and promote the varied dialect of Yorkshire. Articles range from academic linguistics and folklore to original prose and verse in Yorkshire dialect.

Editor Name(s): Dr Arnold Kellett
Address: 22 Aspin Oval, Knaresborough, North Yorkshire HG5 8EL
Mag Frequency: Annually
Single Issue: £4
Payable to: Yorkshire Dialect Society, c/o 61 Moor Lane, Carnaby, Bridlington YO16 4UT
Inserts accepted: No
Circulation approx: 550
Payment terms to contributors: None
Accept/rejection approx times: 6 months

T
TRANSIT

A little magazine all about the beat generation and associated people. Jack Kerouac, Burroughs, Ginsberg, Bukowski, Gary Snyder, Ferlinghetti, Richard Brautigan, Diane Di Prima and many others. We include their writing and writing about them.

Editor Name(s): Kevin Ring
Address: 27 Court Leet, Binley Woods, Nr Coventry CV3 2JQ
Telephone: 024 76543604
Email: kev@beatscene.freeserve.co.uk
Mag Frequency: Quarterly
Subscription: No subscriptions
Single Issue: £3
Overseas: £4 single copy
Payable to: M Ring
Inserts accepted: No
Payment terms to contributors: Copies
Accept/rejection approx times: 1 week

TREE SPIRIT

The magazine of Tree Spirit, charity 801511, includes news and views on all matters related to trees: poems, drawings, stories and articles which are tree orientated. Tree Spirit's aims are to protect trees and woodlands, to create new woods, to promote a greater understanding, awareness and affection for trees, woods and the natural environment.

Address: Hawkbatch Farm, Arley, Nr. Bewdley, Worcs DY12 3AH
Subs to: Emma and Liam Dowling, 82 Kingston Road, Earlsdon, Coventry CV5 6LR
Mag Frequency: 3-4 annually
Subscription: £12 waged/£7.50 unwaged
Single Issue: £1.50
Back Issue: £1
Overseas: £20
Payment in: Cheque/PO/foreign currency
Payable to: Tree Spirit
Inserts accepted: No
Circulation approx: 350-500
Payment terms to contributors: Free copy of magazine
Accept/rejection approx times: 1 month from receipt

T
TREMBLESTONE

Still the best poetry magazine to come out of Plymouth since Terrible Work first appeared in 1993. The first two issues of Tremblestone, November 1999 and March 2001 include work from Josephine Ebert, Helena Ericksson, Carolyn Finlay, Charles Hadfield, Norman Jope, Alexis Kirke, Louise Minton, Ian Robinson, Steve Spence, Sandra Tappenden, Anthony Borden Ward, Liz Winfield, Gordon Wardman and Jay Woodman, amongst others. Tremblestone is an eclectic magazine of roughly eighty pages. I'm not interested in every page being a carbon copy of the one before. Tremblestone publishes long poems, prose poems, medium sized poems and translations. Very fond of slipperyness. Tremblestone welcomes work from new and established writers and also carries magazine reviews from UK and abroad. The third issue of Tremblestone is currently in progress.

Editor Name(s): Kenny Knight
Address: Corporation Buildings, 10F How Street, The Barbican, Plymouth, Devon PL4 0DB
Mag Frequency: Once a year at present
Subscription: £12 for 3 issues - post free. £20 for 6 issues
Single Issue: £4 post free
Overseas: £15 worldwide, post free, for 3 issues. £25 for 6 issues
Payment in: Cheques drawn on UK banks or cash in Sterling
Payable to: Tremblestone
Inserts accepted: No
Circulation approx: 105
Payment terms to contributors: Free copy of Tremblestone
Accept/rejection approx times: 6 - 8 weeks

TRIUMPH HERALD

A Christian poetry magazine with a lively selection of articles, stories, letters, puzzles and Christian arts news. Subscribers often tell us they feel part of a family as we offer a meeting point for Christian poets to share their news and views. We welcome all poems, articles and stories and look forward to hearing from anyone wishing to get in touch. (Please write for a sample copy and subscription details).

Editor Name(s): Sarah Andrew - Managing Editor, Neil Day - Editor
Address: Triumph Herald, Remus House, Coltsfoot Drive, Woodston, Peterborough PE2 9JX
Telephone: 01733 898102
Fax: 01733 313524
Email: triumphhouse@forwardpress.co.uk
Website: www.forwardpress.co.uk
Mag Frequency: Quarterly
Subscription: £15 UK
Single Issue: £3.75
Overseas: £21
Payment in: PO/Cheque/Credit Card
Payable to: Forward Press Ltd
Inserts accepted: Yes
Terms: Small inserts are welcome - write to arrange inclusion
Advertising Rates: None - write to arrange inclusion in magazine
Circulation approx: 1000
Payment terms to contributors: Payments given ranging from £2-£10 for all submissions published
Accept/rejection approx times: 3 months

T
TROGLODYTE: : A CULTURAL MAGAZINE

International magazine in the English language with a special interest in African and Black studies, antiquities, topography, literature and general cultural interests, pro-human and pro-life, seeking short stories in good prose, metrical verse, and bold line drawings of nature, good architecture, and the like - strictly low-technology, and good clean fun.

Editor Name(s): Joseph Biddulph
Address: 32 Stryd Ebeneser, Pontypridd CF37 5PB
Telephone: 01443 662559
Mag Frequency: Irregular, rising to quarterly
Subscription: Can order issues in advance
Single Issue: E=3 Euros, £1.95 UK, $3 US including airmail - or equivalent
Overseas: One unified world price, as above
Payment in: Euros, UK £, Irish £ in any form, IRC's, US cheque, currency cash if risked in post
Payable to: Joseph Biddulph
Inserts accepted: Yes if strictly suitable
Terms: On application - sometimes free
Advertising Rates: On application
Circulation approx: Very low but growing
Payment terms to contributors: None at all
Accept/rejection approx times: 2 - 3 months

ULTIMATE CULT VIDEO GUIDE
(1st Edition)

A guide to all videocassettes released before 1983 (in the UK) and within the sci-fi, horror or cult cinema genres. The guide has a dual rating system showing both quality of film on cassette (ie - how good film is) and also how rare tape itself has become! It will be updated weekly on - line (for accuracy).

Address: The Cottage, Smithy Brae, Kilmacolm, Renfrewshire, PA13 4EN Scotland
Subs to: Submission of pertinent information is to be sent to email address above
Email: graveorc@yahoo.com
Website: www.geocities.com/graveorc
Mag Frequency: On - going (on - line)
Subscription: No subscription
Single Issue: Hard copy *1st editions only £5 (UK)/$10 (RoW)
Payment in: UK = Cheque, RoW = Bank draft
Payable to: G N Houston
Inserts accepted: No
Circulation approx: on-line
Payment terms to contributors: No contributions accepted

𝓊
UNDERSTANDING MAGAZINE

Understanding Magazine includes poems, short stories, translations, parts of plays, book reviews and articles. Understanding Magazine was founded by Denise Smith in 1989.

Editor Name(s): Editor: Denise Smith, Associate Editor: Thom Nairn
Address: 20A Montgomery Street, Edinburgh EH7 5JS Scotland
Telephone: 0131 4770754
Fax: 0131 4770754
Mag Frequency: 1 double issue per year
Subscription: £8 for 2 issues
Single Issue: £4.50
Back Issue: £2.50
Overseas: £10
Payment in: Cash/cheque in sterling
Payable to: Dionysia Press
Inserts accepted: Yes
Advertising Rates: £100 full page/flyer £25/25p per word
Circulation approx: 500 increasing
Payment terms to contributors: Free copy
Accept/rejection approx times: 8 months

UNHINGED

U

UNHINGED Online publishes short fiction (3000 words max), b&w artwork and small press reviews (500 - 700 words) on a tri-annual basis (January, May, September). For each issue there is a reading window of approximately 3 months, during which time submissions will either be rejected outright or shortlisted for further consideration. A final decision on selections from the shortlist will be made approximately one month prior to the official publication date. Any submissions arriving after that time will be held until the issue is published and reading for the next one begins.

All work is shortlisted/accepted/purchased on the understanding that the contributor owns the copyright, s/he is agreeable to publication on this site for a minimum period of four months, and the work is not being submitted elsewhere in the meantime. Each issue of Unhinged Online will be archived when the publication period has elapsed, but any archived work will be removed immediately upon receipt of the owner's written request.

NB these guidelines will be subjected to regular reviews and changed if necessary.

Editor Name(s): Paul J. Lockey
Address: PJL Press, PO Box 279, Keighley, BD20 0AS
Email: unhinged@unhinged1.co.uk
Website: http://www.unhinged1.co.uk
Terms: There is no payment for reviews, though reviewers do get to keep any items they are asked to give opinions on.
Payment terms to contributors: Online pays £5.00 per original (unpublished) story, £2.50 per re-printed story, and £2.50 per original illustration. All payments are by personal Sterling Cheque and sent to contibutors on publication.

U
UPSTART!

Upstart! is a high quality literature magazine that publishes short stories (up to 5000 words) and poetry from all over the UK and further afield. We prefer original, quirky, upbeat writing, and welcome extracts from novels, plays and any other forms. Each issue contains work from writers who live abroad, eg Africa, the Caribbean, Asia. New writers as well as established writers are encouraged to send their work. The magazine is becoming established as a high quality small press upstart!

Editor Name(s): Carol Barac and Alison Woodhouse
Address: 19 Cawarden, Stantonbury, Milton Keynes MK14 6AH
Telephone: 01908 317535
Fax: Same as phone
Email: cro.barac@tesco.net
Mag Frequency: One or two a year
Subscription: £11.90 for 2
Single Issue: £6.95 plus 55p postage = £7.50
Back Issue: £3.95 plus 55p postage = £4.50
Overseas: Add £1 to all prices
Payment in: GBP/bank draft
Payable to: Upstart! Press
Advertising Rates: £25 for quarter page
Circulation approx: 300 (mailing list of 800 plus)
Payment terms to contributors: None yet
Accept/rejection approx times: 6 months

URTHONA

Urthona (founded 1992) is dedicated to exploring the arts from a spiritual perspective. We see beauty in its widest sense as a tool for change - both personal and social. Urthona publishes contemporary poetry, short stories, reviews and indepth articles on artists whose work exhibits a dynamic spiritual vision. We are particularly inspired by the Buddhist tradition of the East and by the work of William Blake - Urthona is his archetypal spirit of the Imagination.

Editor Name(s): Shantigarbha and Ratnagarbha
Address: 3 Coral Park, Henley Road, Cambridge CB1 3EA
Telephone: 01223 472417
Fax: 01223 566568
Email: urthona.mag@virgin.net
Website: www.urthona.com
Mag Frequency: 2 a year
Subscription: £7 pa
Single Issue: £3.50
Overseas: £11.50 pa (airmail)
Payment in: Sterling only
Payable to: Urthona
Inserts accepted: Yes
Terms: POA
Advertising Rates: Full page £80/half page £50/quarter page £30/eighth page £18
Circulation approx: 1,200
Payment terms to contributors: Free copy of magazine
Accept/rejection approx times: 2 months

u
USK VALLEY VAUGHAN ASSOCIATION

Scintilla, the annual publication of the Usk Valley Vaughan Association, is designed to be a place of fruitful confluences. It brings together academic investigations and poetic insights inspired, directly and otherwise, by the writings, ideas and concerns of Henry Vaughan and his alchemist twin brother Thomas. Their holistic vision of man and nature, their experience of spiritual, psychological and material transformation, their dedication to healing, whether through scientific/medical discovery or the therapeutic powers of poetry, - all these shared preoccupations are more than ever current.

Scintilla is therefore not solely concerned with the Vaughans, though their presence remains the sine qua non of an undertaking that sprang from the 1995 tercentenery of Henry's death. Characteristcally the first issue contained academic articles, on his poem 'Distraction', his rhyming technique, and his reaction to civil war; essays on the poetics of healing, on the hermetic philosophy, alchemy and poetry, Vernon Watkins, modern cosmology, the power of language; a short prose fiction; sixty five pages of new poems; and (a regular feature) the work of a visual artist. Each number since has combined articles, essays, poems (now including winners in our annual Poetry Competition) and visuals; with a musical setting of Vaughan verses featuring in our latest issue.

Editor Name(s): General Editor: Dr Peter Thomas
Address: ENCAP, English Literature, Cardiff University, PO Box 94, Cardiff, CF1 3XB
Telephone: 029 20874854
Fax: 029 2087 4647
Email: ThomasPW@cardiff.ac.uk
Website: http://www.cf.uk.//uwcc//encap/ceir/scintilla/scnhome/html
Mag Frequency: Annual
Subscription: £7.50
Single Issue: £7.50
Back Issue: No's 1 and 2 at £6.95
Payment in: Sterling
Payable to: UVVA-SCINTILLA
Inserts accepted: Yes
Terms: By agreement
Circulation approx: 300/400
Payment terms to contributors: Articles/Essays - £40/50, Poems £10
Accept/rejection approx times: Yearly by christmas

VIGIL

Exploration of relationship through poetry and fiction from writers around the world. An international journey into what it means to be human amidst daily threats to freedom from political oppression, the tyranny of hunger and poverty or the chains of technological control systems. Affirmation of the sanctity of the human spirit through the beauty of heart and soul expression in poems and stories of highest endeavour. Above all fellowship in the craft of words to promote greater consciousness of our humanity rejoicing in our cultural diversity yet coming together in the common cause of our inspiration.

Address: Vigil Publications, 12 Priory Mead, Bruton, Somerset BA10 0DZ
Mag Frequency: 2 pa
Subscription: £8 for 3 issues
Single Issue: £3
Back Issue: £1.20 - £2.80
Overseas: £10 for 3 issues
Payment in: Cheque/PO in sterling
Payable to: Vigil Publications
Inserts accepted: Yes
Terms: £25
Circulation approx: 250
Payment terms to contributors: 1 free copy
Accept/rejection approx times: 6 weeks

𝒱
VISIONS

Visions is a non-profit magazine dedicated to bringing you the best in sf/fantasy/horror fiction. I aim to include a wide range of styles/tastes in each issue. All forms of sf/fantasy/horror are more than welcome of any length (up to 10000 words) - but stories over 2000 words are especially welcomed on disk! Printed manuscripts and disks (IBM 720k or Amiga 880k only ASCII or RTF format files preferred) accepted - both if possible. Artists are also welcome to get in touch - write for details.

Editor Name(s): Sean Kennedy
Address: 116 Long Lane, Carlton-In-Lindrick, Worksop, Notts S81 9AT
Email: visions@excite.co.uk
Website: http://start.at/visions
Mag Frequency: Bi-monthly
Subscription: £7.50 (6 issues)
Single Issue: £1.50
Overseas: Subscription: US $20 (Europe)/US $25 (RoW); Single issue: US $4 (Europe)/US $5 (RoW)
Payment in: US $/Francs/DM/Sterling
Payable to: S Kennedy
Inserts accepted: Yes
Terms: Ask
Advertising Rates: Ask
Circulation approx: Rising
Payment terms to contributors: Free copy
Accept/rejection approx times: 2 weeks/2 months

ν

VOICE & VERSE

The magazine for all who love reading or writing poetry, Voice & Verse regularly features work by established names as well as introducing and encouraging those new to the small press poetry scene. Each issue is packed with readers' letters and email; short articles; a wide range of poetry, from the descriptive and the poignant to the comic and the topical; news of events and competitions; reviews of small press poetry publications and much helpful information. Every poem accepted for publication is eligible for free entry to the Top Ten Competition. Ten poems are selected in each issue and a prize of £25 goes to the poem which gets the most votes from readers. Editorial policy is to promote poetry in print, and in performance, and to increase the appreciation of poetry. Submission guidelines are available on request. Readers are offered personal appraisal of their poems (for a small fee), typesetting and promotional services. The editor welcomes enquiries by letter, fax or email.

Editor Name(s): Ruth Booth
Address: Robooth Publications, 7 Pincott Place, London SE4 2ER
Telephone: 020 7277 8831
Fax: Same as phone
Email: robooth@gofornet.co.uk
Website: www.smallpresspoets.co.uk
Mag Frequency: Quarterly
Subscription: £12
Single Issue: £3.50
Overseas: £20 subscription, £5 single issue
Payment in: £ sterling cash/cheque/PO/IMO
Payable to: Robooth Publications
Inserts accepted: Yes
Terms: Exchange for 200 leaflets
Advertising Rates: £5 up to 50 words - free to subscribers
Circulation approx: 120
Payment terms to contributors: 1 free copy of magazine
Accept/rejection approx times: 4 weeks

V

VOYAGE

An eclectic mix of new and established writers of short stories and poems from around the world. Voyage seeks to help writers succeed by giving constructive advice and criticism. Over the last 4 years we have published over 100 first time writers. Now sold in 34 countries.

Editor Name(s): John Dunne
Address: 14 Honour Avenue, Goldthorn Park, Wolverhampton WV4 5HH
Telephone: 01902 652999
Fax: 01902 652999
Email: voyagemag@zyworld.com
Website: http://members.fortunecity.com/regentbooks/VoyageMagazine.html
Mag Frequency: Quarterly
Subscription: 6 issues - £15, 12 issues - £25
Single Issue: £4
Overseas: Europe 6 issues - £18, ROW - £22
Payment in: Sterling or Dollars
Payable to: JGD
Inserts accepted: Yes
Terms: £15 per 1000
Advertising Rates: £50 per page or prorata
Circulation approx: 3200
Payment terms to contributors: Up to £10 per 1000 words on publication
Accept/rejection approx times: 6 weeks

WALKING WALES

The premier magazine for all of those interested in walking in Wales. All associated topics are covered, and there is a strong bias towards good photography and design.
Editor Name(s): Carl Rodgers, Chris Barber, Derek Rees, David Perrott
Address: 3 Glantwymyn Village Workshops, Cemmaes Road, Machynlleth, Monts, SY20 8LY
Telephone: 01650 511314
Fax: 01650 511602
Email: walkingwales@perrocart.co.uk
Mag Frequency: Quarterly
Subscription: £14
Single Issue: £3.25
Payment in: Pounds sterling
Payable to: Gwalia LTD
Inserts accepted: Yes
Terms: Negotiable
Advertising Rates: Contact: Western Mail, Cardiff 029 20583651
Circulation approx: 3000
Payment terms to contributors: Negotiable
Accept/rejection approx times: 1 Month

W
WANDERLUST

The magazine for people with a passion for travel, covering cultural, adventure and special-interest travel. Award winning writing and photography, and annual competitions in both.
Potential contributors must view our guidelines first on the website, or send a SAE for them.

Editor Name(s): Lyn Hughes
Address: PO Box 1832, Windsor SL4 1YT
Telephone: 01753 620426
Fax: 01753 620474
Email: info@wanderlust.co.uk
Website: www.wanderlust.co.uk
Mag Frequency: Bi-monthly
Subscription: £16
Single Issue: UK £2.95 (£3.50 mail-order)
Back Issue: £3.50 UK
Overseas: £20 Europe/RoW surface, £30 airmail
Payment in: UK Sterling
Payable to: Wanderlust Publications
Inserts accepted: Yes
Terms: On application
Advertising Rates: £1575 FPC
Circulation approx: 33,000
Payment terms to contributors: £150 per 1,000 words
Accept/rejection approx times: 3 - 6 months

WASAFIRI

In over eighteen years of publishing, Wasafiri has changed the face of contemporary writing in Britain. As a literary magazine primarily concerned with new and postcolonial writers, it continues to stress the diversity and range of black and diasporic writers world-wide. Wasafiri remains committed to its original aims: to create a definitive forum for the voices of new writers and to open up lively spaces for serious critical discussion not available elsewhere. It is Britain's only international magazine for Black British, African, Asian, and Caribbean literatures. Wasafiri is supported by an impressive group of well known authors and critics, including Michael Ondaatje, Chinua Achebe, Caryl Phillips, Ngugi Wa Thiong'o, Kamau Braithwaite, Marina Warner, Nadine Gordimer, Abdulrazak Gurnah, Merle Collins, Ferdinand Denis, Bernardine Evaristo, Maya Jaggi and Aamer Hussein. Get the whole picture, get Wasafiri, the magazine at the core of contemporary international literature today.

Editor Name(s): Susheila Nasta
Address: Dept of English and Drama, Queen Mary, University of London, Mile End Road, London E1 4NS
Telephone: 020 7882 3120
Fax: 020 7882 3120
Email: Wasafiri@qmw.ac.uk
Website: www.english.qmw.ac.uk/wasafiri
Mag Frequency: Three times a year
Subscription: 1/2/3 year subs: £21/£38/£54 individual; £42/£76/£108 institution
Single Issue: £7(UK)/£9, $14 (Overseas)
Back Issue: £7 (UK)/£9, $12 (Overseas) individual; £14 (UK)/ $18 (Overseas) institution
Overseas: 1/2/3 year subs: £27/£50/£72 individual or £54/£100/£144 institution
Payment in: £ Sterling/Visa/Mastercard/Access
Payable to: Wasafiri
Inserts accepted: Yes
Terms: On application
Advertising Rates: £325 full page/£190 half page/£115 quarter page
Circulation approx: 5000
Payment terms to contributors: Poems - £30, fiction - £50, commissioned articles £50, reviewers - the issue
Accept/rejection approx times: 6 months

W
WEARWOLF

Weird
Esoteric
Allegorical
Remnants
With
Offbeat
Leathery
Fun
... but we'd rather you purchased a sample issue before delugeing us with your unsolcited poetry. God knows it's cheap enough...

Address: Wolfs Head Press, PO Box 77, Sunderland SR1 1EB
Mag Frequency: Sporadic
Subscription: £2.50 for 5 issues
Single Issue: Two 1st class stamps
Overseas: On application
Payment in: UK cheques, POs, stamps, cash at own risk
Payable to: Wolfs Head Press
Inserts accepted: Yes
Terms: On application
Advertising Rates: On application
Circulation approx: Variable
Payment terms to contributors: Free copy
Accept/rejection approx times: About a generation

W

WEYFARERS

Weyfarers has been going since 1972, It contains 28 sides of poetry and 4 of poetry reviews. Submissions judged on merit in the views of the editors, a team of three, with an occasional guest editor. Poetry of all types considered, rhymed or unrhymed, serious or humorous. Editors on the look-out for poems of contemporary relevance with sharpness of observation or language. The magazine has a good reputation for promoting poets with a future.

Editor Name(s): Martin Jones, Jeffery Wheatley, Stella Stocker
Address: Administrative Editor, Martin Jones, 1 Mountside, Guildford, Surrey GU2 4JD
Telephone: 01483 504 556
Mag Frequency: 3 issues per year
Subscription: £6
Single Issue: £2.50
Overseas: £7 (sterling)
Payment in: Preferably in £ Sterling
Payable to: Guildford Poets Press
Inserts accepted: Yes
Terms: Negotiable
Circulation approx: 300
Payment terms to contributors: Free copy of issue of poem
Accept/rejection approx times: 2-3 months

W
THE WOLF'S TALE

A collection of erotic poetry, fiction and art celebrating the joy of sex and sexuality, profiling the work of non-professional writers and artists. Essays, reviews and other non-fiction articles discussing sexuality are also welcome.

Editor Name(s): Michelle Drayton-Harrold
Address: Batcave Publications, F 1/2 10 Atlas Road, Glasgow G21 4TE Scotland
Telephone: 0141 587 1461
Email: cuddles.thebatcave@ntlworld.com
Mag Frequency: Annually (late October/early November)
Single Issue: £4 (approx)
Back Issue: No longer available but compenia of previous editions proposed for 2002 release
Payment in: Personal Cheque or Postal Order
Payable to: Michelle Drayton-Harrold
Inserts accepted: Yes
Terms: Negotiable
Advertising Rates: Negotiable
Circulation approx: 50 - 60
Payment terms to contributors: Free copy of publication
Accept/rejection approx times: Within 1 month

W

THE WORD - LIFE JOURNAL AND POETRY MAGAZINE

The Word magazine is an enquiring life journal that represents an ongoing Romantic Renaissance into the Age of Aquarius and features the best in poetry from today's poets. It is a magazine aimed at the serious writer. The Word only publishes the select few, having become a standard for offering credibility and merit to the serious poet and those who achieve excellence. The benefits to the poets that have so far featured have been increased by the reputation that the magazine has gained among literary establishments. Their aim is to publish on merit, not for vanity. All poetry that is chosen for publication in the Word's Poet Showcase is chosen from entries that feature on the end of every Partners In Poetry competition - top ten places - Honours List. Submissions are only accepted for articles. Previous features include articles from fine writers like Professor Desmond Tarrant, Pamela Constatine, Anthony North etc. They do advise viewing the magazine. If you want easier access to poetry publications and a platform for reviews try their other magazine A Bard Hair Day or The Poet Tree.

Editor Name(s): Ian Deal
Address: 289 Elmwood Avenue, Feltham, Middlesex TW13 7QB
Telephone: Approach in writing please
Email: partners_writing_group@hotmail.com
Website: www.homestead.com/partners_writing_group
Mag Frequency: Bi-annual - April 30th and October 30th
Subscription: England £7, Europe £8 or $12, International £9 or $14
Single Issue: England £3.50 sterling, Europe £4 or $6, International $4.50 or $7
Back Issue: Same - always available
Overseas: £3.50 - include IRCs for return
Payment in: Sterling only - Cheque/PO
Payable to: Ian Deal
Inserts accepted: Yes
Terms: £50 per 1000 or complimentary advertising
Advertising Rates: £50 full page, £25 half page, £10 quarter page - page size 148mm x 211mm
Payment terms to contributors: Complimentary copy to all poets appearing in 'Poets Showcase'
Accept/rejection approx times: Within 2 weeks

W
WORDS

Words sets out to bring new material by both published and previously unpublished authors before a wider audience consisting of all ages and abilties, with the result that the standard of writing is very high indeed! Compiled from entries to our competitions, it is a quarterly magazine specialising in short stories which is sold in aid of the Winnicott Baby Unit (charity Reg No 292668). Before submitting any work authors are advised to study loosely a back issue (available free on receipt of a 40p stamp or overseas 3 IRC's). As the readership is very wide-ranging no work of a possibly offensive nature will be published and all material is strictly edited.

Editor Name(s): Shaun Peare
Address: PO Box 13574, London W9 3FX
Telephone: 0585 399602 (Evenings only 6-9)
Email: wordsmag@clara.co.uk
Website: www.writers.brew.clara.net/words/
Mag Frequency: Quarterly
Subscription: £10 pa (UK)
Single Issue: £2.50
Back Issue: 1 free then £1.50
Overseas: £15 Europe/£20 RoW
Payment in: Sterling only
Payable to: Words
Inserts accepted: Yes
Terms: £20 per 1000 or exchange
Advertising Rates: None in Words (see Words Adverts)
Circulation approx: 1000 plus
Payment terms to contributors: 2 free copies of the issue in which their work appears
Accept/rejection approx times: No unsolicited mss accepted

WORDS ADVERTS

Words Adverts is distributed free with Words Magazine. An A5 size publication it carries adverts from writers, Small Press Magazines and entrepreneurs throughout the world. While still a fledgling admag it reaches a readership in excess of 1500 each quarter. To claim your free 40 word classified advert just send your advert plus your full postal address (for free checking copy) and 50p stamp (UK) or 3 IRC's to the address below.

Editor Name(s): Nikki Dench
Address: PO Box 13574, London W9 3FX
Email: Adverts@wordsmag.clara.co.uk
Mag Frequency: Quarterly
Subscription: Free
Single Issue: SAE or 40p stamp or 2 x IRC's
Payment in: Sterling only
Payable to: Words
Inserts accepted: Yes
Terms: £15 per 1000
Advertising Rates: £10 per page for subscribers to Words Magazine and £15 per page to non-subscribers, classified 5p per word
Circulation approx: 1500 plus

W
WORDSHARE

Creative writing magazine Wordshare welcomes contributions from disabled people, and people past retirement age. It is an A4 format magazine funded by the Eastern Arts Board. Please add brief autobiographical note to your submission telling how you qualify - through disability or retirement. SAE would be appreciated.

Editor Name(s): John Wilkinson
Address: John Wilkinson (Editor), 8 Bodmin Moor Close, North Hykham, Lincoln LN6 9BB
Mag Frequency: As and when sufficient suitable writing comes in
Subscription: Nil
Single Issue: N/A
Inserts accepted: No
Circulation approx: 4000
Payment terms to contributors: No payment. One copy for every submission; two copies for those accepted

WORDSMITH

Following the success of Scribbler!, a writing magazine aimed at young children, we were made aware of the need for a writing magazine for young adults. Wordsmith was born! Launched in autumn 1999, it has proved to be a tremendous success already with issue 1 claiming 2,651 subscribers! The magazine is devoted to helping children aged between 11 - 16 years enjoy the english language in all it's varied forms, and is closely linked to Key Stage 3 of the National Curriculum. Despite being an educational magazine, there are many sections that include elements of fun allowing the subscribers to relax and enjoy the learning process. With the chance for contributors to see their written, drawn and photographic work in print and the opportunity to win fantastic prizes with every issue, Wordsmith is aiming to be the premier writing magazine for young adults.

Editor Name(s): Allison Dowse
Address: Wordsmith, Remus House, Coltsfoot Drive, Woodston, Peterborough PE2 9JX
Telephone: 01733 890066
Fax: 01733 313524
Email: youngwriters@forwardpress.co.uk
Website: www.youngwriters.co.uk
Mag Frequency: Quarterly
Subscription: £16.50
Single Issue: £4.15
Back Issue: £4.15
Overseas: £19.50
Payment in: Cheque, Credit Card, Postal Order
Payable to: Forward Press Ltd
Inserts accepted: Yes
Terms: Available on request
Advertising Rates: Available on request
Circulation approx: 4,000 plus
Payment terms to contributors: Prizes
Accept/rejection approx times: Up to 6 weeks

W
WORLD WIDE WRITERS

Welcomes short stories which must be original and not previously published or broadcast. Length: 2500-5000 words. Runs a regular and annual short story competition offering £3000 and a trophy for the best short story of the year. The winning short story in each issue receives £625, the second £315 and any other printed £125. Founded 1996.

Address: PO Box 3229, Bournemouth, BH1 1ZS, UK
Telephone: 01202 589828
Fax: 01202 587758
Email: writintl@globalnet.co.uk
Website: www.worldwidewriters.com
Mag Frequency: quarterly
Subscription: £25 UK or £40 world - wide (incl. surface mail)
Single Issue: £6.99
Back Issue: £6
Overseas: Price available on request
Payment in: Cheques/PO/major credit cards
Payable to: Writers International Ltd

WRITE ANGLES

Bi-monthly magazine for writers or anyone interested in literature. Features include news, festivals, new regional publications, competitions and events listings.

Editor Name(s): Jane Stubbs
Address: Jill Leahy, YAB, 21 Bond Street, Dewsbury WF13 1AX
Telephone: 01924 455555
Fax: 01924 466522
Email: jane.stubbs@yarts.co.uk
Mag Frequency: Bi-monthly
Subscription: Nil
Single Issue: Nil
Inserts accepted: No
Circulation approx: 2000

𝒲
WRITE TO PUBLISH

Electronic magazine of author.co.uk, the UK site for the business of writing and publishing. Information on all aspects of writing, web space and advice with ecommerce and ebook publishing facilities for authors and small presses.

Editor Name(s): Trevor Lockwood
Address: 61 Gainsborough Road, Felixstowe, Suffolk IP11 7HS
Telephone: 01394 273388
Email: trevor@author.co.uk
Website: www.author.co.uk
Mag Frequency: Fortnightly
Subscription: Free
Single Issue: Free
Overseas: Free
Inserts accepted: Yes
Terms: Negotiable
Advertising Rates: Negotiable
Circulation approx: 40,000 site visitors each week
Payment terms to contributors: Variable
Accept/rejection approx times: Fast

THE WRITE-ZINE

A newsletter for writers and publishers interested in working within the electronic environment. Articles and links to some of the most prolific online writers, interviews, news, events. We believe in taking advantage of the internet and actively encourage interactive forums and online discussions with our readership. We provide market listings, market information and full guidelines for each.

Editor Name(s): G S Powell
Address: 36 Whitgift House, Battersea, London SW11 3TH
Telephone: 020 7223 2660
Fax: 0820 056 7475
Email: info@thewritezine.com
Website: www.thewritezine.com
Mag Frequency: Monthly with weekly updates
Subscription: £20 per annum
Single Issue: £2.30
Payment in: Sterling
Payable to: G S Powell
Inserts accepted: No
Advertising Rates: Advertorial £250, Display £30, Class £18
Circulation approx: 4,900
Payment terms to contributors: Payment upon publication
Accept/rejection approx times: 14 days prior to publication

W
WRITER'S MUSE

The Writer's Muse, now in its second year, accepts short stories, poetry, articles, reviews, biography, or even short plays on any subject matter, in any genre or form. Submission can be printed, on disk (text file) or by e-mail. No individual's submission should exceed 2000 words in length (unless by arrangement with the editor). Science fiction, fantasy, horror, romance, all welcome as long as it's well written. No children's fiction. Occasional feature of a series but usually by commission. Original art work for each cover is also required.

Editor Name(s): Managing Editor: Calum Kerr, Art Editor: Joyce Timperley, Sales and Distribution: Nigel Bent
Address: 151 Brookfield Road, Cheadle, Cheshire SK8 1EY
Telephone: 0161 491 6074
Fax: 0161 491 6074 (by arrangement)
Email: editor@writersmuse.co.uk or calum@cheadle.u-net.com
Website: www.writersmuse.co.uk
Mag Frequency: Bi-monthly
Subscription: £12 per annum (incl p&p)
Single Issue: £2 plus 50p p&p
Overseas: £15 per annum (incl p&p)
Payment in: Sterling
Payable to: C K Publishing
Inserts accepted: Yes
Terms: Negotiable
Advertising Rates: Ring for details
Circulation approx: Approx 100 per issue
Payment terms to contributors: Complimentary copy
Accept/rejection approx times: 1 month - 6 weeks

WRITERS BREW PRESS NEWSLETTER

A5 - minimum of 16 pages - Writers Brew Press latest news always opens the newsletter with News, Competitions, Reviews, Markets and just about anything of use to a writer filling the rest. Originally used to promote Writers Brew Press, it grew in demand until it became its own entity. Reviews accepted from current magazine subscribers only and only used when space allows. Market news and reports welcome from anyone. We include as much information as we can each quarter.

Editor Name(s): Amanda Gillies
Address: PO Box 241, Oakengates, TF2 9XZ
Telephone: 01952 277872
Email: Newsletter@writers.brew.clara.net
Website: http://www.writers.brew.clara.net/club/
Mag Frequency: Quarterly
Subscription: Free to all magazine subscribers
Single Issue: 33p stamp
Overseas: Us only $10 Dollars payable to - Dreamwalker Press and sent to PO Box 720862, Orlando, FL 32872-0862, USA (Please note, US cheques only to this address, no mss. All enquiries to the UK office with a minimum of 2 IRC's for a reply)
Payable to: Writers Brew Club
Inserts accepted: Yes
Terms: £10 per 100 - or reciprocal (100 only)
Advertising Rates: £25 full page, £15 half page, £12 quarter page
Circulation approx: Growing
Payment terms to contributors: None
Accept/rejection approx times: Publication waiting time 3 months no material held over

W
WRITERS' BULLETIN

Markets and news information for writers. Resouces, courses, book reviews, advice on writing and selling. All markets verified shortly before going to press. No second-hand or out of date information. No guesswork.

Editor Name(s): Shelagh Nugent
Address: Linden Cottage, 45 Burton Road, Little Neston, Cheshire CH64 4AE
Telephone: 0151 353 0967
Fax: 0870 165 6282
Email: helicon@globalnet.co.uk
Website: www.cherrybite.co.uk
Mag Frequency: Bi-monthly
Subscription: £2 per no of issues required
Single Issue: £2
Overseas: £2.40 (EU)/£3 (RoW) per no of issues required
Payment in: Sterling or dollar bills
Payable to: Writers' Bulletin
Inserts accepted: Yes
Terms: Usually reciprocal, otherwise £5 per 100
Advertising Rates: £30 per full page
Circulation approx: 500
Accept/rejection approx times: N/A

W

WRITERS' CAULDRON

A5 - minimum of 56 pages - Soon to be produced in black and white only, but for the foreseeable future it will remain colour inside and out. Contains all types of stories from new and established authors. Competition winners and short listed entries are also included. We only accept rhyming poetry. No surreal stories or ones that leave the reader guessing. No swear words or sex. New submission protocol with submission form only, 2001-Nov, 2002-Feb, 2002-May, 2002-Aug, 2002-Nov. Send SSAE (19p) for free guidline leaflet. No material held over.

Editor Name(s): Amanda Gillies
Address: PO Box 241, Oakengates, TF2 9XZ
Telephone: 01952 277872
Email: Cauldron@writers.brew.clara.net
Website: http://www.writers.brew.clara.net/club/
Mag Frequency: Quarterly
Subscription: £15 per year UK or £18 RoW
Single Issue: £5 sterling only or 18 IRC's
Overseas: US only $35 Dollars payable to - Dreamwalker Press and sent to PO Box 720862, Orlando, FL 32872-0862, USA (Please note, US cheques only to this address, no mss. All enquiries to the UK office with a minimum of 2 IRC's for a reply)
Payable to: Writers Brew Club
Inserts accepted: Yes
Terms: £10 per 1000
Advertising Rates: £50 full page only - 2 adverts per magazine only
Circulation approx: Growing
Payment terms to contributors: Free copy
Accept/rejection approx times: Publication waiting time 3 months. Subscribers are given preference - but we publish at least 3 non-subscribers each magazine

$\mathcal{W}$
WRITERS' FORUM

Writers' Forum is a major resource for writers, from beginners to established authors. It covers the who, why, where, what and how on the craft of writing. Fiction, faction and feature writing. Scripts for television. Comedy and biogaphy plus a website for writers. It costs just £18 a year for six issues and if you would like a free sample copy send us a SAE (80p) 12 x 9 inches to the address below and we'll post you a back issue.

Editor Name(s): John Jenkins, Mary Hogarth - Assistant Ed
Address: PO Box 3229, Bournemouth, BH1 1ZS
Telephone: 01202 589828
Fax: 01202 587758
Email: writintl@globalnet.co.uk
Website: www.worldwidewriters.com
Mag Frequency: Bi-monthly (six issues per year)
Subscription: £18 per year
Single Issue: £3.00
Back Issue: same
Overseas: £25
Payment in: Cheque/credit card
Payable to: Writers International LTD
Inserts accepted: Yes
Terms: Inserts £35 per 1000 (1 sheet A4 folded) includes a FREE half page colour advert inside
Advertising Rates: Covers £1400, Full Page £995, Half £525, Third £400, Quarter £300, 1/6 £200, 1/8 £160, Notice board £85, Mini ads £50, Web Directory (series) £275 (single) £85. Plus, 10% discount for pre-payment, notice board - max 40 words, mini ads - max 20 words.
Circulation approx: 25,000
Payment terms to contributors: one month following publication
Accept/rejection approx times: 2 - 3 weeks

WRITERS' NEWS & WRITING MAGAZINE

The news magazine that no writer can afford to miss, Writers' News is the very home of writing. With its associated Writing Magazine, automatically sent to members, its coverage of everything the writer needs to know, its practical help and inspiration, and indeed its sheer depth and variety, it is in a class entirely of its own; and not surprisingly, its readership is more than twice that of all other titles for writers put together. Ingredients include: News of market and other opportunities, events, legislation and trends affecting the writer; its own extensive range of competitions plus full coverage of other people's; and a monthly diary of events; personal helpline answering individual questions; in-depth interviews and profiles with practical tips for writers; coverage of all the main genres of writing; regular columns, letters, book reviews and much more; the most complete advertising service for writers. Writers' News is only available by direct subscription. Writing Magazine is available from all good newsagents.

Editor Name(s): Derek Hudson
Address: PO Box 168, Wellington Street, Leeds LS1 1RF
Telephone: 0113 2388333
Fax: 0113 2388330
Email: writersnews@ypn.co.uk
Website: www.writersnews.com
Mag Frequency: Writers' News - Monthly/ Writing Magazine - Bi-monthly
Subscription: £44.90/ £39.90 by DD
Single Issue: Writing Magazine price £3.00
Back Issue: £3.50
Overseas: £49.90/44.90 by DD/CC
Payable to: Writers' News
Inserts accepted: Yes
Terms: £35 loose/£50 bound-in per 1000
Circulation approx: Writers News - 21000 plus
Writing Magazine - 45500 plus

y THE YELLOW CRANE

Interesting new poems from South Wales and beyond...

Address: J. Brookes, 20 Princes Court, Plasnewydd, Cardiff CF2 3AU Wales
Mag Frequency: Quarterly
Subscription: £7
Single Issue: £1.50
Overseas: £10
Payment in: IMO/Cheque/PO
Payable to: J Brookes
Inserts accepted: No
Circulation approx: Growing
Payment terms to contributors: 2 copies of magazine
Accept/rejection approx times: Goodness knows

YORKSHIRE JOURNAL

Yorkshire Journal is an outstanding publication based on the quality journals that were popular until the early part of this century. We have re-established this fine tradition with an attractively designed and well-produced quarterly periodical of 120 pages about Yorkshire, its history, culture, landscape, customs and people, produced in the heart of the county - and all for only £2.95 an issue. From a wide range of writers, photographers and illustrators, many of them experts in their fields, come substantial articles on folklore, art, current events and architecture; and short stories and poetry. Topics vary from the informative, the illuminating and the controversial to the not-so-serious and downright light-hearted. Send synopsis in first instance.

Address: Ilkley Road, Otley, West Yorkshire LS21 3JP
Telephone: 01943 467958
Fax: 01943 850057
Email: (editorial): mwhitley@smith-settle.co.uk, leverington@smith-settle.co.uk or (sales): sales@smith-settle.co.uk
Mag Frequency: Quarterly
Subscription: £12
Single Issue: £2.95
Overseas: £16
Payment in: Visa/Mastercard
Payable to: Smith Settle Limited
Inserts accepted: Yes
Terms: On application
Circulation approx: 3000
Payment terms to contributors: Poems - complimentary copy/Articles - varies
Accept/rejection approx times: 2-4 weeks

Z
ZENE

Zene is the only British writers' magazine dedicated to the small and independent press (worldwide!). Every issue features detailed contributors' guidelines for markets you will not find elsewhere, and many of these publications pay very well. You'll learn about new magazines, anthologies, comics, novels, etc, which are looking for all kinds of writing including fiction, poetry and non-fiction of all genres. Zene also lists current competitions, news and views of writers, including feedback on how they've been treated, plus changes of address/circumstance/requirements of publishers. Zene is never out of date! We publish regular articles on all aspects of writing but are never patronising. Finally, our comprehensive reviews section covers about 100 further titles - and, often controversially, we tell it like it is! Unsolicited submissions are welcome for all sections as long as they follow standard ms format and are accompanied by SAE and covering letter. Guidelines and review copies are also welcome from all publishers, including those in this book. Zene also runs a printing scheme for the benefit of independent publishers, getting the best prices for various types of printing including quality short run books and magazines.

Address: TTA Press, 5 Martins Lane, Witcham, Ely, Cambs CB6 2LB
Email: ttapress@aol.com
Website: www.tta-press.freewire.co.uk
Mag Frequency: Bi-monthly (6 issues pa)
Subscription: £12 (6 issues)
Single Issue: Subscription only
Back Issue: Sold out
Overseas: Europe £15/USA and Canada US $24/RoW £18
Payment in: Cheque/PO/Eurocheque etc
Payable to: TTA Press
Inserts accepted: Yes
Terms: Negotiable
Advertising Rates: Query with SAE
Payment terms to contributors: Negotiable
Accept/rejection approx times: 1 month

Z

ZINE ZONE

Zine Zone is a 'courant de pensees' publication primarily aimed at creative youth. We have developed a production style in keeping with the photocopied 'zine' tradition. This gives the magazine an edge that appeals to visual, print and design makers, as well as writers and musicians. The language and commentary reflect the cream and mud of creativity left out by media moguls. Increase in demand and contribution lead Zine Zone to publish an unpredictable and chaotic mix of illustrative work including poetry, reviews, short stories. We also organise events. Work can be sent in black and white prints. Clear handwritten texts are accepted. We also take work on 3.5 inch Macintosh formatted floppy disks. Save text as 'Text' file. Contact ZZ for further details. Add details to reviews: ie band/artist, titles, formats, venue, contact, issue #, dates, prices, ISBN etc. No slides/CVs necessary. London-based Zine Zone is distributed mainly in the UK (70%) and in a dozen countries including South Africa, China, Greece, Japan and the USA!

Address: 47 Retreat Place, London E9 6RH
Fax: 0181 525 1466
Email: zine.zone@ndirect.co.uk
Website: www.ndirect.co.uk/~zine.zone
Mag Frequency: Every 41 days
Subscription: £12 (8 issues/1 year) £8 (4 issues/6 months)
Single Issue: £1.95
Back Issue: Varies, write for details
Overseas: £15 Europe/£18 RoW
Payment in: Cheque/PO/IMO
Payable to: Zine Zone
Inserts accepted: Yes
Circulation approx: 2000
Payment terms to contributors: Negotiable, payment is only made for commissioned work
Accept/rejection approx times: 3 months

Z
ZINE-ON-A-CD

We began as Super Trouper, then became Zine-on-a-Tape, and now we have been promoted to Zine-on-a-CD! Yes, we are a small press magazine published on an audio CD. So you can pop us in your hi-fi and listen to the poetry, reviews, interviews, stories and music! You can also check out Zine-on-the-Web and Zine-on-an-Email!

Editor Name(s): Andy Savage
Address: Andy Savage, 19 Downside Road, Whitfield, Dover, Kent, CT16 3NS
Email: andy@andysav.free-online.co.uk
Website: http://www.andysav.free-online.co.uk/zine.htm
Mag Frequency: One or two a year
Subscription: £5 for 2 issues post paid
Single Issue: £3 post paid
Overseas: $10 post paid
Payment in: Cheque/PO or concealed cash
Payable to: Andrew Savage
Advertising Rates: No adverts
Circulation approx: Around 100
Payment terms to contributors: Complimentary copies
Accept/rejection approx times: 4 weeks

Z

THE ZONE

The Zone is the last word in science fiction magazines; with excellent short fiction, big name interviews, insightful criticism and incisive articles - plus complete coverage of SF in the media, with illustrated review columns in every issue... The Zone publishes original SF stories alongside genre poetry and experimental or stylist prose of the highest quality. Non-fiction is of vital importance too, and so The Zone features interviews, articles, essays and regular review columns - covering all manner of relevant (and irrelevant) science fictional topics and themes in the media. Unsolicited mss are welcome. We are looking for high quality, speculative fiction, with plenty of ideas and imagination - but it does not have to be 'hard-SF'. We are not interested in 'epic fantasy quest sagas' (with wizards and warriors, etc) or any traditional or contemporary horror (satanism, werewolves/needless gore of serial killers, respectively). However, subtle SF-fantasy may be acceptable. Fiction for The Zone should be of approximately 1000 to 5000 words. SF poetry is published in The Zone, by invitation only. The work of one genre poet will be featured in the magazine's poetry showcase. However, science fictional prose-poems of 60-70 lines (approximately) are always welcome. Non-fiction: original articles on any aspect of science fiction (retrospective or topical) will be considered. Please write first, outlining your idea. Several special projects are ongoing and others are in development - send an SAE/IRC if you want details of these. Length of any non-fiction works, by arrangement with the magazine's editors, but articles of 1000 to 5000 words (or longer if serialised), will be considered. Book reviews (approximately 250 to 500 plus words) by arrangement with editors. Send samples of your published reviews and list of your favourite SF authors. Designed for the discerning readers of SF fandom. The Zone aims to please the lifetime enthusiast and the genre newcomer alike.

Address: Pigasus Press, 13 Hazely Combe, Arreton, Isle of Wight PO30 3AJ
Email: pigasus.press@virgin.net
Website: http://freespace.virgin.net/pigasus.press/index.htm
Mag Frequency: Irregular
Subscription: £12 for 4 issues
Single Issue: £3.20
Back Issue: £2.50
Overseas: Write for details, enclosing IRC
Payable to: Tony Lee
Inserts accepted: No
Advertising Rates: Available on request, send SAE/IRC
Circulation approx: Unknown
Payment terms to contributors: Token payment (currently £5/$10) plus free copy, paid on publication
Accept/rejection approx times: 4-6 weeks

£IVERS GUIDES WRITERS' DIRECTORIES

From page to stage, novices to novelists, whether starting out or seeking a new way of writing, all the advice and info you ever needed to know (probably) in one invaluable booklet - Saving you a fortune in phone calls and postage, saving you time and energy, and the trouble of wading through the publication jungle: Markets; Useful Sources, including the Internet; Literary Events; Competitions; Recommended reading. Information welcome from organisers (events; competitions etc), publishers and editors. Current titles: The Compleat Short Story Writer; The Compleat Poet.

See also, Competitions Bulletin. £ivers Guides compiled by Carole Baldock. Mailing list details: Editorial Director of www.poetext.com (also, www.fictionette.com for short stories, online shortly); Editor of Competitions Bulletin; Associate Editor of Orbis Markets annd Competitions editor for the Woman Writers Network (WWN) Co-ordinator for Liverpool's Dead Good Poets Society.

Editor Name(s): Carole Baldock
Address: 17 Greenhow Avenue, West Kirby, Wirral CH48 5EL
Telephone: 0151 625 1446
Email: carolebaldock@hotmail.com
Website: www.poettext.com and www.fictionette.com
Mag Frequency: Annual
Subscription: £5
Overseas: £6
Payment in: Sterling
Payable to: Carole Baldock
Circulation approx: 500 plus

Organisations and resources of interest to Poets and Writers

Association Of Little Presses
32 Downside Road, Sutton, Surrey SM2 5HP

The Society Of Authors
84 Drayton Gardens, London SW10 9SB
Phone 0171 3736642

The Poetry Library
Level 5, Royal Festival Hall, South Bank Centre, London SE1 8XX
Phone 0171 9210943
Huge holdings of little mags and poetry titles. Issues current awareness lists of poetry publishers, organisations, magazines and competitions.

The Little Magazine Collection And Poetry Store
Mss & Rare Books Room, University College of London Library, Gower Street, London WC1E 6BT
Phone 0171 3807796
Geoffrey Soar and David Miller's collection of more than 3500 poetry mags.

The Poetry School
130c Evering Road, London N16 7BD
Phone 0181 9850090
Tuition in reading and writing poetry; courses, workshops, readings and events. Provides a practitioners' forum.

2003 Edition

Writers' Bookshop invites entries for the Small Press Guide 2003

Entries or enquiries before 1 June 2002 to:
Editor, Small Press Guide
Writers' Bookshop
Remus House
Coltsfoot Drive
Woodston
Peterborough
PE2 9JX

Tail Piece

Writers' News Magazine, see page 351, have launched a regular feature identifying websites of interest to writers.

Small Presses with their own sites should contact Martyn Morrison on 0113 238 8333 for full details and a cost of appearing in this feature that reaches over 20,000 writers on a monthly basis.